CONSTITUTIONAL FATE

CONSTITUTIONAL FATE

Theory of the Constitution

Philip Bobbitt

New York   Oxford
OXFORD UNIVERSITY PRESS

Copyright © 1982 by Oxford University Press, Inc.
First published by Oxford University Press, New York, 1982
First issued as an Oxford University Press paperback, 1984

Library of Congress Cataloging in Publication Data
Bobbitt, Philip.
Constitutional fate.
Includes bibliographical references and index.
1. Judicial review—United States.   I. Title.
KF4575.B63   1984   347.73′12   83-17343
ISBN 0-19-503422-8 (pbk.)   347.30712

Printing (last digit): 9 8 7 6 5 4
Printed in the United States of America

To Rebekah Johnson Bobbitt

I would like to say "This book is written to the glory of God" but nowadays that would be chicanery, that is, the trick of a cheat, for it would not be rightly understood. I mean simply that it came at an end of another's suffering and is intended to serve a value I cannot name that is other than mere self-regard. Insofar as I have failed to be in harmony with this value, my book will fall short of the vision it is an attempt to express.

ACKNOWLEDGMENTS

There are many persons to whom I have shown the manuscript that preceded this book, so many in fact that a lawyer might say publication has long since occurred. Those faithful and responsive readers know who they are; I know who some of them are. One group of students, my seminar in the 1978–1979 terms, earned my enduring affection so patient were they with my efforts and so willing to test theoretical approaches at a time and in an environment that can scarcely have encouraged these approaches. The members of this group were Gary Amsterdam, Parker Folse, Barbara Lipscomb, Olin McGill and Richard Pappas. The Dean of the University of Texas Law School, Ernest Smith and his Associate Deans George Schatzki and Michael Sharlot, collaborated to contrive writing time and financial support for me. At an important time the Russell Sage Foundation supplied additional funds to support my work, interrupted by service in Washington in 1980–1981. Douglass Cater and Joseph Slater, of the Aspen Institute, and Marshall Robinson and Peter DiJanosi of Russell Sage, cooperated in this generous effort. I ought also to mention letters from my teachers, Grant Gilmore and Gilbert Harman, that came at times when I was convinced that no serious, sensitive reading of my work was likely and that publication ought to be abandoned. Professor Barbara Aldave, my colleague, has been my companion in countless conversations whose benefit has been almost wholly mine. Susan Rabiner, of the Oxford University Press, has been a hopeful but not intrusive editor. Mark Sagoff, of the Center for Philosophy and Public Policy at the University of Maryland, has been helpful.

The first draft of this manuscript was written in Austin, Texas. Since then work on this book has proceeded in Washington, London, Vienna and Oxford; it leaves my hands as I have just returned to Austin and my house where the initial work was done. In all these places there have been persons, unacknowledged here, who have assisted me. There is another, however, without whom that first draft could not have been done. Miss Katherine Burghard, careless of her many sacrifices and efforts on my behalf, was my indispensable ally and support. If there is merit in the result, it is merit that she has helped bring into being.

Excepting these acknowledgments, I have had doubts about providing a preface. My aim in this book is to plunge the reader into a world, the experience of which will cultivate a particular sensibility toward the Constitution so that, at least as to the fundamental question of the legitimacy of judicial review, the matter can be debated with a sense of fitness and not hollowly. A preface is of course likely to detract from this experience because it must be constructed out of the stylistic materials it wishes to do away with. But I have become convinced that, without some introductory guide, the book is likely to be misunderstood and it would be irresponsible of me to allow a misplaced popularity to stand uncorrected out of vanity.

This book presents a general theory of Constitutional decision. It is not written in a conventionally theoretical manner. The way in which this theory is presented is naturally determined by some of the assumptions of the theory itself and, like it, differs from the standard models in this subject. This is a difference in kind and therefore it is to be expected that the mode of presentation is different also. The standard models are presented in a standard way. The difficulty arises because the method of presentation cannot prevent the contemporary reader from assimilating it into the standard modes. For example, one might conclude from the sketches in Book I that these personal histories, written in a depictive way, suggest a biographical determinism in the ideas with which the characters are associated, readers being accustomed to such suggestion, when in fact it is my aim to show the very opposite of this, that the characters become actual in the living out of the necessity of their ideas. This is one example among a great many; indeed a reader might finish the entire book and be surprised to learn that any theory at all had been presented. Accordingly I offer this brief guide.

Book I shows how the legitimacy of judicial review is achieved. This is a matter of various corridors of argument. Book II is an extended treatment of one of these ways of argument. It does not represent a preferred way; indeed the very idea of such a preference is incompatible with the general theory. Book III is concerned with judicial review, a topic treated distinctly from the subject of legitimacy. An account of judicial review is given in terms of functions, which do not offer a means of establishing legitimacy. Instead a functional mapping of judicial review makes clear that legitimacy is not a matter of review *per se* but is related to it as the various channels of argument derive from the functions of review, i.e., review, in the context of the features of our Constitution, must use them. A more extensive and detailed Afterword follows the body of this book in a similar effort to organize what must be, if it is to be successful, a guideless and list less treatise. I apologize for the oblique tone of the present preface; of course my apology can only be provisionally accepted.

Austin, Texas   Philip Chase Bobbitt
December 1981

CONTENTS

Chapter 11   Applying Ethical Argu-
              ments   157
Chapter 12   Constitutional Conscience   168
              Conclusion   176

Book III   CONSTITUTIONAL EXPRESSIONISM

              Introduction   181
Chapter 13   Constitutional Review   182
Chapter 14   Functions of Review   190
Chapter 15   Expressive Function   196
Chapter 16   Arguments and the Expressive
              Function   220
Chapter 17   Change and the
              Constitution   224
Chapter 18   The Genealogy of
              Arguments   230
Chapter 19   Legitimacy and Review   233

              Conclusion   241
              Afterword: *Amor Fati*   243
              Notes   251
              Index   279

I

CONSTITUTIONAL ARGUMENT

CHAPTER 1

A TYPOLOGY OF CONSTITUTIONAL ARGUMENTS

The central issue in the constitutional debate of the past twenty-five years has been the legitimacy of judicial review of constitutional questions by the United States Supreme Court. This issue is thought to have been given heightened attention owing to the Court's historic decision in *Brown* v. *Board of Education of Topeka, Kansas*[1] and thereafter to have achieved status as the question of the hour in the legal academy with Judge Learned Hand's Holmes Lectures at the Harvard Law School in 1958.[2] Throughout the sixties the activism of the Warren Court kept the issue of this legitimacy alive, and interest was intensified by the controversial decision in *Roe* v. *Wade*[3] in the seventies. I think it is fair to say that the question of the legitimacy of judicial review has claimed more discussion and more analysis than any other issue in constitutional law. This book is an examination of the question of such legitimacy. It may strike some, however, as going about an answer in a rather odd and roundabout way.

For it is customary among essayists in constitutional law to address such questions in one of two ways. Judges and academic lawyers tend to examine the events surrounding the adoption of the Constitution, its homely but interesting text, the political relationships the Framers were trying to establish and those they sought to make impossible,[4] even sometimes what the Court itself has said about its own role.[5] And from a competition among the arguments arising from such examinations, critics purport to determine the proper scope for the Court's role. On the basis of such arguments it has been artfully argued that to legitimate the acts of Congress the Court must have the power of review, since the power to affirm necessarily predicates the power to strike down.[6] Elsewhere it has been noted that parts of the text, for example the Supremacy Clause, authorize the Court's review of acts of the state legislatures.[7] Others following a different reasoning have said that the legitimacy of review is confirmed by a study of discussions at the Constitutional Convention addressed to whether or not to include the justices of the Supreme Court in a Council of Revision whose duty it would have been to review all laws before they became effective—since all the arguments for and against this proposal appear to share the assumption that the courts were empowered to determine the constitutionality of those laws they encountered in the process of deciding cases.[8] Correspondence among the Framers regarding a Bill of Rights also appears to reflect this assumption.

Still others have argued that institutional features of the Court arising from precisely that insulation from political reaction that is often thought to make the Court ill-suited for final review, actually fit the Court to be the conservator of constitutional principles, the development and preservation of which take place by means of judicial review.

These various arguments all constitute one sort of analysis and come mainly from academic lawyers who are the priestly critics and opening-night reviewers of the legal profession.

The second kind of examination begins a little farther back. Judicial review of legislative acts, it is said, is proper because it is likeliest to assure just accommodations. This is so, on one view of the matter, because the terms of the original social contract would inevitably be varied by political majorities with the power to do so, so that these majorities, and their agents the legislatures, must be restrained in the same way that courts must often prevent the coercive renegotiation of contracts between private parties of unequal bargaining power.[9] But since only a long dead majority can be said to have originally agreed to such a contract, the full force of this argument can perhaps be avoided.[10] It may instead be offered, however, that courts are the best final arbiters of the sort of hypothetical contract that would be agreed to by all citizens at any time (in ignorance of any particular personal advantage), since legislatures must respond to the powerful and to shifting majorities within their constituencies[11] and do not have to justify their decisions by appeals to the principles of such an "original contract."[12] This argument depends on the acceptance of the idea that those rules one would have agreed to without reference to one's own position in life do, in fact, reflect and will yield a condition of disinterested justice. Philosophical argument of this kind for judicial review will depend on an assumption that the Constitution is, or can be interpreted to be, this sort of original contract. This throws us back on legal argument. Thus the usual philosophical bases for judicial review take us only to the doorstep of legitimacy, since it must still be shown that a particular use of the Constitution actualizes the role for which review is justified.

And yet legal argument—the analysis of the Constitution to which so many able minds have devoted themselves this last quarter century—cannot establish independent legitimacy for judicial review, for its debates and its analyses are conducted by means of arguments that themselves reflect a commitment to such legitimacy. So although a general theory of constitutional law may appear to establish the legitimacy of certain kinds of arguments—as when a social contract theorist might wish to confine courts to a textual analysis of the Constitution[13]—it is in fact the other way round. It is because we are already committed to the force of an appeal to text that such an argument can be used in support of a court's role. When one argues that a court's experience with parsing documents, or its time for reflection, or its relative insulation from political pressure, and so forth, fit it as an institution for the task of assessing the constitutionality of legislation, one is already committed to the view that enforcing rules derived from the constitutional text is the legitimate task at hand.

In the ensuing pages therefore I will not take the conventional tack of raising arguments that appear to define the scope of legitimate review. Instead, in Book I, I will present a typology of the kinds of arguments one finds in judicial opinions, in hearings, and in briefs. Each kind of argument must be one with which each of my readers could agree, though each may of course differ as to its force.

In this task it is not necessary to appeal to rules. You cannot *decide* to be convinced by any of these arguments; nor, of course, need you decide whether they are convincing. There is a legal grammar that we all share and that we have all mastered prior to our being able to ask what the reasons are for a court having power to review legislation.

If you doubt this, imagine for a moment some of the arguments that will not appear in this constitutional typology. One does not see counsel argue, nor a judge purport to base his decision, on arguments of kinship; as for example, that a treaty should be held to be supreme with respect to a state's statute because the judge's brother has a land title that would be validated thereby. Nor does one hear overt religious arguments or appeals to let the matter be decided by chance or by reading entrails. These arguments and a great many others are not part of our legal grammar, although there have been societies and doubtless are still societies within whose legal cultures such arguments make sense.

This suggests that arguments are conventions, that they could be different, but that then we would be different. This is evident in Orwell's description of the revolutionary whose house is searched without a warrant. "They can't do this to me," he says. "I've got my rights."

This point is not always appreciated. Indeed some commentators are inclined to ignore the significance of constitutional argument altogether, as when a political scientist boasts that he can predict the vote divisions in Supreme Court cases and coolly concludes that political bias decides most cases. It is not relevant for the time being whether constitutional arguments decide cases or *are* the decision itself, by which I mean that they form the structure of meaning the case ultimately achieves as precedent. What is now important is that the Court hears arguments, reads arguments, and ultimately must write arguments, all within certain conventions.

In Book I, I will explore the various types of constitutional argument. I shall begin by saying that there are five types. As will become clear, these five are really archetypes, since many arguments take on aspects of more than one type. Eventually I hope to persuade the reader that these five types are not all there are.

Historical argument is argument that marshals the intent of the draftsmen of the Constitution and the people who adopted the Constitution.[14] Such arguments begin with assertions about the controversies, the attitudes, and decisions of the period during which the particular constitutional provision to be construed was proposed and ratified.

The second archetype is *textual argument,* argument that is drawn from a consideration of the present sense of the words of the provision. At times textual argument is confused with historical argument,[15] which requires the consideration of evidence extrinsic to the text. The third type of constitutional argument is *structural argument.* Structural arguments are claims that a particular principle or practical result is implicit in the structures of government and the relationships that are created by the Constitution among citizens and governments. The fourth type of constitutional argument is *prudential argument.* Prudential argument is self-conscious to the reviewing institution and need not treat the merits of the particular controversy (which itself may or may not be constitutional), instead advancing particular doctrines according to the practical wisdom of using the courts in a particular way.

Finally, there is *doctrinal argument,* argument that asserts principles derived from precedent or from judicial or academic commentary on precedent. One will not find in the text of the Constitution the phrases "two-tier review" or "original package" or any of the other necessary and ephemeral modes of analysis by which the Constitution is adapted to the common law case method, yet these doctrines are every bit as potent as those phrases originally printed in Philadelphia.

To an exploration of these five types of argument—historical, textual, structural, prudential, and doctrinal—I shall devote the remainder of Book I. It will become apparent that what is usually called the *style* of a particular judge, as well as the very different notions of style in particular eras, can be explained as a preference for one type of argument over others.

My typology of constitutional arguments is not a complete list, nor a list of wholly discrete items, nor the only plausible division of constitutional arguments. The various arguments illustrated often work in combination. Some examples fit under one heading as well as another. For example, the constitutional argument that a particular sort of question is best suited to be decided by one institution of government and ill-suited to another, may in some cases be thought of equally plausibly as a prudential argument or a structural one. For that matter, structural argument itself contains a prudential component just as arguments of any kind may be said to be "doctrinal," since the various approaches and kinds of constitutional arguments are embodied in constitutional doctrines. A different typology might surely be devised through some sort of recombination of these basic approaches, and there can be no ultimate list because new approaches will be developed through time.

CHAPTER 2

HISTORICAL ARGUMENT

Historical arguments depend on a determination of the original understanding of the constitutional provision to be construed. At first, one must notice how odd it is that the original understanding in any field of study should govern present behavior. Certainly no one proposes an historical argument in physics: for example, that we should try to discover what Democritus had in mind when he used the word *atom* so that we could use the term properly when confronted with, say, problems associated with electron spin. Nor is anyone in the arts likely to argue that a particular artist must conceive his problem in terms dictated by his precursors. Indeed we reserve the epithet 'derivative' for artists who do precisely this. While it is true there is no text in the arts and sciences of the mid-twentieth century, to notice this is scarcely to explain the phenomenon. There may be no text simply because of our doubt that exegesis will work in the sciences or the arts.

The very decision to produce a Constitution in writing presupposes a different faith. This faith finds expression in John Adams's view that "frequent recurrence to the fundamental principles of the constitution . . . [is] absolutely necessary to preserve the advantages of liberty and to maintain a free government. . . . The people have a right to require of their law givers and magistrates an exact and constant observance of them."[1] This states the basis for the idea that an original understanding has force: that the Constitution *bound* government and that the People had therefore devised a construction by which they could enforce its limits and rules. But what was the original understanding of the use to be made of this original understanding? That is, how did the Framers and ratifiers intend their intentions to be determined and applied? We do not know this and we cannot know it.

There was no preexisting written constitution of whose application the Framers and ratifiers spoke, either in contemporary documents or in the text of the Constitution itself. And, of course, the adducement of contemporary British canons of statutory interpretation is largely beside the point. Moreover, the Constitution was not, despite the charter of the Convention, an amendment to the Articles of Confederation.

We do not have an original commitment to a particular form of historical argument. To what source are we to refer for an authoritative understanding? To statements of members of the Convention who proposed a particular provision? To the debate surrounding its adoption on the Convention floor? To earlier language which had been superseded? Or should we look, not to the Constitutional Convention, which we must remember was not authorized to propose a new constitution, but instead to the various ratifying state conventions? James Madison wrote that an appeal to historical argument requires us to "look . . . not in the General Convention, which proposed, but in the State Conventions, which accepted and ratified the Constitution."[2] But if to the state conventions, do we look to what they were promised—as, for example, by the Federalist Papers—or to what they independently took the various provisions to mean? The latter would be more in keeping with Thomas Cooley's observation that "the object of construction, as applied to a written constitution, is to give effect to the intent of the people in adopting it."[3]

If this method is decided upon, then must each of the thirteen ratifying conventions—or perhaps the first nine—have been in agreement on any point at issue?[4] And what would count as agreement, since an up or down vote on the construction of a

particular provision could not occur in these contexts as it might
have in the drafting convention?

Suppose we turn back to the Constitutional Convention. As
early as 1838—two years, after the death of James Madison, the
last living member of the Convention—the Supreme Court announced that construction of the Constitution must rely on "the
meaning and intention of the convention which framed and
proposed it for adoption and ratification."[5] In 1869 the Court
again examined the "intention of the Convention" and decided
that the Framers had intended to confer a comprehensive taxing power on Congress. It therefore upheld a federal tax on
state-issued banknotes even though the effect was to drive such
notes out of circulation, a context not explicitly considered by
the Convention and one, we may speculate, that the state conventions were unlikely to have contemplated with indiffer-
ence.[6] The Court has since resorted to examination of the debates at the Convention to determine what uniformity is
required by the indirect tax provision,[7] to let stand a President's removal of executive officers without congressional consent,[8] to decide whether the treason clause prohibits the impu-
tation of incriminating acts when uncorroborated by two
witnesses.[9] The Court has relied on this sort of historical argument to support its view that congressional districts must have
a roughly equal population[10] and its ruling that Congress could
not augment the constitutionally required qualifications for
membership in its chambers.[11] The list might be expanded considerably, in part perhaps because garnishing an opinion with
historical arguments is usually considered an expression of good
form. But an interesting feature of such reliance by the Court
on historical arguments is that in all these cases there is not one
instance in which it may be said that the Court has definitively
established the intent of the Convention on any important issue. Usually when this has been attempted it has subsequently
been refuted.[12]

The records of the debates are so scanty that full discussion
of any point has been lost; more importantly, the Convention
met in secret without official minutes in an atmosphere that
concealed dissent and put a premium on achieving agreement
to a document that was unglossed or unexplained in any way

that might disclose or provoke fissures in the coalitions that proposed it. There were to be no future sessions; everything was subordinated to the adoption of the Constitution. Consequently, much language is without comment in Madison's notes. The debates that were recorded are fragmentary and indicate little more than highly particular or highly general positions that can scarcely be said to have been endorsed by the adoption of specific language for which the position had been used as support. It happens, in fact, that even in the brief records we do have, we encounter the phenomenon of delegates urging the adoption of the same language for disconsonant purposes.[13] It is rare that the debate surrounding the adoption of particular language can provide a decisive historical argument for a provision being construed in a particular way. At most such study is likely to indicate only the concerns of the more voluble or more forceful members of the Convention. Finally, the debates cannot operate affirmatively to establish the correctness of a particular construction because they can't establish why a coalition of state delegations adopted a particular measure. At most, the debates can falsify a particular reading, not simply through recourse to a single exchange, but by describing the evolution of a provision through the rejection of particular language.

Thus when called upon to determine the scope of its original jurisdiction, the Court observed that a proposal which would have allocated to the Senate the question of disputes between the states was voted down by the Convention.[14] Thus also Justice Brandeis, dissenting from a holding that the President could remove a postmaster without congressional consent, parried the majority's observation that the Convention records did not directly answer the matter. "Nothing," he wrote, "can be inferred from the silence of the Convention of 1787 on the subject of removal. For the outstanding fact remains that every specific proposal to confer such uncontrollable power upon the President was rejected."[15]

Most recently, constitutional lawyers have been called upon, in their proper role as citizen-lawyers discussing the Constitution in their communities, to consider the question whether a President may be impeached for acts that are politically repugnant to Congress, though not of constitutional impact. The historical approach to this question might frame the question: "Did the Framers intend the phrase 'high crimes and misdemeanors' to include matters of political dispute between the branches?" A study of the debates would seem to reject such an interpretation because this very proposal was put forward by Mason at the Convention, was the subject of controversy in an exchange between Madison and Mason, and was voted down.[16] But suppose it had been adopted. Then we would not have such assurance in determining intent. For while a debate and vote can make clear that a particular provision was severed from a rejected meaning, regardless of the delegates' reasons, when a passage was *adopted* we are thrown back on the puzzle of varying and sometimes incompatible intentions left unexpressed or, in the case of trade-offs for votes on other matters, indecisive and embodied in language chosen to satisfy objectives other than clarity.

I am simply describing the topological features of such arguments. I am not questioning the jurisprudential and epistemological assumptions made by those who employ historical arguments. I am not trying to deprive them of the word 'intent' nor would I rule out any specific sources, including influential collateral sources like the Federalist Papers, as useful both in setting the general spirit of specific provisions and, in the way I have suggested, in actually ruling out particular readings.

But this has seldom been enough for the full-bore historicist in constitutional law. He wants what none of the historical arguments I have drawn can give, and that is the authoritative reading in a particular context. Such scholars have always been a part of our constitutional history; they are a reflection, I think, of both the liberal hostility to the federal judiciary and the American desire for a certitude that is technological in its freedom from dependence on judgment. It is worth spending a moment on one particular variant of historical argument that promises such certitude. This is the approach that says, with Holmes, "We ask, not what this man meant, but what those words mean in the mouth of a normal speaker of English, using them in the circumstances in which they were used."[17] This method, which Contracts scholars quite misleadingly call an "objective" method, frees us from the difficulties of determining intention, difficulties which are enhanced by the paradoxes encountered in a decision by a group said to reflect a certain intent even though this is likely not shared by most of its members who, in turn, make proposals that are then adopted by yet other groups of decisionmakers themselves not necessarily sharing a particular intention. At a stroke all of these problems are brushed aside, and with them the negative, asymmetrical limitation of historical argument. Instead, there is a true meaning, discernible and objective, an object whose contours we may trace by consulting the maps and photographs of that day. It is an idea that has roots in Spencer Roan and Luther Martin,[18] but in our own day has been principally associated with William Winslow Crosskey.

Crosskey was by all accounts an unusual, even an eccentric, man. He was, according to Harry Kalven, "the stuff from which legends are made"[19] and was perhaps not unconscious of his effect. I remember his portrait on the walls of the Yale Law Journal office—a balding head over a truculent scowl, his large heavy-set frame crammed into a small officer's chair. He obviously dominated that editorial board as he dominated the photograph. He had been older than the rest of his classmates—thirty when he entered the Yale Law School—because he had taken eight years to graduate from Yale College, interspersing his terms there with periods during which he sold aluminum siding to support his family.

At law school, Crosskey refused to keep notebooks and let it get around that he never read cases in preparation for class. When Charles Clark called on Crosskey one day to recite the facts in a case, the class dissolved in muffled sniggering which Crosskey silenced by saying "Professor Clark, if you can control your class, perhaps we could get somewhere with this case." Of course, Crosskey excelled as a law student. Decades later Robert Hutchins, Karl Llewellyn, and Roscoe Steffen were able to compete with stories chronicling Crosskey's formidable manner and abilities when he was their student.[20]

After Yale, Crosskey clerked for Chief Justice Taft and then went on to a Wall Street practice with Davis, Polk. He was immediately made personal assistant to John W. Davis, and Davis is reported to have said later that Crosskey's brain was the best piece of legal equipment he had ever encountered.[21] In 1935 Crosskey accepted an offer from the University of Chicago Law School where it was thought he might add a note of "professionalism" to a strongly theoretical faculty. The faculty was shortly disabused of any such notions when his first course, Federal Income and Estate Taxation, resolved into a study of exclusively constitutional issues. For Crosskey was one of those brilliant men who is obsessed by the conviction that life is far simpler than the nitwits running the world perceive it to be; with such iconoclasm it was idle to suppose that he would attempt anything less than a revolution in constitutional scholarship.

As his last task on Wall Street, Crosskey had drafted a lengthy memorandum on the jurisdictional reach of the then-new Securities Act. With lawyerly economy he planned to convert this into his tenure piece. The legend is that this initial search for the boundaries of the commerce power lengthened into the investigation which, sixteen years later, resulted in the two volumes we know as *Politics and the Constitution*.

Politics and the Constitution is, I think all agree, a remarkable work. Its central thesis is that the Constitution established a government fully empowered to accomplish the broad charter of the Preamble and not, as has been generally thought, a government of limited enumerated powers. The Supreme Court was to be the final authority on all matters of state and federal law, but with a sharply circumscribed role of review regarding congressional acts. The President was endowed with plenary authority to insure domestic tranquility just as Congress was empowered to pass all laws necessary and proper in its judgment for the general welfare. It was, in short, the Constitution Franklin Roosevelt would have written in 1935.

How did Crosskey reach these surprising conclusions? Let me give one example. In determining the scope of the commerce power, the Supreme Court has construed the word 'states' in the phrase from Article I

to regulate commerce with foreign nations and among the several States and with the Indian tribes to mean "territorial divisions of the country" and has thus contrived the doctrine of *interstate* commerce. Crosskey argued, with dozens of accompanying citations, that the word 'states' in the Commerce Clause was understood in 1787 to refer to the "people of the states" and that the term 'commerce' meant "all gainful activity." In Crosskey's words, the Commerce Clause was understood in the late eighteenth century as a "simple and exhaustive catalogue of all the different kinds of commerce to which the people of the United States had access: Commerce, that is, *with the people* of foreign nations, commerce *with the people* of the Indian tribes, and commerce *among the people* of the several states."[22] Therefore, Crosskey concluded, Congress was granted plenary power to regulate all gainful activity regardless of its scope or character.

Using similar methods, relying on examples of word usage drawn from eighteenth-century newspapers, pamphlets, letters, diaries, articles, and other documents, Crosskey tried to recreate the legal and linguistic context within which the Constitution was drafted. He expressed scorn for the idea that the Constitution should change through time. "Did you ever see a 'living' document?" he would ask his classes.

How could these meanings have been so utterly lost during the first decades of constitutional construction by the Supreme Court? Crosskey proposed this startling answer: James Madison, converted in old age from the nationalistic Father of the Constitution to a Jeffersonian states' rightist, had tampered with the notes he kept of the constitutional debates and had released them only when all other members of the Convention had died. This deception was advanced by the complicity of Jeffersonian justices on the Supreme Court who, from a date early in Marshall's tenure, began to systematically paint glosses on the true meaning of the constitutional text.

Similarly, the Federalist Papers, the chief guide to the meaning of the constitutional text, were dismissed by Crosskey as a mere political document, designed simply to lure ratification by the reluctant states. Its use thereafter by the Court was a disingenuous, indeed a mendacious, ploy. So it was that the true Constitution became in Crosskey's phrase the "unknown" Constitution.

What was the reaction to these charges and this wholesale

attack on constitutional argument as practiced? Initially, the reaction was very favorable. "This remarkable work sweeps away
acres of nonsense that have been written about the Constitution," wrote the eminent historian Arthur Schlesinger, Sr. "It
is, " he continued (without irony), "perhaps the most fertile
commentary on that document since the Federalist Papers."[23]
Arthur Krock reported that among Crosskey's "earnest students are members of the Supreme Court."[24] "For those
doubters who find it hard to believe in the fact of actual, intentional distortion of the Constitution," Max Rheinstein wrote,
"Mr. Crosskey produces irrefutable evidence."[25] And even Arthur Corbin, who had taught us all that the intention of the
parties was but a single element in the complex decision whether
or not to enforce a disputed contract, approved of the great
length Crosskey devoted "to the language of the time in which
the Constitution was written and first interpreted."[26]

For a year the publication of the first two volumes of *Politics
and the Constitution*—two more were projected—was the major
event in constitutional scholarship. The books were reviewed in
thirty-two law reviews and journals; the University of Chicago
Press went into a second printing. But then the pendulum began to return.

A favorable review by Malcolm Sharp in the Columbia Law
Review[27] was followed by a bewildered notice in the same journal by Irving Brant, Madison's biographer. "In spite of appall-
ing misrepresentations," Brant wrote, in a placating, if wary,
tone, "there is a vast amount of sound reasoning in Mr. Crosskey's work."[28] Next came a review by Julius Goebel, a distinguished legal historian. "Let it be said at once," Goebel began,
"that Mr. Crosskey's performance, measured by even the least
exacting of scholarly standards is . . . without merit." Allowing
that "it is of course possible that what seem to be extraordinary
perversions of fact . . . are actually the result not of design but
of mere blundering," Goebel launched a devastating thirty-page
attack on Crosskey's representation of the state of Anglo-American law in 1787—an important, indeed crucial, element in
Crosskey's rationale, since many of the terms for which he
sought definitions were legal terms sprung from legal contexts.[29] This was in March of 1954.

In June of that year two more reviews appeared in the Har-

vard Law Review, which had hitherto been silent. The first, by
Ernest Brown,[30] proceeded on several fronts. The notion that
the Crosskey Constitution could have erupted full-grown without
political development was ridiculed; contemporary letters by
Washington and Jefferson were quoted to establish the Federalist Papers as true reflections of the Convention's understanding. Singularly damning was Brown's use of Crosskey's own
method. The words 'among' and 'several' as well as others were
examined for their eighteenth-century usage and shown, pre-
dictably, to have had several meanings, some of which were
compatible with the conventional Constitution and none of
which compelled the Crosskey revision.

Most damaging, however, was the review that followed
Brown's, a lengthy analysis by Henry Hart of Crosskey's thesis
about judicial review. Professor Crosskey, Hart wrote, "[is] a
devotee of that technique of interpretation which reaches its
apogee of persuasiveness in the triumphant question, 'If that's
what they meant, why didn't they say so?' " With this remark
Hart served notice that he had no intention of adopting the
variant of historical argument Crosskey had used. The remainder of the review is revealing for the way in which Hart used a
different approach—one I have called doctrinal argument—to
attack Crosskey's thesis.

Crosskey had argued that judicial review was a right of
courts and, as such, had to be explicitly provided for, in the
same way that the President has the right to be commander-in-
chief or the Congress has the sole right to declare war. But
Hart replied that judicial review is instead a power merely incident to the judicial process, that is, to the obligation of a court
to dispose of a case according to law.[31] As such, a court's decision as to the unconstitutionality of a statute is merely a decision not to give it effect in this and in future cases; it does not
purport to control the judgment of Congress or of the President in their discharge of their own functions.[32]

Now compare this approach of Hart's—the derivation of a
general principle from the judicial process of case decision,
precedent-setting, and precedent-following—with Crosskey's
approach to the same issue.

Crosskey introduces a pamphlet circulated in Philadelphia
just as the Convention began proposing an Equalizing Court to

umpire between Congress and the States and to decide appeals brought by Congress against a state for disobedience to federal acts or by a state against Congress for passing them in the first place. Taking this function to be similar to the present-day functions of the Court, Crosskey contrasts the composition of the proposed Equalizing Court with that actually provided in Article III. "The Supreme Court is set up in so very different a way," Crosskey writes, "as, on this basis alone, to make difficult the belief that it was intended to have any such function." Similarly, Crosskey refers to the various proposals for a Council of Revision and determines that if judicial review had truly been intended, some apparatus less cumbersome than a Supreme Court functioning in a common-law mode would have been chosen.

How foreign this is to Hart's approach, which grounds judicial review precisely in the common-law method of adjudication and treats it as a necessary by-product. Indeed, in discussing this section of *Politics and the Constitution* Hart says that the principle derived from Crosskey's objections—taking, one might say, a doctrinal approach even to book reviewing—would apply as well to the review of state statutes, regarding which there is not much dispute even in Crosskey.[33]

Notice once more the difference of methods. Crosskey takes the phrase 'judicial power' and asks whether this phrase, used in its usual way in 1787, assumed the power of judicial review. This question is answered by looking at the post-Independence, pre-Convention practices in those states with limited constitutions. There being few examples of the exercise of such a power, Crosskey rests his case. But this is where Hart begins. On a different reading of the precedents Hart concludes that of the nine cases Crosskey discusses at least three are holdings squarely in support of a power that is repeatedly asserted and never, in any of the cases, flatly negatived. Read the way one might read precedent, Hart uses Crosskey's cases to buttress a conclusion that the reviewing power was present in the American legal culture of that period.

There are many examples of these differing approaches in the review. I will content myself with one more. Crosskey does provide a role for judicial review, albeit a limited one. Courts are to determine the constitutional issue for themselves, re-

gardless of congressional acts, when the matter concerns a provision in the Constitution directly addressed to the judiciary.
Article III is one of these, though there are at least two provisions within it addressed to Congress. The Eleventh Amendment is another. The First Amendment is not. And so on.

But beyond these clarities lurk considerable difficulties. The
Fourth, Fifth, Sixth, Seventh, and Eighth Amendments, Crosskey says, "taken together" are of a similar "substance" as Article
III, but they are not, by their terms, addressed to judicial competence. Indeed the prohibitions against unreasonable searches
and seizures and against the taking of private property without
just compensation would seem to be directed toward executive,
not judicial actors. If, by "substance," one means that these prohibitions are enforced by the judiciary, then the same thing
would of course be true of the First, Ninth, and Tenth Amendments, which Crosskey excludes.

After exposing other difficulties in Crosskey's prescription,
Hart delivers his final assessment of Crosskey's work. "The root
difficulty," Hart writes, "is not that [Crosskey's analysis] is vague
or hard to apply but that it is unintelligible in the profound
sense that it is incapable of explication in terms of any principles worthy of the ideals of Constitutional government."[34] As
shall be observed in a subsequent chapter, this criticism from a
doctrinal point of view amounts to a charge that Crosskey's approach will not function doctrinally, that is, will not generate
neutral, general principles for appellate application.

And this must be right, not just because confinement to a
piecemeal slotting in of chosen meanings for specific words is
likely to yield an incoherent charter, but because the very
method of growth by which principles emerge has been cut off,
stunted at the base.

After the Hart review much of the furor around Crosskey
subsided. He had promised two more volumes which would
vindicate his analyses and further substantiate Madison's per-
fidy, but advancing years and illness prevented his finishing
them. Nothing came of Max Rheinstein's claim only a year before that "Lawyers will use [Crosskey's book] in argument,
judges will have to discuss it, historians will have to test it, politicians will draw upon or inveigh against it."[35] Crosskey's book
has only been cited once in the text of an opinion for the Su-

preme Court and this for a trivial point.[36] It has, with its brilliant and eccentric author, sunk beneath the waves of our constitutional consciousness. Why did this happen?

In part it happened because the problem with which Crosskey began in 1937—the frustration of the New Deal Congress by the Court—was largely solved by the very methods which Crosskey despised and by the institution whose role he wished to limit.

Also, new problems engaged the legal culture, not least those stemming from a case—*Brown* v. *Board of Education of Topeka, Kansas*—handed down at about the same time that Henry Hart's review appeared. In *Brown,* after the Court had requested and received briefs on the question of the Original Understanding of the Fourteenth Amendment, it devoted only a single paragraph to the subject in its opinion. The historical arguments were, Chief Justice Warren wrote, "at best, . . . inconclusive."[37] Crosskey's enterprise, the escape from inconclusiveness, was doomed. He died without fanfare in 1962 in Connecticut, not far from the place of his early triumphs.

But the class of argument—a variant of that I have called the historical approach[38]—lives on, promising a renunciation of generations of wrong living and a return to simple rules straightforwardly applied. Thus it was with recognition that I read the dustjacket copy of Raoul Berger's *Impeachment,*

> An admirable and powerful book,
> [It is] valuable and illuminating.

signed by the eminent historian Arthur Schlesinger, Jr.

If Crosskey's program and the work of his successors ultimately fails, it will be because it has to fail. The variant of historical argument that seeks to evade the asymmetricality and tentativeness of conventional historical argument—its ability to negative a particular interpretation but not to establish a single meaning conclusively—also forsakes its power. Historical arguments can be most powerful when severed from the text, rather than when married to it as Crosskey urged.

This can be seen in the singular and interesting history of the Eleventh Amendment. That text reads,

> The judicial power of the United States shall not be construed
> to extend to any suit in law or equity, commenced or presented

against one of the United States by Citizens of another state, or
by Citizens of any Foreign State.

The history of the adoption of the amendment is well known.
In 1793 the Supreme Court, reading Article III's text literally,
had accepted original jurisdiction in *Chisholm* v. *Georgia*, a suit
brought against Georgia by two South Carolina citizens to collect a debt.[39] The resultant fury in the states, who feared suits
based on Revolutionary War debts and expropriations, was reflected in a bill passed by the Georgia House of Representatives
providing that "any Federal Marshal, or any other person"
seeking to execute the mandate in *Chisholm* would be "guilty of
felony, and shall suffer death, without benefit of clergy, by being
hanged."[40]

This outraged reaction was not without some justification.
Campaigners for the Constitution's ratification, including Hamilton, had given assurances that sovereign immunity would not
be abrogated by Article III.[41] The Court, however, had limited
its view to the text alone, a text silent on the matter of immunity.

At the first meeting of Congress following the decision, the
Eleventh Amendment was proposed by an overwhelming vote
of both houses and passed, in Justice Frankfurter's phrase, with
"vehement speed."[42] It was framed precisely to cover the situation in *Chisholm*, in which a citizen of one state had brought
an action against a state other than his own in federal court.

Then in 1890 a citizen of Louisiana sued that state in an
attempt to recover the interest on state bonds which had been
repudiated by a subsequent state constitution.[43] Since the plaintiff was suing his own state he alleged, as Justice Bradley put
it, that he was "not embarrassed by the obstacle of the Eleventh
Amendment, inasmuch [as it] only prohibits suits against a state
which are brought by the citizens of another state."[44] "It is true,"
Bradley conceded, that "the amendment does so read."[45] But
the amendment reflects a larger act, he wrote, namely the rejection by the People of the Supreme Court's decision in *Chisholm*. At this point Bradley might simply have stopped and said
that, with *Chisholm* out of the way, the original Constitution
standing alone did not authorize such a suit in the federal

courts. But he went further. The People, Bradley reasoned, in rejecting the *Chisholm* majority, were agreeing with the principles of the dissent in that case; therefore in ratifying the Eleventh Amendment's narrow text the People in fact were adopting much broader views. Can one imagine, Bradley asked in a variation of the rhetorical question posed by the *Chisholm* dissent, what would have been the outcry if the Eleventh Amendment had qualified its prohibition by adding that the United States judicial power may nevertheless extend to suits against states brought by their own citizens?[46] And so Bradley construed—no, *construed* is the wrong word—*reconstructed* the Eleventh Amendment to govern suits by a corporation created by Act of Congress, suits by persons of whatever citizenship in admiralty, and suits by a foreign state. In other words the Eleventh Amendment governed all those situations for which the draftsmen of the Amendment were too shortsighted to provide. Ever since Bradley's decision in *Hans* v. *Louisiana,* the Court has not hesitated when confronting similar situations to read the Eleventh Amendment in precisely this way.[47]

This example shows yet another form of historical argument. It avoids the pitfalls of the asymmetrical phenomenon I have noted previously because it doesn't attempt to establish a meaning for a particular phrase. It is forceful yet fraught with difficulty because it requires us to create the concept from which a particular conception is drawn when the Constitution has given us only the latter. Professor Dworkin,[48] like Bickel before him,[49] has observed that the Constitution often provides general *concepts*—of equal protection or due process, for example—to which each generation must affix particular *conceptions*—for example, promoting integration in the public schools or providing competent counsel to indigents. This illuminating turn of phrase is, however, the opposite face of the dark, largely featureless side of Bradley's variant of historical argument. It is a variant that risks an easy elision into a sort of imaginative legal anthropology. There is, for example, Justice Rehnquist's sarcastic charge that "if those responsible for [the Bill of Rights and the Fourteenth Amendment] could have lived to know that their efforts had enshrined in the Constitution the right of commercial vendors of contraceptives to peddle them to unmarried minors through such means as window displays and vending machines located in the men's rooms of truck stops . . . it is not difficult to imagine their reaction"[50] when actually, it *is* difficult to imagine their reactions, much more difficult than to imagine their reactions to events contemporary with their own lives.

Such imagining is also historical argument, in another of its variations. This variation depends also on assumptions about intention, but in a peculiar way: that the whole life of an eighteenth-century agrarian society should govern us since the Founders were of that special day and that we, from our very different lives, can know what those people would have thought in situations within which they would have been, of course, very different people. It is easy to see that such arguments are better for dissent than for the Court because, as will be argued in Books II and III, they express a particular moral point and are therefore more effective as rhetoric than as decision procedure.

CHAPTER 3

TEXTUAL ARGUMENT

In contrast to, but often confused with, historical arguments are textual arguments. Justice Joseph Story shows the distinction ably.

> Mr. Jefferson has laid down [what he deems a perfect canon] for the interpretation of the Constitution. . . . On every question of construction [we should] carry ourselves back to the time, when the Constitution was adopted, recollect the spirit manifested in the debates and instead of trying what meaning may be squeezed out of the text, or invented against it, conform to the probable one, in which it was passed . . .
>
> Now who does not see the utter . . . incoherence of this canon. . . . Is the sense of the Constitution to be ascertained . . . by conjecture from scattered documents, from private papers, from the table talk of some statesmen . . . ? It is obvious, that there can be no security to the people in any constitution of government if they are not to judge of it by the fair meaning of the words of the text.[1]

Why is this? Why should we be limited to recourse to a text when collateral sources may identify the intention of the Framers or ratifiers? We should be limited because, as Story put it, "Constitutions . . . are instruments of a practical nature, founded on the common business of human life, adapted to

25

common wants, designed for common use, and fitted for common understanding. The people make them; the people adopt them; the people must be supposed to read them . . . ; and cannot be presumed to admit in them any recondite meaning . . ."[2]

Historical arguments draw legitimacy from the social contract negotiated from an original position, textual arguments are sometimes mistaken for similar contractual arguments with the parol evidence rule strictly applied. Instead, textual arguments rest on a sort of ongoing social contract, whose terms are given their contemporary meanings continually reaffirmed by the refusal of the People to amend the instrument.

Story believed that this obligation to apply contemporary meanings constrained judges: one cannot appeal to superior learning to establish the meaning of a common phrase. To the textualist, an eighteenth-century dictionary is as illegitimate as a twentieth-century Brookings pamphlet. Moreover, as we have observed, historical arguments can often be found to support, if not establish, a great variety of positions. But a consensus is usually available as to the common use of a particular term in a particular context.

In my lifetime the principal exponent of this view was Hugo Black, long the Senior Associate Justice of the Supreme Court. Justice Black was of a type not infrequently seen in American law. Hostile to academics and corporate businessmen at the same time, he regarded himself as a self-made man. He read the classics—by which he meant the Greek historians and Shakespeare—and, again true to type, doted on Jefferson and Madison. Largely self-educated, he relished telling the story of how he had pinned an opposing member of the Senate with a passage quoted from the "Fallacies of the Anti-Reformers," Volume 27 of the Harvard Classics.[3] Like other men the South has produced, he appears to have held intensely a Hobbesian view of the conflicts in life and, at the same time, passionately idealized the common man.

Yet Hugo Black was not merely a type, for in addition to his manic self-improvement and invincible provincialism, Black had one thing none of his colleagues had: Black had genius, a grasp of the effect of simplicity in the law and of the need for it and an understanding of how to make his contemporaries feel that need. It was this understanding that animated and gave to textualism a power that it had not had since the Marshall Court. It was Hugo Black who led constitutional argument out of the wilderness of legal realism. He accomplished this by his remarkable use of textual argument and his creation of a constitutional grammar for this use.

That he was caustic in his distaste for self-consciousness and introspection, indeed modernism in any form, aided him in his course because, as we shall see, it was pragmatism applied to law that produced the Constitutional crisis in 1937. It was this crisis that put Hugo Black on the Court and thereby made possible its own resolution.

It is generally held that the crisis of legitimacy for judicial review occurred in the years 1932–37 when the United States Supreme Court, in a number of reactionary 5–4 decisions, struck down important parts of the New Deal program as unconstitutional. In response to this frustration of national purpose, Crosskey began *Politics and the Constitution* and President Franklin Roosevelt proposed the Court Plan, which would have added new members to the Supreme Court and, presumably, changed the outcome of future cases. The events of that spring and summer are familiar, culminating in the dramatic shift by Justice Roberts in *NLRB* v. *Jones-Laughlin* that began the series of validations of New Deal legislation. The death of the Court Plan followed quickly, having served, many observed, its purpose. Regarding the Court crisis of 1937, Thomas Reed Powell quoted Fielding: "He would have ravished her if she had not, by a timely compliance, prevented him."[4]

Actually the crisis had a different form from that usually recognized. The real constitutional crisis of the 1930s was begun by Holmes, not by Sutherland. It consisted principally in the tension between legal realism, which held that there were no discernible, non-formal legal rules of any significance, and the American faith in law, which depended on political conflict being transmuted into legal conflict when issues of constitutional importance were involved.

The widely perceived constitutional crisis, heightened by the cynicism and boldness of the President's proposed remedy, was largely a crisis in perception. The Court's restriction on President Roosevelt's programs was scarcely total. The Tennessee Valley Authority (TVA) was upheld, as were the President's monetary and banking policies; most of the programs of the 100 days were implemented without obstacle. Few persons now think that the incoherent National Recovery Act (NRA) would have been a success, and indeed its provisions had been hurriedly drafted to coopt then-Senator Black's more radical thirty-hour work week bill. As for the drama of the Court Plan, on the very day that the Judiciary Committee reported out the Court Plan with a negative vote, Justice Van Devanter retired, giving President Roosevelt the decisive appointment he needed. While President Roosevelt insisted on pressing the Court Plan even after *Jones-Laughlin*, it met a ritualistic end in the Senate, recommitted shortly after the death of the majority leader who had been promised the next seat on the Supreme Court as a reward for his sponsorship of the Plan. Few people think the Senate would have gone along with the Plan in any case.

The real constitutional crisis arose neither from a judicial tourniquet on effective progressive legislation nor from the institutional confrontation that time would assuredly have rendered moot. Instead, the critical pathology must be understood as developing in the disillusion that came with the realization that law was made by the Court. "Now with the shift by Roberts [in *Jones-Laughlin*]," Professor Frankfurter had written President Roosevelt, "even a blind man ought to see that the Court is in politics and understands how the Constitution is being judicially construed."[5]

Senator Black had done his share to precipitate this crisis. He had insisted on voting against confirming either of President Hoover's nominations to the Court on the ground that their background had so shaped their views that they would necessarily act in political opposition to the policies Black favored. The Court Plan itself, a naked exercise of political power, hardly reflected any illusions as to the provenance of Court decisions. Only twenty Senators opposed the motion to recommit the Court plan, but one was Senator Black. In 1935 Black had introduced a bill to eliminate circuit court consideration of statutes challenged on constitutional grounds. He had begun campaigning for the direct election of federal judges.

With what can now be seen as intricate if bitter irony, President Roosevelt chose Black for the Court as a way of punishing both the institutions that had frustrated his plans. He chose the most radical, most despised member of the Senate, knowing that the Senate could not refuse to ratify the nomination of one of its own. Of the various men in the Senate, only Minton of Indiana had been more vitriolic and personal in his attacks on the Court. Indeed, when the president had approached Minton as a potential nominee he had demurred, saying that his remarks would be an insuperable barrier to working with the current justices. Concealing his membership in the Ku Klux Klan and allowing his one friend in the Senate, Borah, to humiliate himself by permitting him to believe that no such membership had occurred, Black joined the Court in 1937. He thus became the holder of the seat that was to have gone to the sponsor of the Court packing plan.

If the real crisis in constitutional law had been the frustration of New Deal legislation by the Supreme Court, then Justice Roberts's changeover to join the liberal four that made them a majority and the concomitant shelving by the Senate of the Court bill would have ended the crisis. Black's appointment would have merely provided the coda.

It was, in fact, only the opening phrase. We may appreciate this now by recalling the theoretical background against which Black's appointment was made. A few months before, Roberts had spoken for the old, apolitical forms. It was Roberts who had claimed to be a mere conduit for constitutional rules when, in striking down the Agricultural Adjustment Act, an important piece of New Deal legislation, he had written

> The judicial branch of the government has only one duty,— to lay the article of the Constitution which is involved beside the statute which is challenged and to decide whether the latter squares with the former.[6]

Ridiculous, said Thomas Reed Powell, in his Charpentier Lectures at Columbia, and he was indiscreetly quoted in a college newspaper as saying that such men were either stupid or crooked.

> It's the judicial heads that count. For years now, the newspa-
> pers have been giving the line-ups of Justices as they give the
> line-ups of legislators. Yet in spite of all this there is frequent
> reiteration of the myths that somehow the Justices are the mere
> mouthpieces of an oracle not themselves. . . . [T]he plain man
> can dispel the fancies with his simple knowledge of what ac-
> tually happens.[7]

This was the voice of the new understanding, the shattering of the old forms by a disciple of Holmes.

At the time, Black's appointment must have seemed a final shot in the victory over the old forms, a victory in which even Roberts appeared forced to collaborate. But this was not so. To see how far this was not so, we have only to read Black's own Charpentier Lectures given twenty-three years after Powell's. In these Black urged a theory of textualism which forbade the use of prudential or political judgment by judges and required that they give absolute affect to the words of the Constitution. He spoke, that is, for the apostolical, dutiful measurer rather as Roberts had. And this time it was Black whom Powell felt compelled to rebuke; indeed we can see in Powell's criticism how fundamentally anti-realist this approach is. Powell wrote,

> We may invoke some twentieth-century official remarks from
> some Supreme Court justices who seek to impress upon us in
> effect that it is not they that speak but the Constitution that
> speaketh in them. Somehow this reminds me of the biographer
> who wrote of Gladstone that his conscience was not his guide
> but only his accomplice. . . . [S]uch judicial denials of personal
> power [make] me doubt either the capacity or the candor of
> the men who [make] them.[8]

Black later referred to this passage when he said, "Some people have said that I'm either a knave or a fool" for defending tex-tual absolutes, echoing Powell's original canard against Roberts.

What could have happened in the intervening years to ar-ray Black against Powell and the realists in this way? It is sup-posed that Roberts, the naive formalist, saved the country from crisis by taking the expedient, realist's route and switching his vote. Does this mean that Black was simply an apostate, a throwback to the disingenuousness with which Powell, and Black himself, had earlier taxed Roberts but of which even he had freed himself? I think not—if the true constitutional crisis is perceived. In that crisis, Powell, Roberts, and Black—the academy, the Court, and the politician—each had a hand. But only Black devised a theoretically satisfactory means of averting constitutional breakdown. This is how he did it.

Black developed the textual argument, and a set of supporting doctrines, with a simplicity and power they had never before had. His view was that the Constitution has a certain number of significant prohibitions which, when phrased without qualification, bar any extension of governmental power into the prohibited areas. A judge need not decide whether such an extension is wise or prudent; and as such a non-decider, he is a mere conduit for the prohibitions of the Constitution. He is not, as the realists charged, enforcing his own views; indeed he may sometimes be in the exquisite position of affirming legislation hostile to his own views. Moreover, he is doing so on a basis readily apprehendable by the people at large, namely, giving the common-language meanings to constitutional provisions. This allowed Black to restore to judicial review the popular perception of legitimacy which the New Deal crisis had jeopardized.

Here is a scene of Black. In the following passage we will see Black espousing the approach of textual argument, as well as expressing some corollaries that follow from it and aid its implementation in constitutional law. CBS News is the interlocutor (the last time a sitting Justice had appeared in his study for a prime-time broadcast had been the ninetieth birthday radio greetings by Holmes in 1931). The CBS reporter asks what reason Black has for arguing that there are absolute prohibitions on government. Black replies,

> Well, I'll read you the part of the first amendment that caused me to say there are absolutes in our Bill of Rights. I did not say that our entire Bill of Rights is an absolute. I said there are absolutes in our Bill of Rights. Now, if a man were to say this to me out on the street, "Congress shall make no law respecting an establishment of religion"—that's the first amendment—I

would think: Amen, Congress should pass no law. Unless they
just didn't know the meaning of words. That's what they mean
to me. Certainly they mean that literally.[9]

Notice that the reply to the question "What is your reason?" is
a textual appeal. And the interpretation of the text is the one
given by the man in the street.

A little later in the same answer Black contrasts textual argument with prudential argument in the context of the Fifth
Amendment. Justice Frankfurter had offered as a reason for
barring coerced confessions from admission at trial that his
construction of the due process clause of the Fourteenth
Amendment barred all fundamentally unfair procedures. Black,
by contrast, developed the doctrine of the "incorporation" of
the Bill of Rights into the Fourteenth Amendment, and thereby
was able to apply the specific prohibitions of the Fifth Amendment to the situation of coerced confessions in state trials. The
doctrine of incorporation is crucial to the textual approach, since
the language of the Fourteenth Amendment by itself is too
sparse to provide the common phrases on which the textualist
relies. Indeed, one may say that the development of this doctrine was driven by the theoretical requirements of textual argument. Here is Black, defending this incorporation; we may
observe his larger motives.

> I subscribe to the doctrine that the Fifth Amendment, which
> says that no person shall be compelled to be a witness against
> himself. [I apply the Fifth Amendment's self-incrimination clause
> directly; I do not need to give additional meaning to its due
> process clause, nor the similar clause in the Fourteenth Amend-
> ment applying against the states.] And the theory—opposite to
> mine—has been the fact that that's bad, and it's unlawful, the
> Constitution prevents it, is not because it's in the Fifth Amend-
> ment. Well, if it's not because it's in the Fifth Amendment, where
> does it come from? Is it the mind of the judge? In other words,
> is he going to fix limits to the Constitution? I don't see that. I
> don't think I have that power. And I wouldn't do it. . . . I've
> sustained laws as constitutional that I was bitterly against—didn't
> agree with them.[10]

By this method Black is able to avoid the realist dilemma,
which is that the mere recognition that legal rules are simply

the product of judge making provides no guide to the judge himself. Because realism doesn't distinguish between good law and rightly decided cases, on the one hand, and wrong cases on the other, it provides no rule for decision. It can, therefore, provide no basis for legitimacy. By his textual method, Black sought to resolve the constitutional crisis of the 1930s and restore legitimacy to judicial review.

One corollary of the textual approach is a disregard of precedent. Thus, Black says,

> I think it's my obligation to take this Constitution—I don't care what anybody else has decided—that's immaterial. Our system of government puts different people on the Court. People with different views. I think it's their business to try to read these words, silly as it may sound, to some people. Some people have said that I'm either a knave or a fool, because if I was not dishonest I couldn't say that there are absolutes. Well, I just don't agree with them. I think I can—and do.[11]

After all, not only can a Justice today give as valid a reading to a text as one twenty years ago, but today's reading is perhaps a better one in the sense that it better comports with the construed term as commonly understood today. It was at this point, as if to dramatize the textual perspective, that Justice Black produced from his coat pocket a small copy of the Constitution.

The reporter asks,

> Mr. Justice, I would think you'd know the Constitution by heart at this time. Why do you always carry that little book of the Constitution?

Black replies:

> Because I don't know it by heart. I can't—my memory is not that good. When I say something about it, I want to quote it precisely. And so I usually carry it in my pocket.[12]

And, of course, in answer to the question,

> Could a non-lawyer possibly be a judge of the Supreme Court of the United States?

Justice Black replies,

> I don't see why he shouldn't. Not at all.[13]

Then the reporter asks,

Now, suppose that you were to find in some case which you were considering, that there was a difference between what you thought was fair, what the heart says, and what the law provides. How would you decide?[14]

And Black replies with the textual approach:

I would follow what I thought the law provided. Undoubtedly. Just there. That's it. You see, you have laws written out. That's the object in law, to have it written out. Our Constitution—I would follow exactly what I thought it said at the time.[15]

There is no mention, you observe, of collateral sources to interpret the text. There are no discussions of the controversies which swirled around particular passages at the time of their adoption or of the inconvenient fact that racial segregation and school prayer were ongoing and unchallenged at the time when the amendments by which they are challenged were adopted.

Of course, Justice Black did not rely on textual arguments to the exclusion of all others; his *Adamson* dissent,[16] in which he argues that the Fourteenth Amendment extends the Bill of Rights to the states, is well known. But ask yourself this question: What made the legal conclusion in *Adamson,* arrived at by an historical route generally thought to have been discredited by Professor Fairman,[17] so powerful and irresistible that by 1969, although no historian had yet come forward to defend this position and many had announced it untenable, the Court had adopted it in almost every area of civil rights and civil liberties?[18] The answer lies in the overwhelming simplicity of Black's approach and the illusion this simplicity preserves that judges take their charter from a text and do not have to rely on themselves to make up a rule. The answer is not that liberal, nationalistic presidents appointed Justices more willing to intervene in state matters. There are a number of ways such intervention might have been accomplished, and one way—a due process rationale—is far more inviting to interventionists and seems to have some historical support, to say nothing of the available precedents and the aura of Cardozo's prose cadenzas. Instead the Court chose a different route, pulled by the theoretical requirements of textual argument.

Indeed, it was the textual approach in the construction of another clause of the Fourteenth Amendment that ultimately resolved the constitutional crisis begun in the 1930s in a case twenty years later. That case was *Brown* v. *Board of Education of Topeka* and the question answered was not whether an application of *Plessy* v. *Ferguson* might be used to upset the system of educational segregation, a doctrinal approach urged by some members of the Court and the approach used in *Sweatt* v. *Painter* to integrate the classrooms of the University of Texas Law School. [In its simplest terms, *Plessy* had established that a state might lawfully provide separate facilities for blacks and whites so long as the facilities were roughly equivalent; in *Sweatt* the Court found a separate law school by virtue of its separation unequal and hence a violation of the Constitution.] Nor did the Court linger over the question of whether the original understanding of the Fourteenth Amendment required integration or whether it did not, at least in the understanding of its contemporaries, tolerate state-enforced segregation. Instead the Court asked whether the system of segregation existed to benefit blacks or to harm them. This question required only that the Court, and the nation, understand what is meant by the words 'equal protection,' and know that the Southern states were not protecting their black citizens from and were indeed helping to inflict on them a caste system that would have been intolerable and unlawful if applied to whites.

Listen, then, to the CBS interview again and notice how the question put to Justice Black is phrased in terms of the realist crisis.

There was one historic shift by the Court that seems to relate to this point. In 1898, in *Plessy* v. *Ferguson*, the Court held that separate could be equal in interstate transportation. Yet in 1954, in *Brown* v. *School Board*, it held that separate could not be equal in the school education. Now, the law hadn't changed. What appears to have changed is the judges' opinion of how the law should be interpreted. In other words, did they not relate to the temper of the times?

Justice Black:

The judges had changed. That's right. The judges had changed. As far as my opinion is concerned—my agreement to that case; I would have agreed to it in *Plessy* v. *Ferguson*, I would have agreed to it at the time those amendments were first adopted. My view was, we had a simple question: Does that give to the colored people of the nation equal protection of the law? Now, that means were they being treated any better [or worse] because you gave them different schools, and separated them? And if so, was it as those civil war amendments provided, given on account of race? Well, I've lived in the South all my life, practically, until I came up here. And of course, I knew what it was.[19]

Thus one power of the textual argument is that it provides a valve through which contemporary values can be intermingled with the Constitution. The contemporary understanding of the word 'commerce,' for example, is far more comprehensive and hence a more promising source of national power than the understanding of a century ago, reflecting our more interconnected economy as well as our awareness of that interconnectedness. At the same time, we need only to recall Justice Black's consistent dissents from the Court's efforts to include wiretaps within the Fourth Amendment[20] to observe the stultifying rigidity of textual arguments.

Similarly, some words no longer convey any very potent meaning. The shocking example of *Nixon* v. *General Services Administration*[21] was possible, I suspect, simply because the word 'attaint' no longer has much meaning for us. In that case, a congressional statute that provided for the seizure of President Nixon's papers, while exempting both those of his predecessors *and* his successors, was held to create a "legitimate class of one" and was not therefore a bill of attainder.

In a related way, textual arguments are inappropriate vehicles for accommodating arguments in areas where conceptual change has outpaced absorption into everyday language. Economics is one such area. It was, one should note, T. R. Powell, who despised textualism, who asked Justice Holmes, "What would you do if just once counsel said, 'I don't know whether this statute poses a direct or an indirect burden on commerce, and the history of its adoption is unclear, but let me argue the

efficiencies, the sense of the matter.' " And Holmes replied, "By
God, I wish they would!"[22] Textual arguments also do not allow the mid-course corrections that are the indispensable navi-
gational devices of common law development; language simply
does not change that quickly.

Nor is language use, by itself, a guide. It is thrilling to see
Justice Black taking a swing at the Gordian Knot of economic
due process by suggesting that corporations are not "persons"
within the Fourteenth Amendment.[23] Certainly, the man in the
street would be inclined to agree. But would a lawyer, accustomed to the distinction between natural and nonnatural persons, agree? And if a lawyer would not, why wouldn't he? Isn't
it because the uses to which lawyers have put the word "person" include purposes for which they wish to treat corporations
as responsible entities with all the liability and proprietary characteristics of natural persons? And if this is so, it surely represents a choice about how to use the law, a choice from which
the meaning of the word follows, not one the meaning antici-
pates. It was no idle sneer when in the mid-forties T. R. Powell
said that Justice Black "is said to write his opinions for the intelligent layman."[24] This was the fundamental criticism leveled
by the realists: words, like rules, can't lead to a decision by those
who are themselves required to give content to the words.

There are, of course, other kinds of textual argument. When
a Supreme Court Justice, trying to embarrass those who urge
that capital punishment is unconstitutional by virtue of the
Fourteenth Amendment,[25] refers to the fact that the amendment's text explicitly qualifies the circumstances under which
life may be taken or when a similar argument claims that § 1
of the Fourteenth Amendment could not have been meant to
bar the disenfranchisement of felons since § 2 expressly refers
to disenfranchisement,[26] these arguments are often taken as
historical arguments, indicating what the Framers of the
amendment had in mind. They are historical arguments, but
they rely on a textual approach, as was conceded in the case
from which I drew the last example. Rejecting the offer of a
conventional historical argument, the Court wrote that § 2 of
the Fourteenth Amendment "is as much a part of the [Consti-
tution] as any of the other sections, and how it became a part

of the [Constitution] is less important than what it says and what
it means."[27]

I say this argument is mainly textual because its force derives from the reaction against the inconsistency that would result if the plain words of some portion of text—even one not
devoted to the particular problem—were ignored and the Court
sanctioned an interpretation that was incompatible with the
words of the text.

In this case we see the watermark of textual arguments—
their ability to make opponents squirm, the aura of facticity
they shed on those who oppose them. And we see also something of their limitation. Every word in the Constitution is not
equally significant, and some of its most explicit texts are also
its most trivial. More important, in a Constitution of limited
powers what is *not* expressed must also be interpreted.

CHAPTER 4

DOCTRINAL ARGUMENT

Did the threat of the Court Packing Plan, following Franklin Roosevelt's overwhelming victory in the 1936 election, cause Owen Roberts to abandon the Court's conservative bloc and vote to uphold New Deal statutes and social welfare legislation in the states? Was his, in T. R. Powell's cruel phrase, "the switch in time that saved nine"?

Roberts was greatly stung by Powell's accusation. The substance of the charge is this: Roberts joined the five-man majority in the *Tipaldo*[1] case which reaffirmed the holding in *Adkins*,[2] one of the old Court's most retrograde decisions, and thereby struck down New York's minimum wage law in June 1936. Chief Justice Hughes and Justices Brandeis, Stone, and Cardozo dissented. Then in March 1937, Justice Roberts changed sides in *West Coast Hotel Co.* v. *Parrish*.[3] His vote gave the *Tipaldo* dissenters a new majority which flatly overruled *Adkins* and sustained minimum wage legislation for the first time.

Roberts was a large, handsome man of genuine modesty. On leaving the bench, he wrote, "I have no illusions about my judicial career. But one can only do what one can. Who am I to revile the good God that he did not make me a . . . Holmes, a Brandeis or a Cardozo?"[4] But he was deeply hurt by the accepted gossip that he had switched sides in response to Roose-

velt's threats and successes and prepared a memorandum for
Felix Frankfurter, doubtless intending that it be published at
his death (as it was), in which he endeavored to exculpate himself. First, Roberts said that he had been willing to overrule
Adkins in *Tipaldo,* but because counsel for New York had merely
tried to distinguish *Adkins* Roberts had decided simply to concur in an opinion that said no more than that *Adkins* controlled;
then, when Justice Butler's draft reaffirmed the *Adkins* principle, Roberts simply neglected to file a special concurrence.

Second, Roberts stated that when the *Parrish* case arose, he
had voted for probable jurisdiction because there *Adkins* was
"definitely assailed and the Court was [being] asked to recon-
sider or overrule it." This, he recalled, was a vote against the
remaining members of the *Tipaldo* majority who voted to dismiss the appeal. This vote, plus the fact that Stone's illness delayed an opinion until after the election, made it evident that,
in Roberts's words, "no action taken by the President had any
causal relation to any action in the *Parrish* case."[5]

But since the Washington Supreme Court had sustained the
minimum wage statute, Roberts's vote to note probable jurisdiction would appear to have an opposite import to the one he
remembered. While it is true that the conference vote on the
merits of the case in December did antedate Roosevelt's sub-
mission of the Court Plan to Congress, the vote followed by a
month and a half the election and the President's public declaration that *Tipaldo* was "the final irritant."[6] Even to a sympathetic reader, Roberts's memorandum is inconclusive.

But the important point for us is: Why did Roberts care one
way or the other? The answer is that Roberts was committed to
the type of constitutional argument that I have called doctrinal
argument, and a judge devoted to applying law derived from
those principles which precedent develops is certain to feel most
keenly any charge of expediency.

This commitment to doctrinal argument and the difference
in the two men's approaches are made clear by Roberts's dispute with Black in *Smith* v. *Allwright.*[7] Responding to Black's
suggestion in *Smith* that *Grovey* v. *Townsend*[8] need not be followed since it had been overruled *sub silentio* by the cloudy
opinion in *United States* v. *Classic,*[9] Roberts's dissent charged that

this was not the manly and frank way to do things. He likened Supreme Court decisions of this kind to "a restricted railroad ticket, good for this day and train only."[10] This statement is said to have outraged Black's supporters, who considered it hypocrisy coming from Roberts, the man who had so recently rejected recent precedent to such profound effect. Both of these reactions betray misunderstandings of the constitutional approaches of the two men.

Black's variant of textual argument gives no status to precedent, since one justice can read the words of the Constitution as well as his predecessor, or any number of them for that matter. Roberts's doctrinal argument, however, is almost wholly based on precedent and is derived from the doctrines that have accreted around various constitutional provisions. This attachment to doctrinal argument makes plausible Roberts's otherwise absurd refusal to vote to overrule *Adkins* despite his later protest that he would have done so had the question been properly presented. It explains the depth of his reaction to the widely held view that he had switched his vote for prudential reasons. This is why Roberts was enraged by the cavalier treatment given precedent and at the same time so stung that he should be accused, or even praised in some quarters, for the same thing. There is an ethical aspect to Justice Roberts's aesthetic jurisprudential convictions.

In the Anglo-American tradition this ethic is subsumed in the phrase "the rule of law." It is addressed principally to judges and depends on at least two clear distinctions. First, legislative policy making must be distinguished from judicial rule applying. (This distinction may be somewhat easier to maintain in a system which doesn't allow its courts to overturn legislative acts.) Second, judicial rule applying must be a reasoned process of deriving the appropriate rules and following them in deciding any practical controversy between adverse parties without regard to any fact not relevant to the rules, such as the status or ultimate purposes of the parties.

The aesthetic, when applied to courts functioning in constitutional decisionmaking, I will call the *doctrinal* approach. One of the by-products of this approach is that scholars operating according to its paradigms tend to focus on the distinctive characteristics of common law courts concluding that only doctrinal arguments are legitimate. This approach reflects not simply the rule of law, but the rule of reasoned, appellate-produced, written-opinion-governed law.

The doctrinal approach determines a view of legitimacy to which Henry Hart and Albert Sacks are committed in their influential work, *The Legal Process.* They have stated their judgment

> that decisions which are the duly arrived-at-result of duly established procedures ought to be accepted as binding upon the whole society unless and until they are duly changed.[11]

And what is "due" is the process of reasoning from general principles:

> [A]djudication is meaningless unless the decision is reached by some rational process . . . [and] if a decision is to be rational it must be based upon some rule, principle or standard.[12]

Roberts's switch for political reasons would have violated the canons of doctrinal argument. It would have been motivated by policy considerations whose outcome was determined by a political assessment; it would not have been based on neutral principles of general application to a legal, rather than political, context. But where do these general principles come from? The answer to this question had determined the unique character of doctrinal argument in our day, for the legal realists had erased the background of assumptions that was supposed to yield such principles by showing that general principles could not be satisfactorily derived simply by the use of *stare decisis* and that substantive law was, if it was to be rational, necessarily purposive and selected, rather than derived. Doctrinal argument as we know it today seeks to preserve the aesthetic of the rule of law in the new context created by realism. The late Professor Hart was its chief theoretician, and his great works have dominated the discussion of constitutional law for the last quarter century.

Hart's answer to the realist question and his reformulation of doctrinal argument have changed the matrix from the application of precedential, substantive rules to the application of rules of precedential process. It's not *what* judges do, Hart told us, it's *how* they do it. Granting that substantive fairness is a matter of ideology, the doctrinal approach holds that fairness will result, regardless or even in spite of the judges' biases, if methods of judging which all concede to be fair are followed scrupulously. These methods include adherence to traditional standards of dispassion and disinterest,[13] the elaboration of convincing reasons for deciding one way or the other, the mutual opportunity for persuasion. For substantive rules to achieve the same status as controlling precedent they must be similarly neutral with respect to the parties and general rather than specific in their application to the cases. Thus judicial rules are distinguished from the unprincipled *ad hoc* acts of the legislature that need not give reasons for its decisions, may legislate for one situation only, is not confined to a factual record, and so forth.

Paradoxically, doctrinal argument in Constitutional law can be distinguished from textual argument in two ways with respect to generality: on the one hand, the doctrine applied is likely to be more general than the textual provision applied, and on the other hand the doctrine will be more specific because it is the mere outline of a single puzzle part of the provision's application. Thus, for example, the doctrinal argument that recent Commerce Clause precedent governs a particular case and must therefore be distinguished, applied, or overruled is broader than the commerce clause itself since the principle of *stare decisis* is more general; at the same time, it is narrower since the doctrine of the earlier decision—say the distinction between direct and indirect burdens on commerce—is more specific than the text of the clause.

The ideology of doctrinal argument in Constitutional law finds fullest expression in Hart and Wechsler's *Federal Courts and the Federal System,* the most influential casebook in Constitutional law. Naturally enough, the book focuses on the methods by which state and federal courts decide who will decide, how decision is to be reached, what authority it will have, etc. This extraordinary work is perhaps the most influential casebook ever written. It is the book most frequently cited by the Supreme Court both generally and in constitutional opinions.[14]

Yet contemporaneous with the book's astonishing success, the Supreme Court has moved farther and farther away from the principal premise of doctrinal argument and of the Hart and Wechsler casebook: the notion that the judicial function with respect to the Constitution is essentially a common law function, arising from the court's common law process respecting litigants. The various process doctrines that flow from this conception of the Court's role—justiciability, mootness, meticulous attention to *stare decisis*—have been less observed in the Court's work. This drift away from doctrine has been the cause of frequent, by now almost customary, attacks on the Court by commentators. Hart's own Supreme Court Foreword in 1959 in the Harvard Law Review provided the model for these assaults.

Hart's essay, "The Time Chart of the Justices,"[15] is divided into two sections. The first section is a sort of armchair accounting of the hours available to the justices for discussion and opinion writing in which Hart counts up the numbers of cert. petitions and dissents and holidays and so on. He arrives at a hypothetical allocation of the 1,532 hours in each Justice's working year (for example, 372 hours are devoted to "collective deliberation") and concludes that the justices are much overworked. What is the point of this odd exercise? It is to excuse the justices from the second portion of the essay, which is a savage attack on the intellectual and moral quality of their opinions. These opinions, Hart writes, "lack the underpinning of principle . . . necessary to . . . exemplify . . . the rule of law. . . . Only opinions which are grounded in reason" can be applied by lower courts. Furthermore, only such opinions will win popular acceptance. He reminds us that the Court

> does not in the end have the power either in theory or in practice to ram its own personal preferences down other people's throats. Thus, the Court is predestined in the long run not only by the thrilling tradition of Anglo-American law but also by the hard facts of its position in the structure of American institutions to be a voice of reason, charged with the creative function of discerning afresh and of articulating and developing impersonal and durable principles of constitutional law. . . .[16]

This is a powerful exposition of the doctrinal position. Let us see how it operates in one class of cases about which Hart is particularly displeased, the Federal Employers Liability Act (FELA) appeals.

The Supreme Court had been indulging in the independent assessment of evidence after appellate courts had stripped plaintiffs of their jury awards in FELA cases:

> The Court's action in agreeing to review such cases [was] in irreconcilable conflict with the unmistakable policy of the statutes which confer its jurisdiction on certiorari, . . . with the Court's own former pronouncements that review on certiorari 'is in the interest of the law, not in the interest of particular parties,' [and] with the Court's position in the institutional structure. [The Court] has not been able to formulate generalized guides to decision of such questions which are intelligible to state-court or lower-federal-court judges or usable by them, and at the 1956 Term the Court retreated to open assertion that case-by-case policing of decisions in this field is one of its proper functions. . . . The conclusion seems inescapable that what the Court is doing in these cases is a misuse of power.[17]

What Hart is complaining about is the failure to follow correct process, to apply the doctrinal distinction between law and fact. But it is more than that. It is also that the Supreme Court was overturning appellate decisions arrived at by doctrinal routes, while itself refusing to provide alternative doctrinal maps. This easily led to the charge that the Court was "result oriented." What better proof could one have that a decision was made on some unprincipled basis than the author's refusal to offer a principle?

But Hart does not go so far. He attributes such Court opinions to a lack of time for collective deliberation. From this Hart turns to a lengthy, one might say, Thomistic analysis of *Irvin* v. *Dowd*[18] in which he concludes that the two most significant aspects of the case are that it leaves a rather delicate question of adequate state grounds undecided and fails to respond to a dissent by Justice Harlan. Seeing these two features as significant is itself significant. The first aspect is important because it so contrasts with prudential arguments, as we shall see. The second aspect illuminates the doctrinalist reliance on reasoned interplay and illustrates another tenet of doctrinal arguments both before and after realism—namely, the notion of the one true rule of law. In the following passage, Hart, having described the dissent, concludes that the majority must not have had the time to consider it or they would *necessarily* have been convinced or required to reply.

> [T]he merits and respective implications of the differing interpretations were never open-mindedly and thoroughly examined by the whole Court prior to the decisive vote on the outcome [it would appear] [f]or it would seem to be psychologically difficult if not impossible for any judge to emerge from this kind of consideration of an able and subtle analysis and then to explain his own reasoning in arriving at a different decision without having some hint of the possibility of the alternative analysis creep into the explanation.[19]

In each of the main features of this essay—its insistence on general principles, its tacit acceptance of a single, legitimate approach across which a dissent may put a roadblock, its aloof dismissal of political considerations—Hart shows the superstructure of doctrinal argument.

Hart's remarkable essay has been the model for much of the scholarly criticism of the Court which has appeared since. It shares, with Wechsler's celebrated Holmes Lectures of 1959,[20] the powerful critical tools of doctrinal argument. But the essay also reveals something of the flaws of the doctrinal approach.

Doctrinal argument assumes the Court has but one function, when in fact the Supreme Court properly exercises a family of functions. I will have a greater opportunity to consider later this family of functions—the cueing function, about which I have lectured, the expressive function, to which much of Book III is devoted, and others, but I think it is plain that the doctrinal approach treats the United States Supreme Court as though it were the last, best appellate tribunal.[21]

Recall, for example, Hart's complaint that the Supreme Court of that period insisted on granting certiorari in FELA cases. In these cases Circuit courts had been reversing jury findings of liability on the basis that negligence "in whole or in part," as required by the statute, had not been shown. The Court repeatedly overruled such cases, holding that any negligence, even the slightest, would justify a verdict for the employee.[22] From a doctrinal perspective this is unsatisfying on at least two grounds: First, the Court took several cases without announcing a general principle applicable to a larger class, thus deciding on a case by case basis. Second, the Court gave no good reason why the statute should be read as imposing virtually strict liability on employers. It looked as though the only principle was "employees win."

It looked this way because the commentators, and the appellate courts who refused to follow the new rule, looked at the rule through the doctrinal glasses of classical negligence law.[23] The statute, as the Court read it, really could not be fit within conventional negligence doctrine. This does not mean, as doctrinalists would suggest, that there is no principle. It means that radical departure from doctrine necessarily appears unprincipled[24] from the perspective of the doctrine it replaces. "Employees win" is a principle; indeed it is a key principle in the doctrine of strict liability. Moreover, the Court was required to continue taking cases until its cue was finally acceded to by the intermediate courts, although there was no truly new doctrinal development after the *Rogers*[25] construction.

The "Time Chart" reflects other biases of doctrinal argument. It depends on descriptions of both the world and the constitutional world that are far from evident. Doctrinal argument assumes dispassionate, disinterested justices who arrive at decisions by a process of reason applied to doctrine—by which I mean precedent, institutional doctrines, and doctrines of construction. This partly explains why doctrinal argument is supported by, as we saw in Justice Roberts, an ethical as well as a jurisprudential conviction. At the same time, however, it is a description of the world, and it is as a description of the world that doctrinal argument falls short. Justices of the Supreme Court, as Thurman Arnold pointed out,[26] are far *more* likely to be committed on the political issues of the day than are the rest of us. And although, as one would expect, the doctrinal ideology seeks to keep cases of political significance out of the courts, no one can doubt that the Court is one of our principal political actors. If the FELA cases reflected a shift in favor of the workingman, this was in turn a reflection of Roosevelt's legislative programs and his appointments to the Court.

Hart held, consistent with a doctrinal position, that Congress cannot remove various constitutional matters beyond the jurisdiction of the federal courts. This was the view of his famous "Dialogue," reprinted in the Hart and Wechsler casebook.[27] His argument follows naturally enough from the distinction between legislative and judicial decisionmaking. Only the courts, by virtue of the process which they are to follow in reaching a result, can adhere over time to enduring principles. But this is wrong. There is no reason why a congressional party cannot take constitutional principles as its charter. There are indeed many moving examples of such fidelity and Congressmen, as well as judges, are required by the Constitution to swear to uphold its principles. But it is said that neutrality supposedly distinguishes the judiciary from other branches of government. And yet, as the brilliant and opaque Professor Deutsch has shown, neutrality is in the eye of time and no class of deciders, judges or otherwise, can better predict what will come to be perceived as truly neutral. Thus the facially neutral doctrine of "separate but equal" fell to the facially nonneutral, color-conscious decision to integrate schools, although most of us hope that integration will be perceived some day as wholly neutral with respect to race. We perceive bastardy as an impermissible basis on which to distinguish litigants; but this was not always so. Age is now considered a fair basis of distinction; it may not always be so. A mass intelligence test is now seen by many as a neutral criterion for admission to college, and we consider wealth as nonneutral. Yet both intelligence testing and wealth appear to be largely the result of inheritance and chance. In other words, insofar as a rule can decide an issue, it is nonneutral; yet it will be perceived as neutral to the extent that the non-favored class is perceived as sharing some trait on the basis of which we could discriminate.

Ignoring this aspect of neutrality accounts, in part, for the absolute confidence with which Hart writes. Like lawyers of the late nineteenth century, conclusions inescapably emerge for him. This certainly is accomplished only if one's focus is greatly narrowed and the kinds of legitimate argument are reduced to one. Thus, Hart's process of collective decisionmaking does not sound like the description we have of the Court's Friday conferences. Hart's Court sounds more like the world of the Harvard Law Review: a group of industrious but largely convictionless students arriving at results.

The powerful display of and devotion to doctrinal argument that Hart epitomizes has also found its voice in a peculiar legal institution, the American Law Institute (ALI). Indeed, without an appreciation of the ideology of doctrinal argument and of the true constitutional crisis of the 1930s, one can scarcely believe that the ALI could have been organized in the very teeth of the realist revolt. A brief review of the development of the ALI will illuminate the features of doctrinal argument.

In the early 1920s a group of quite distinguished judges, lawyers, and scholars met in New York, first at the Association of the City Bar and later at the Harvard Club. The principal intellectual force behind these meetings was William Draper Lewis, a professor at the University of Pennsylvania Law School and later the first director of the ALI. (Since 1962 the director—the ALI has had only three directors in its history—has been Professor Herbert Wechsler, Hart's distinguished coauthor.) Lewis was able to interest Elihu Root in a project which would bring together the most distinguished members of the three branches of the law, and by their collective, reasoned efforts produce "restatements" of the mass of inconsistent common law rules announced and applied by the various jurisdictions in the states. Root was known as the dean of the American Bar; he recruited the Committee—a remarkable group. It included Harlan Stone, Samuel Williston, Learned Hand, Julian Mack, Arthur Corbin, Roscoe Pound, and John Wigmore as well as the most prominent members of the New York Bar—C. C. Burlingham, John W. Davis, George Wickersham, and James Byrne; Benjamin Cardozo came on later. Supported by funds from the Carnegie Corporation, the Committee met throughout the summer of 1923 and in February 1924 submitted a report. Drafted mainly by Lewis, it began:

> There is today general dissatisfaction with the administration of justice. The feeling . . . is not confined to that radical section of the community which would overthrow existing social, economic and political institutions. . . . It is unnecessary to emphasize here the danger from this general dissatisfaction. It

kneads disrespect for law, and disrespect for law is the corner-
stone of revolution.[28]

The source of this dissatisfaction was peculiarly lawyerly. It
was not alienation or class revolt; it was that the law had become uncertain and complex. "When the law is doubtful," the
report went on, "persons are inclined to adopt the view most
favorable to their own interests." The result "undermines the
moral fibre of the community. . . . [T]he most important task
that the bar can undertake," the Report concluded, "is to reduce the amount of the uncertainty and complexity of the law."
This was to be done by the preparation of a set of legal ency-
clopedias to be called the Restatements, which would not merely
collect the various rules and cases as other treatises had done
but would state authoritative rules as they should be. The sum-
maries would provide, according to subject matter, a statement
of a set of governing principles followed by an analysis and the
supporting reasons for those principles.

It is astonishing, is it not, that even after having eaten of
the realist fruit of self-knowledge, such an eminent segment of
the bar should attempt this task? Of course, not everyone was
entranced. Holmes was invited to the meeting and given the
report to study. That evening, he wrote the next day to Sir
Frederick Pollock, he had his clerk read aloud to him not the
Root Committee Report but the detective novel *Bull Dog Drum-
mond.* And of the meeting he wrote,

> The eminent in the law have been gathering here, yearning for
> the upward and onward—specifically for the restatement of the
> law, I presume by the members of this body. On earnest exhor-
> tation I showed up for a few minutes yesterday to the extent of
> looking in while Root was delivering a somewhat flamboyant
> address; but I am an aged skeptic and was pleased with Bran-
> deis' remark "Why I am restating the law every day."[29]

Nevertheless, the American Law Institute was organized and
promptly began the preparation of nine broad studies organized by subject matter—by *doctrine* that is—into agency, property, torts, contracts, and the like. The first round was largely
completed by the early 1940s. Almost at once, supported by
money from a Mellon Trust, work was begun on a second round

of Restatements. Not long thereafter, in the early 1950s work commenced on two model statutes, the Model Penal Code and the Uniform Commercial Code (UCC), supported by the Rockefeller and Falk foundations. These model codes, like the Restatements, were shaped by committees headed by a distinguished scholar whose drafts were amended by the committees and sent to the membership for debate and adoption. Wechsler was the chief reporter for the Penal Code and Karl Llewellyn, seemingly ironically, was reporter for the UCC.

The success of the ALI has been remarkable. The UCC has been adopted in forty-nine states. Virtually every state's Penal Code has provisions lifted from the Model Penal Code and it is this model that every self-respecting law school teaches its students. The Restatements have been no less influential. In Pennsylvania alone, a study of the Restatement of Torts from 1939 to 1949 found that three of four cases of first impression relied on the Restatement. Past cases in conflict with the Restatement were repudiated. Only once in the ten years studied did the Supreme Court of Pennsylvania cite a section of the Restatement without following it.[30] Another study noted that up to April, 1981, the Restatement had been cited by appellate courts more than 72,000 times.[31] Finally, the ultimate adoption of these common law rules, arrived at without benefit of court, came when a Presidential Executive Order provided that American trust territories, such as the islands in Melanesia, should take as rules of decision the rules of the Restatements.[32]

I have recounted this extraordinary history for the sake of our study of doctrinal argument, a theology for which the ALI is something like the Vatican. Notice that no Restatement has been attempted for Constitutional law.[33] There are many reasons for this, not the least of which is that unlike the common law of the various states there is only one authoritative decisionmaker as to the common law construction of the Constitution. It would strain belief, or even threaten cognitive dissonance as the psychologists say, to maintain that the one true rule of law recognized in the commonwealth of the ALI could coexist, side-by-side and nowhere applied, with what is in fact done by operation of law, namely the decision of the United States Supreme Court. Where Hart was able to sidestep the

realist dilemma by focusing on doctrines of process, the ALI
met the challenge head on and simply declared various substantive doctrines in those areas of confusion and dissipation of
authority where it did not have to face authoritative contradic-
tion.

This highlights another facet of doctrinal argument: it
functions best when the purposes behind the doctrine are generally agreed upon. This in part accounts, I think, both for the
power and persuasiveness of Hart's essay on the criminal law,
a field in which Professor Wechsler has made distinguished
contributions. Similarly, I think it accounts for the almost universal embrace of the UCC. But where there is no such consensus—and the purposes of the provisions of the Constitution are
always a ready topic for controversy—doctrinal argument in
either its ALI-substantive or Hart's-process variant loses its authority.

Yet another shortcoming of doctrinal argument is its dis-
guise of preference in policy. When most successful, this mask-
ing tricks its own masters and is perhaps responsible for the
self-righteous tone that pervades so much doctrinal commentary. Of course it is misleading to say we are deceived by masks
of our own manufacture; and yet the custom by which such
fabrication takes place tends to mask us as the fabricators from
each other. Consider the following sociology. Of the thirty-four
presidents of the Harvard Law Review from the early 1920s
when the ALI was founded until 1960, twenty-five were members of the Institute. There have been four presidents of the
ALI: George Wickersham was the senior partner of Cadwal-
lader, Wickersham and Taft, One Wall Street. George Pepper,
senator from Pennsylvania, was the founding partner of what
is now Pepper, Hamilton and Scheetz, one of the most prominent corporate firms in Philadelphia. Harrison Tweed was for
many years the head of Milbank, Tweed, the Wall Street firm
of the Chase Manhattan Bank and the Rockefeller interests.
Norris Darrell, the urbane corporate partner of Sullivan and
Cromwell, married Judge Learned Hand's daughter, Mary. And
so on. This is a small world. And like every small world it has
a cohesive set of preferences.

The ideology of doctrinal argument reflects the preferences

of sophisticated, well-to-do Wall Street lawyers. Among these prejudices are a distrust of juries, an abiding attachment to the legal status quo, a preference for uniform and clear rules that inhibit local and personal discretion, a willingness to rely on extended procedural inquiry, a preference for appellate decisionmaking rather than legislative rule making, and an attention to form. These are by no means preferences shared by the rest of the bar. It is no coincidence that Derek Bok's tribute to Henry Hart begins by praising him as someone who could lure a man from Wall Street, nor that Hart's phillipics against the Supreme Court always included a dire reference to the opinion of what he called "first-rate lawyers." Much could be done on the sociology of law professors and attorneys, and I do no more here than suggest that a particular approach to the Constitution or to law generally may be animated, even constructed, by the very groups for whom it appears to express a timeless ideal, beyond construction and pre-existing animation.

Doctrinal argument—the ALI's and Hart's method—rarely appears in pure form in appellate opinions. Judges with the enormous gifts required to adapt the doctrinal approach to the infinitely variegated facts of life and thereby to avoid formalism are almost as rare as Hand and Friendly, the two finest examples of doctrinal Circuit judges. It is, I think, notable that the achievements of these two great judges have been principally in crafting common law, and most impressively, a common law of statutes. For a pure doctrinal approach to Constitutional law we have to look mainly to the academy. This is not to deride the influence of this approach: none of us could think of law without the organizing influence of the analytical modes of law schools. Indeed the list of subjects of the ALI Restatements themselves largely duplicate the list of required courses at the Harvard Law School in the 1930s. Accordingly, to the doctrinalist other approaches appear to be lawless.

One such collision of approaches may be observed in Professor Hart's criticism of Justice Black's opinion in *Youngstown Sheet and Tube*,[34] widely known as the Steel Seizure Case. Black, working from the Constitutional text, asks simply whether that text provides the President with the power to direct the secretary of commerce to take possession of and operate most of the nation's steel mills. This power, Black says, must stem from the Constitution or from an Act of Congress pursuant to Constitutional authority. There being neither express nor implicit statutory authorization, Black then considers the constitutional basis of such authority: "It is clear that if the President had [such] authority . . . it must be found in some provision of the Constitution."[35] The argument, plainly textual, goes this way.

1) Since there is no express constitutional power, it must be fairly implied from an express power. There are two possibilities.

2) One possibility—the President's power as commander-in-chief—will not serve despite, Black notes, the current expansion of the concept of war. That common meaning has not yet gone so far as to include labor disputes.

3) The other possibility—the provisions that "the Executive Power be vested in a President" and that he "take care that the Laws be faithfully executed"—cannot serve, either. The latter text refutes, in the way I have mentioned earlier with respect to internal textual arguments, the notion that the President can act as lawmaker. There being no Congressional Act which the Executive power can execute, the order cannot stand. Finis.

Of this textual opinion Hart and Sacks are sharply critical. The real issue, they write, is who takes the initiative in dealing with a dramatic national emergency. Does the Constitution require Congress to anticipate the crisis or to deal with it as it arises? Or can the President act subject to a congressional veto? We are to resolve this problem by looking to the relative processes of the three branches: "Is a legislature well-equipped to function as our agency of frontline adjustment of private relationships?"[36] Would judicial review serve as an effective check? "Could the courts have administered a doctrine requiring" that Presidential action be limited to national emergencies? and so forth.[37] This program highlights the shape of contemporary doctrinal argument. Not only do we see the utter rejection of a textual or historical approach, but we see the resort to process doctrine as the basis for deriving the new rule.

Despite such creativity doctrinal argument can easily sink into mere formalism because the doctrine is severed from the animating text. I am inclined to think this has happened to the

Equal Protection Clause, whose words are seldom used except as cant and whose application and commentary revolve around "three tiers," "compelling state interests," "fundamental rights," and "suspect classification" to such an extent that one very able author has made a chart[38] by which a justice could locate the constitutionality of a challenged statute or "unconstitutionality" by following columns of "significant interest" and the like down, and rows of "governmental interest" and so forth across.

Doctrinal argument faces its true crisis when the old purposes for the development of the doctrine have been obscured or mooted, or have simply withered away, or when there is no consensus as to the discernible purpose. It is reasoning from purpose that gives doctrinalism its power; it can't provide purpose.

The difficulty is that the debate over constitutional purposes is generally the issue in Constitutional law. Even if we agree, for example, that an attentiveness to the institutional capacities of the three branches would yield us a neutral principle of decision from which to derive rules for future disputes, how do we know that the Constitution is committed to making sure that the most efficient agency act in national emergencies? This seems plausible enough, but the design of the Constitution— not least in its reliance on literal omission as a way of limiting governmental authority—as well as its imposition of various cumbersome requirements on governmental action, suggests that a good many values are to be preferred to the calculus of administrative efficiency.

A poignant example of this dilemma of purpose occurred, not in a judicial opinion, but in one series of the Holmes Lectures at Harvard. I don't mean Wechsler's famous Neutral Principles lectures,[39] though I will refer to them later, nor Judge Friendly's Holmes Lectures, appropriately titled the "Need for Standards in Administrative Law,"[40] but Hart's own lectures delivered in 1963. He shared many characteristics with one other formidable doctrinalist: like Judge Friendly, he had been a summa cum laude graduate of Harvard College, then President of the Harvard Law Review, then clerk to Justice Brandeis. The invitation to have Hart deliver the Holmes Lectures was, however, unique; he remains the only member of the Har-

vard faculty honored in this way. Reminiscent of his "Dialogue"
and the whole test match of doctrinal process, the lectures were
entitled "Conversations on Law and Justice."

Hart began by examining the premise of much social science that estimations of value and fact should be separated.
This premise, he charged, would condemn any legal theory to
futility since we would not then be able to decide whether decisions were sound, who ought to make them, or what values
they should reflect. This was Hart's *cri de coeur* against legal
realism. The second lecture was devoted to a sort of meta-
anthropological essay. Reasoning from the assumption that Man
is a social animal whose wants can be satisfied only in association with others, Hart concluded that a legal system is necessary
to secure the benefits of social living. While reason can play a
part in the determination of law only when there is an awareness of the underlying purpose, we may nevertheless deduce
that an operating society, with the purpose of securing to itself
the benefits of social living, requires mutual forbearance of
aggression, some faith in the promises of others, some minimal
recognition of the security of property—in short, the basic subject matter of the common law.

Hart began his third lecture by discussing the appropriate
roles for legislatures and courts. He then emphasized the necessity of reason in judicial decisions and called for more attention to this quality. All this is the doctrinal ideology as I have
described it. Then Hart said,

> Suppose we were to decide that the commitments in the Con-
> stitution mean that every American is entitled, within the limits
> [of conditions], to an equal opportunity to develop and to ex-
> ercise his capacities as a responsible human being who is also a
> social being; and that the overriding purpose of all actions taken
> by the authority of society as a whole through the processes of
> government and law is to make that opportunity as meaningful
> as possible.[41]

If we accept this value, it then becomes possible to solve the
subsidiary problems of choosing the means of reaching this end
through reason.

Then Hart paused and when he continued he said he had

realized on the very eve of the lecture that he could not offer a general resolution, that he could give no principle by which such values could be justified. He said that his answers were, he now saw, less conclusive than he had hoped. And then, in a hushed and crowded Ames courtroom, he sat down.

In this we confront the integrity and the impotence of doctrinal argument.

Doctrinal ideology requires that decisions be based on premises of general applicability, otherwise they would be *ad hoc* or "legislative." At the same time the doctrinal method requires that adjudication be neutral, thereby claiming the allegiance of litigants through a tacit arrangement of reciprocity. In short, doctrinal argument is the ideology of the common law tradition of deciding appeals.

It is interesting that the oral traditions of the academic and the appellate judge are question asking. Similarly, the Hart and Wechsler casebook model presents largely undigested case materials followed by a series of searching and leading questions. This passive style suggests not only that there is a right answer but also that the neutral method of questioning—can a question be wrong?—will lead the correct answer to pop out. Doctrinal argument does not depend so much on how the drafters actually intended a specific passage to be applied as on the application of doctrines which serve or can be assumed to serve general purposes sought by the drafters. It is true that doctrinal argument has the not-incidental feature of making a virtue of those things likely to be favored by the well-educated and well-financed bar. I have in mind not only the intense focus on issues of jurisdiction and procedure, which only the industrious and well-to-do and the highly trained and intelligent recruited by the well-to-do can afford to exploit, but also the moral sense that such questions are essentially value-free and hence discarded only by the unprincipled. I am not, of course, discrediting such an approach nor, even if it were possible, as I believe it is not, urging its rejection.

Rather I wish to draw attention to two features that will have greater importance as our study continues. First, doctrinal argument, like other approaches, reflects an ideology of inter-related views. Second, each of the various constitutional approaches represents a different conceptualization of the Constitution. Thus we may account for the phenomenon of opinions and commentary which do not seem to mesh with each other and do not join issue on a common ground according to common rules. We will encounter other conceptualizations in the remaining types of constitutional argument to be examined.

CHAPTER 5

PRUDENTIAL ARGUMENT

In his Charpentier Lectures at Columbia[1] Justice Hugo Black sketched the caricature of a particular approach to the Constitution that was antithetical to his own textual method, deriding the approach as subversive of the Constitution. I will call this approach "prudential." Referring to the text of the last clause of the Fifth Amendment—the prohibition against taking private property without just compensation—Justice Black constructed an imaginary opinion which he attributed to "Judge X." Judge X's opinion, in pompous and convoluted tones, came to the conclusion that a family farm might be seized by the Defense Department without compensation being paid, since the takings clause of the Fifth Amendment must be *balanced* against the provision for the war power in Article I. The opinion reasoned that given such competing texts, prudence required that a balance be struck between a calculation of the necessity and great benefits of the official act and the small harm incidentally worked.

> This case presents an important question of constitutional law. The United States is engaged in a stupendous national defense undertaking which requires the acquisition of much valuable land throughout the country. The plaintiff here owns 500 acres of land. The location of the land gives it a peculiarly stra-

tegic value for carrying out the defense program. Due to the
great national emergency that exists, Congress concluded that
the United States could not afford at this time to pay compensation for the lands which it needed to acquire. For this reason
an act was passed authorizing seizure without compensation of
all the lands required for the defense establishment.

Plaintiff contends, however, that the Fifth Amendment's
provision about compensation is so absolute a command that
Congress is wholly without authority to violate it, however great
this nation's emergency and peril may be. I must reject this
contention. We must never forget that it is a constitution we
are expounding. And a constitution, unlike ordinary statutes,
must endure for ages; it must be adapted to changing conditions and the needs of changing communities.

When two great constitutional provisions like these conflict—as
here the power to make war conflicts with the requirements for
just compensation—it becomes the duty of courts to weigh the
constitutional right of an individual to compensation against the
power of Congress to wage a successful war.
    While the question is not without doubt, I have no hesita-
tion in finding the challenged Congressional act valid.
Weighing as I must the loss the individual will suffer because
he has to surrender his land to the nation without compensation against the great public interest in conducting war, I hold
the act valid. A decree will be entered accordingly.[2]

The kind of argument Justice Black is ridiculing here is
prudential argument even down to satirizing the prudentialist's
favorite passage from Marshall, and Judge X is, if anyone
doesn't know, Justice Frankfurter. While textual arguments are
best appreciated when contrasted with historical arguments, with
which they are often confused, prudential arguments are most
easily contrasted with textual approaches like Black's but are
usually confused with doctrinal arguments.
    The contrast with text is sharp, as Black's acid pen and
pointed reference to textual absolutes make clear. In constitutional questions, competing texts can almost always be found;
if a prudential approach is used to decide between texts, then
the texts themselves really count for nothing in the decision.

For example, if the constitutional question is whether the exercise of a particular power transgresses some limitation on government, there will, when measuring congressional statutes against the Bill of Rights, usually be an enumerated power—a text—of which the actual statute is said to be an implied exercise. There being *competing* texts, and no text which states the priority to give one over others, there will be no textual argument that can resolve the balance. It becomes then a matter of prudence, a calculation of the necessity of the act against its costs.

Prudential argument is constitutional argument which is actuated by the political and economic circumstances surrounding the decision. Thus prudentialists generally hold that in times of national emergency even the plainest of constitutional limitation can be ignored. Perhaps others share that belief; but the prudentialist makes it a legitimate, legal argument, fits it into opinions, and uses it as the purpose for doctrines, and it is this that makes him interesting to us.[3]

In our time the most eloquent and creative exponent of prudential argument was Alexander Bickel. Like his mentor, Felix Frankfurter, Bickel was short and slight and dressed in a dapper, elegant way. Like Frankfurter, he had been brought to the United States as a child, had excelled at City College, and had gone on to excel at the Harvard Law School. It is fair, I think, to characterize Justice Frankfurter, for whom Bickel clerked, as Bickel's jurisprudential progenitor. But the line really begins—as does the modern era of prudential argument—with Louis Brandeis. Therefore it is pleasing to observe the first significant expression of modern prudential argument in consitutional law in a memorandum by Brandeis, collected in a volume by Bickel (his first book), to whom Brandeis's papers had been entrusted by their executor, Frankfurter.

In 1916, after an unsuccessful campaign in the states to outlaw child labor, Congress passed a statute excluding from interstate commerce any article manufactured by child labor.[4] Probably only congressional action would have been effective, since only a virtually unanimous rule among the states would have prevented the more scrupulous states from conferring a competitive advantage on those states that refused to prohibit child labor. The federal act was promptly challenged and less than two years later, in the familiar case of *Hammer* v. *Dagenhart*,[5] the Court struck down the 1916 statute as being beyond the scope of the commerce power. Casting about for another approach, Congress then passed the Child Labor Tax Act,[6] which imposed a tax on the products of child labor. It was 1922 before the *Child Labor Tax Case*[7] reached the Supreme Court and Congress' effort was again struck down. That case is also required reading for first-year law students. What is seldom questioned by them, though, is why Holmes and Brandeis failed to dissent in the latter case as they had in *Hammer* and as seemed predictable given Holmes's undiscriminating use of commerce and taxing power cases to support his view that Congress may effect indirect social benefits.

The answer, or at least a partial answer, can be found in *Atherton Mills* v. *Johnston*,[8] a little-known case decided the same day as the *Child Labor Tax Case* and presenting the same statute for construction, but handled in conventional terms of mootness in a brief opinion by Taft.

Atherton Mills had arisen in this way. The father of a child employed by a mill had complained that the mill was about to discharge the boy to avoid triggering the 10% tax on profits derived from child labor. The father argued that the Child Labor Act damaged him by threatening to deprive him of his son's earnings. Claiming that the Act was unconstitutional, he sought an injunction in the federal district court. The defendant mill admitted everything except the unconstitutionality of the statute. The District Court granted the injunction; the case came to the Supreme Court on appeal and was argued late in 1919.

In a draft opinion labeled a memorandum to the Court, Brandeis urged dismissal of the case for lack of jurisdiction on the following grounds. First, the suit was collusive while the jurisdiction of the Court ought to be limited to suits between truly adverse parties. Second, even if he had a bona fide suit the plaintiff should be held to lack standing since regardless of the Act's constitutionality the employer had the right to discharge the boy on any grounds whatsoever. Thus, even a decision striking down the Act would not ensure that the claimed harm would not occur anyway. The federal courts should not pass on constitutional issues at the instance of parties without a genuine stake—that is, something to lose other than the argument—in the outcome.

What arguments did Brandeis offer to persuade his colleagues that the Constitution required such self-discipline? He used not arguments drawn from the Constitution itself but from the institutional consequences of deciding:

> For nearly a century and a quarter Federal courts, as an incident to deciding cases rightfully before them, have necessarily exercised at times the solemn duty of declaring acts of Congress void. But the long continued, uninterrupted exercise of this power has not sufficed to silence the doubt originally expressed whether the framers of the Constitution intended to confer it. On the contrary, the popular protest against its exercise has never been as vehement, nor has it ever secured the support of so many political thinkers and writers, as in the last decade. At a time like the present, when the fundamental principles upon which our institutions rest are being seriously questioned, those who have faith in their wisdom and desire to preserve them unimpaired, can best uphold the Constitution by careful observance of the limitations which it imposes.[9]

Accordingly, a court's first responsibility is to decide whether it should decide. Brandeis believed the Court should avoid constitutional decision in order to safeguard the Court's own position and to activate the political processes of the legislature. These are not textual or historical or even doctrinal reasons, though they are sometimes embodied in doctrine. They are prudential reasons.

Why then did Brandeis not dissent in the *Child Labor Tax Case?* Brandeis's reason was not, I want to emphasize, the same reason that Holmes didn't dissent. Holmes, the greatest modern doctrinal justice, likely chose not to dissent for purely doctrinal reasons. Once Holmes had registered his dissent in a case whose authority controlled a later one, he felt bound *a fortiori* for the same reasons of similarity of issue that in another approach would have led one to anticipate a further dissent.[10] He often did not press the point once he had his say on the subject.

By contrast, Brandeis the prudentialist, refrained on prudential grounds: he believed that the decision would reinvigorate
drives in the states to institute anti-child-labor laws[11] and that
holding out hope for a favorable Court decision would only
dissipate these movements. But it is more interesting than this.

With the *Atherton Mills* memorandum Brandeis had gained
a foothold for a position of considerable importance on a Court
in which he was doomed to sit in the minority. The Court determined not to decide *Atherton Mills* that term. Even on re-
argument, when the Solicitor General intervened to urge the
constitutionality of the Act but refused to press the jurisdictional issue, the Court still did not decide. Finally, young Johnston reached age sixteen, the Act no longer applied to his employer, and the case was mooted. But the groundwork had been
laid for Brandeis's development of the jurisdictional doctrines
by which prudence was brought to bear in determining when
the Court should act. Indeed, afterward Brandeis would cite
the Taft opinion in *Atherton Mills* for this very point,[12] inexpli-
cably to the observer limited to the pages of the U.S. Reports.[13]

So one suspects that Brandeis may have chosen not to dissent in the *Child Labor Tax Case* for tactical reasons. The majority, after all, could just as easily have chosen *Atherton Mills* as
the vehicle for striking down the tax. It is at least as important
for the development of prudential argument that Bickel *thought*
Brandeis had chosen not to dissent for tactical reasons,[14] for it
is in Bickel's work that the prudential approach is most explicitly severed from the doctrinal.

Brandeis's campaign for prudentialism culminated in his
majestic concurrence in *Ashwander*[15] fourteen years later. Quoting Cooley, he wrote:

> It must be evident to anyone that the power to declare a legis-
> lative enactment void is one which the judge, conscious of the
> fallibility of the human judgment, will shrink from exercising
> in any case where he can conscientiously . . . decline the re-
> sponsibility. The Court will not pass upon the constitutionality
> of legislation in a friendly, non-adversary, proceeding, declin-
> ing because to decide such questions 'is legitimate only in the

last resort, and as a necessity in the determination of real, earnest and vital controversy between individuals. It never was the
thought that, by means of a friendly suit, a party beaten in the
legislature could transfer to the courts an inquiry as to the constitutionality of the legislative act.'[16]

"The most important thing we do," said Brandeis, "is not
doing."[17] The means of avoiding decisions are crucial for
prudential method and for the Court's role Bickel wrote of
this famous phrase "because [they] are the techniques that allow leeway to expediency . . ."[18]

Thus we see the unique position the *Atherton Mills* memorandum and the later *Ashwander* opinion occupy in constitutional law. The former is a prudential argument such as are
common in all conferences at all times cast in the form of a
draft opinion. The latter is an opinion seized as an opportunity, as concurrences often are. By this route, prudential argument became legitimate constitutional argument. It moved from
the cloakroom and the private conversations of worldly men
into opinions, as reasons that might be explicitly used to support a judicial decision.[19]

Bickel gave the fullest expression of the prudential approach to constitutional law in his celebrated essay, "The Passive Virtues."[20] This subtle and ingenious work detailed the use
of various jurisdictional doctrines as mediating devices by which
the Court can introduce political realities into its decisional process. Recall the discussion a few pages ago of Professor Hart's
approach to the *Steel Seizure Case*[21] and the contrast that approach presented with the method taken by Justice Black for
the majority. In "The Passive Virtues," Professor Bickel gave
the *prudential* approach to the *Steel Seizure Case.* In Bickel's view,
prudential considerations, "having to do chiefly with the need
to maintain pressure on the parties for a settlement that would
allow [steel] production to continue," should properly have been
decisive for the Court, directing it to abstain from judgment on
the constitutional merits.[22] Bickel points out that Frankfurter
dissented from what he saw as a precipitate grant of certiorari
with the allusion to prudential argument that "the time taken"

in letting the case wind its way up through the appellate path
would be "available also for constructive consideration of the
parties of their own positions and responsibilities."[23]

Readers should turn to Bickel's essay for a rich display of
prudential constitutional techniques. It would be impossible to
summarize these because Bickel develops the categories of prudential techniques—and the considerations that determine their
employment—through detailed factual accounts of the cases in
which they were, or should have been, used. And this feature
is notable for our study, since prudential approaches are efforts to bring to constitutional decisionmaking "the impact of
actuality," in Frankfurter's words.[24] It is instructive to contrast
this feature with doctrinal argument, which is typically used in
an effort to escape the impress of peculiar facts to get to the
high ground of principle.[25] One thinks of the factless rules of
the Restatements in this regard. In reproving the pre-realist
doctrinalists, Professor Frankfurter wrote, "Every tendency to
deal with constitutional questions abstractly, to formulate them
in terms of barren legal questions, leads to dialectics, to sterile
conclusions unrelated to actualities."[26] (And of course we observe the dialectical style in Hart's "Dialogue," his Holmes Lecture "Conversations" and, most influentially, in the leading
questions of the Hart and Wechsler casebook.)

In contrast to the doctrinal approach, Bickel set forth in
"The Passive Virtues" a general statement of the prudential position.

> The accomplished fact, affairs and interests that have formed
> around it, and perhaps popular acceptance of it—these are ele-
> ments . . . that may *properly* enter into a decision to abstain
> from rendering constitutional judgment or to allow room and
> time for accommodation to such a judgment; and they may also
> enter into the shaping of the judgment, the applicable principle
> itself.[27] (emphasis added)

The devices that Bickel contended the Court had used and
should continue to use in the service of prudence include discretionary standing, the grant of certiorari and the dismissal of
appeal, the doctrines of vagueness, ripeness, and political ques-

tion, and others. It naturally follows that Bickel objected to the Rule of Four by which a minority of the Justices can bring a case before the Court; he considered the question of whether to decide a case to be at least as important as the other "constitutional merits." Contrast this attitude with Henry Hart's bitter attack on the Supreme Court's recent policy of treating the dismissal of appeals similarly to its certiorari policy; that is, as "dismissals for the want of a convenient, or timely, or suitably presented question."[28] For Bickel, such a development was natural and prudent. The discretionary device was expanding to its useful bounds. For that, it was unprincipled.

By the same measure, these prudential techniques depend on ignoring the word "all" in the Article III phrase "all Cases, in Law and Equity, arising under this Constitution." No strict textualist would permit this, though he might be willing to argue over the meaning of the phrase "judicial power" in the same passage. The differences in approach are profound. It is characteristic of Bickel and Frankfurter and other exponents of prudential argument that they never quite believed textualists like Black actually meant what they said. Guido Calabresi has reported, in his Holmes Lectures, that Justice Black responded to Charles Black's attempted reformulation of the absolutist position along heuristic lines (surely, Professor Black said, Justice Black is willing to make concessions to *some* events, as in the hypothetical bending of the Bill of Rights to protect thousands of lives from nuclear blackmail) not, as was thought, by a straightforward rejection but by replying, "Guy, I can't *say* that." Perhaps Calabresi's prudentialism determines even his account of this exchange. The textual approach is not only not a calculus, its claims refuse to admit calculation, and this was what made Justice Black so maddening to prudentialists.

A prudentialist is likely to deride a doctrinal approach as being as naive as the textual approach is disingenuous. After a Saturday conference in 1943, Frankfurter wrote in his diary that a position taken by Black was "a perfect illustration . . . of Brandeis' remark to me, [that] 'Black hasn't the faintest notion of what tolerance means, and while he talks a lot about democracy, he is totally devoid of its underlying demand which is tolerance in his own behavior.' "[29] This remark is illuminating only if we imagine the discomfort Black sought to inflict in conference by forcing his colleagues to respond to simple absolutist textual arguments. It was not "tolerant" in the sense that it was not worldly and was self-righteous. Then turning in the same entry to confront an exponent of doctrine just as he had finished with the exponent of text, Frankfurter ridiculed Justice Roberts. Roberts's "innocence," he said, reminded him of Judge Julian Mack, a great, largely unremembered doctrinal judge—through whom, Frankfurter said, experience passed without stopping.[30]

We may count it either a shortcoming or a valuable asset that the prudential approach assumes it *must* be served and that textualists or doctrinalists are therefore either lying or are naive[31] when they profess uninterest in prudentialism.

For Bickel, prudential argument was a device to enable principled, doctrinal decision. Acutely sensitive to the fragility of democratic institutions, Bickel thought that by prudently avoiding some controversies and by handling others in subtle, indirect ways the Court could preserve its independence and authority for those few cases that should be decided on the merits and therefore as to which a neutral doctrine should be crafted and applied. Of course determining which cases deserved this treatment was foremost a matter of prudence (an anti-miscegenation statute, for example, ought not to be taken up during the school desegregation controversy, a reckless Congressional investigation ought not to be legitimated even if this was the result a decision on principle dictated). Yet Bickel was stung when, following the publication of an expanded version of "The Passive Virtues" in his book, *The Least Dangerous Branch,* he was sharply criticized in the Columbia Law Review by Gerald Gunther,[32] who in the 1970s was the principal proponent of doctrinalism in constitutional law. Bickel, Gunther wrote in a telling and brilliant phrase, demanded "100% insistence on principle, 20% of the time." Gunther correctly saw that Bickel's approach "would endorse conjecture about the complexities of political reactions as a primary ingredient of court deliberations,"[33] and he thought this was intolerable. "Doctrinal integrity," he said, "must be more than a sometime goal [if] devotion to principled adjudication is [to be] taken seriously."[34] And Gunther rejected the idea that Brandeis was a precursor of Bickel.

Gunther's assessment of Brandeis is open to doubt. While asserting that the *Ashwander* principles are compatible with the doctrine of a narrow construction of jurisdictional discretion, Gunther neglects to show where these principles themselves come from. They can be derived—with one exception—from the doctrinal justification for judicial review that the determination of constitutionality is merely concomitant to the judicial process. A discretionary use is however quite incompatible with the derivation. Indeed, even the facts of the *Ashwander* case scarcely compel a refusal to accept jurisdiction by the Court. If they had, Brandeis would not have urged that the Circuit Court decision stand but would have asked that its judgment be vacated. Finally, by ignoring Brandeis's original and provocative constitutional approach, we assimilate his style into the very different approach of his great contemporary and friend, Justice Holmes.

It may aid in drawing the contrast between the doctrinal and prudential approaches to contrast for a moment the views of the great Justices Holmes and Brandeis, who are often mistakenly thought to have held substantially similar opinions. Holmes was a profound and ardent skeptic and was therefore no crusader. He once sharply rebuked a correspondent who had referred to him as a "statesman," Holmes feeling that the word had connotations too political to be properly applied to a proper judge. Holmes never read the newspapers, and was a passionate student of philosophy well into his nineties. One often comes across references to *Mind* in his letters, but there are seldom references to any current political fight. There is beauty and style in Holmes's words that come from a highly refined aesthetic sensibility.

Brandeis's words have no such beauty, though they do have power. It is useful to recall Brandeis the crusader, the campaigner for Zionism, the "statesman": "Wherever, for example, legislation sought to protect or encourage unionism, the Brandeis vote was predictable."[35] And Brandeis, like Frankfurter after him, was a frequent presidential counselor and advisor on proposed legislation.

Reflecting his political commitments, Brandeis favored legislative experiment as a means of reform. Holmes entertained
no such thoughts, indeed he regarded them as illusions. But
these different views actually placed Holmes and Brandeis together in opposing the Court's intervention in such experiments, Holmes thinking that the Court was just as deluded as
the legislature but hadn't the guidance provided by election to
be free to impose the particular delusions they happened to
prefer. In this way, the doctrinalist and the prudentialist often
intersected at that peculiar time in our history when both were
opposed to pre-Realist, reactionary law-finding in the Constitution. But we should remain mindful of the profound differences of two men's approaches. Recall, for example, Holmes's
famous letter to Pollock, written during the recess of 1919.
Holmes, summering at Beverly Farms, reports that Brandeis
has urged him to go into the factory towns and see conditions
firsthand and to immerse himself in the facts and data of modern industrialism. Holmes refuses to do this and tells Pollock,
"I hate facts."[36] This remark displays both the aloof, aristo-
cratic charm and the dated weakness of doctrinal argument; it
is utterly foreign to the fact-dependence of prudence.

We can observe the differing contours of the doctrinal and
prudential approaches to the Constitution in those cases before
the Court on which Holmes and Brandeis differed while in
fundamental agreement as to so much else. Thus, in *Olmstead*[37]
Holmes was willing to invent a common-law doctrine somewhat
like our exclusionary rule to govern official wiretapping, while
Brandeis read the Fourth Amendment to guarantee privacy
from such intrusions, although there is no specific textual or
historical support for such a view. Brandeis's view reflects a
policy choice of the kind which, when made constitutional and
hence beyond the reach of the legislature, Holmes and doctrinal judges generally have not regarded as within their powers.

In *Gilbert* v. *Minnesota*[38] Holmes and Brandeis also split over
a constitutional issue which Holmes regarded as involving determinations which were essentially "legislative." Holmes felt
compelled to concur in sustaining the conviction of a pacifist
who had discouraged enlistment in the armed forces, while
Brandeis's criticism of the statute for the "overbreadth" of its

reach foreshadowed some prudential decisions of later decades. Similarly, if more prosaically, because Holmes was willing to rely on the doctrinal rule that the defense of entrapment must be raised at trial, he upheld a conviction in *Casey* v. *United States*[39] in which Brandeis would have had the Court direct an acquittal on its own motion.

Holmes dissented, as Brandeis did not, in *Meyer* v. *Nebraska*[40] from the Court's holding that a statute prohibiting the teaching of foreign languages to children in and below the eighth grade was unconstitutional. Nebraska had urged, at oral argument, that such statutes were necessary to acculturate newly arrived immigrants. Twenty-two states had enacted similar laws. Holmes felt that the matter was "one upon which men might reasonably differ" and determined, therefore, that the Court must respect such a legislative judgment as to social fact. Brandeis joined the majority, finding that a fundamental, personal right had been infringed despite the Court's refusal to ground this specific right in historical, textual, or doctrinal arguments. (It is interesting, for our study, that Holmes's immediate judicial heir to preeminence in the doctrinal position in American Constitutional law, Judge Learned Hand, could find no justification for cases like *Meyer* and indeed eventually concluded, in his dramatic series of Holmes Lectures,[41] that judges not responsible to an electorate simply had no warrant whatsoever to strike down legislation of this kind. Such austere detachment is a function of the doctrinal approach to the Constitution which I have mentioned earlier. It is in part what a prudential approach can remedy—if the cure is preferred to the disease—by admitting into the arena of argument those preferences of policy which arise in the political world.)

These famous cases cast doubt, then, on any synonymy of approach between Holmes and Brandeis. Bickel had good reason to believe that Brandeis could be claimed as a forebear of the prudential approach. Of course more than genealogy was at issue in Gunther's attack on Bickel and prudence. To the defense of the general position that had been assaulted by Gunther, Hand's former law clerk and the author of the constitutional casebook that most reflected the approach of Hart and Wechsler, Bickel addressed his Holmes Lectures of 1969.[42] There he reviewed the work of the Warren Court and

stood detached for a moment from the momentum and direction of constitutional prudential argument.

Bickel argued that the most important decisions of the era—
in school segregation, discrimination in housing, the poll tax,
racially-limited juries, and others—could not be justified by resort to doctrine or to any truly neutral principles. Wechsler had
confessed as much in his Holmes Lectures ten years earlier.
The Warren Court found its justification instead in a particular
political vision of progress. If that Court had calculated rightly,
then, as Jan Deutsch has pointed out, history will ratify their
decisions, and these will come to be seen as resting on "neutral"
principles. Their decisions will be perceived as applying rules
whose preferences can be explained without reference to groups
that have a political identity. There may come a time, that is,
when to exclude a child from school on the basis of his race
will be thought as arbitrary as excluding him on the basis of his
height. Or, to take the other side of neutrality, there may come
a time when the relationship of blacks to the Civil War amendments will be perceived as unique in the way that state discretion is perceived unique with respect to the Twenty-First
Amendment.

But Bickel would not take this course, though he was scarcely
insensitive to its appeal. Instead, he wrote,

> For myself, I continue to believe with my teacher, the late Pro-
> fessor Henry M. Hart, Jr., that if judicial supremacy is at all
> justifiable, then it is because the Court is 'predestined in the
> long run not only by the thrilling tradition of Anglo-American
> law but also by the hard facts of its position in the structure of
> American institutions to be a voice of reason, charged with the
> creative function of discerning afresh and of articulating and
> developing impersonal and durable principles.'[43]

The words quoted by Bickel are, of course, from Hart's "Time
Chart of the Justices."

And what of prudential argument? Bickel could only say
that his use allowed the Court to avoid going in the direction
that unalloyed principle might take it when this course was
dangerous to the institution and that it allowed accommodation
with other branches that customarily act prudentially. He ap-

parently arrived at this rather modest defense of prudential approaches because, even though he doubted the Court could always develop neutral constitutional principles when needed, he also came to believe that judicial supremacy—which is to say judicial constitutional review—was unworkable in broad areas of social policy. He rightly saw that even a modest prudentialism was an invitation to such activity. This assessment is to be distinguished from the doctrinal view *simpliciter*. Bickel clearly saw the futility of much doctrinal argument as applied to constitutional rather than statutory construction. And he just as clearly continued to put forth prudential arguments and advocate their use. Bickel's recantation, like Galileo's and recalling the latter's remark that it would be "a terrible detriment for the souls if people found themselves convinced by a proof of something that it was made then a sin to believe," was hardly a rejection of his past work. Indeed, from Gunther's point of view, it may have made matters worse than the mere 80% figure of unprincipled decisions had suggested, since now it became clear that the very deciding which cases belonged to the 80% or to the 20% was itself prudential. Bickel, however, would not go beyond this. He wished to be principled even if, as he wrote of Burke, "one of his principles was the principle that on most occasions in politics principles must not be allowed to be controlling."[44] He would not support affirmative, rather than passive, programmatic rather than institutional, prudentialism. This next step was left to his successors, the most prominent of whom are Guido Calabresi, who dedicated his Holmes Lectures[45] in 1977 to Bickel, and Bruce Ackerman, whose *Private Property and the Constitution*[46] is an extended treatment of a constitutional issue from a prudential perspective and is itself dedicated to Bickel.

What Bickel recognized—and what Gunther was at pains to dispute—was that the Court has an enormous influence on events when it declines to strike down a law and that this influence is by no means the same as when the Court declines to discuss the issue. This insight, as Bickel frankly acknowledged, came from his remarkable colleague, Professor Charles L. Black, Jr. It is to Black's contribution to Constitutional argument that I shall next turn.

CHAPTER 6

STRUCTURAL ARGUMENT

Structural arguments are inferences from the existence of constitutional structures and the relationships which the Constitution ordains among these structures. They are to be distinguished from textual and historical arguments, which construe a particular constitutional passage and then use that construction in the reasoning of an opinion. And they are also quite different from prudential arguments, which in themselves alter the flow and character of information going to the judge. Thus, to apply the Fifth Amendment's "takings" clause[1] Ackerman's preferred judge requires economic data, data that to a judge alienated from prudential approaches would seem at best irrelevant and at worst corrupting.

Structural arguments are largely factless and depend on deceptively simple logical moves from the entire Constitutional text rather than from one of its parts. At the same time, they embody a macroscopic prudentialism drawing not on the peculiar facts of the case but rather arising from general assertions about power and social choice. Let me give you a current example of structural argument.

In *National League of Cities* v. *Usery*[2] the United States Supreme Court struck down an amendment by Congress to the Fair Labor Standards Act which would have brought state employees within certain wage-and-hour guidelines. The reasoning supporting the holding in *Usery* provides a paradigm of structural constitutional argument that runs roughly as follows:

1) The Constitution sets up a federal structure necessarily providing for states;

2) States must perform those functions integral to being a state without Congressional regulation or the relationship established by the Constitution between the federal and state structures would become the assimilation of one structure into the other;

3) it is plausible to conclude that determining the wages and hours of its employees is one of those fundamental state activities as to which state authority should be sovereign, within the various prohibitions of the Constitution. It is possible that choosing whether to elect or appoint certain state officials or where to locate the state capital, and so forth, are other such activities; or it may not be so. But it follows from the very structure of the sort of federalism created by the United States Constitution that there must be at least some such activities.

I think a reasonably close reading of *National League of Cities* will support the view that the case rests on such a structural argument and not, as is sometimes suggested, on arguments drawn from the text of the Tenth Amendment.[3] Indeed, it is a measure of how habitual our recourse to the text has been that the most important structural case in Constitutional law, *McCulloch* v. *Maryland,*[4] is commonly thought to base its holding on two textual passages on which the opinion does not in the main rely—the Necessary and Proper Clause and the Supremacy Clause. We shall return to *McCulloch* and to a contrast of the different analyses of it from a structural and a doctrinal point of view, but first I should like to emphasize by example that we are held captive by the idea that a specific text or doctrine engrafted onto text is the only sure guide to constitutional decisionmaking, even when structural argument is doing the real work of resolving the issue.

In 1941, in *Edwards* v. *California,*[5] a state statute was invalidated which attempted to prohibit the immigration of indigent

persons to California. Anyone who has read the *Grapes of Wrath*
can guess the reason for the statute. But I defy any reader not
already familiar with the case to guess the reason given by the
United States Supreme Court for striking down the statute. The
grounds chosen were preemptive doctrines of the Commerce
Clause, which limit the extent to which a state may inhibit interstate commerce. This reason is as vulgar as it is preposterous, since it treats the indigent, Edwards, as though he were
chattel in the commerce of the well-intentioned brother-in-law
who had brought him into the state. This absurd approach is
most interesting, for it reveals one deep basis for doctrinal
analysis, namely that sheer text does not address many situations which the constitutional sense of judges tells them must
be addressed. It also shows the deliberate rejection of structural
argument, since the Court had cited to it in a concurrence the
case of *Crandall* v. *Nevada*,[6] which having been decided before
the adoption of the doctrinally prolific Fourteenth Amendment
had upheld on purely structural grounds a right to travel and
had invalidated a head tax on exit from a state. The reasoning
in *Crandall* relies on this structural argument: The structure
relevant for the decision is the national polity and the important relation that structure establishes between individual citizens and their elected representatives. It follows from this relation that representatives to the national government must
travel to Washington and that if citizens should seek to approach the seat of government to urge particular causes they
too must travel out of their states. From this and the relation
of the national government to its constituent states, it follows
that states may not restrict travel by penalizing it. This opinion
displays an approach to constitutional law deliberately refused
by the *Edwards* majority.

The cases of *Crandall* v. *Nevada* and *McCulloch* and *Carrington* v. *Rash*, which I shall presently discuss, are analyzed from
the structuralist point of view in a book entitled *Structure and
Relationship in Constitutional Law*, the Edward Douglas White
Lectures, by Charles L. Black, Jr.[7] Insofar as Professor Black's
reconstruction of the rationales of these cases is correct, he did
not originate structural argument in these famous lectures. And
yet I think it is fair to say that for our generation of lawyers

and commentators he did invent them, and in doing so created his own precursors by giving us a systematic way in which to read them.

In the introduction to an edition of Seneca, T. S. Eliot wrote, "Few things that can happen to a nation are more important than the invention of a new form of [you'll never guess] . . . verse."[8] This is, as Bronowski characterized it, "a startling remark,"[9] but one that has no doubt considerable justification. Far less justification is required for the assertion that few things that can happen in the life of this nation are more important than the introduction of a new form of constitutional argument. For such an introduction we are all indebted to Charles Black.

Black created anew the structural form at the very time when doctrinal argument was showing the considerable strain I have argued it must bear when new law is being written. This came at the time of the Warren Court, and it is important to realize that Black was one of the few insistent academic defenders of that Court's opinions at the very time when he was constructing more satisfying rationales.

Consider his reconstruction of *Carrington* v. *Rash*,[10] for example. In 1965, the Texas constitution provided that a member of the armed forces was only permitted to vote in the county of his or her residence at the time of entering the service. Carrington, who had enlisted at eighteen in Alabama, was stationed in El Paso and wanted to vote there, where his present home was. With only one member dissenting, the United States Supreme Court upheld his claim, saying the statute denied Carrington the equal protection of the laws. *Carrington* was typical of a number of doctrinal opinions in the area of equal protection. It blithely ignored a perfectly plausible, rational purpose for the statute—as the Court must often do in applying the rational basis standard, since what statute does not bear *some* rational relationship to *some* legitimate legislative purpose— which here was simply to prevent small rural communities from being taken over by transients with no ties or interests in the locality other than perhaps a certain resentment at having landed far from home in a "dry" county. Doctrine in the equal protection area has a singularly fantastic aspect, and I assure you that this example is no more remarkable than many. But of interest to us is Black's reconstruction.

> Carrington [Black would have had the Court hold] was a federal soldier, recruited by the national government to perform a crucial national function. Conceding that in every way he qualified to vote, Texas said that, solely upon the showing that he was in performance of that function, he was not to vote. [This is] a distinctive disadvantage based solely on membership in the Army . . . [I]t ought to be held that no state may annex any disadvantage simply and solely to the performance of a federal duty.[11]

Black grounds his rationale in the "structure of the federal union and in the relation of federal to state governments."[12] His explanation would be as sound whether or not a Fourteenth Amendment existed.

Only one's law sense can determine whether this approach is more satisfying than the application of the two-tier doctrine of equal protection review. For myself, structural argument is the most potent and potentially satisfying recent development in constitutional argument, although it is not without its shortcomings. One of the shortcomings is not, however, that structural argument is not doctrinal argument. Often particular opinions are commonly criticized and advertised as being hopelessly inadequate when in fact all the critic succeeds in demonstrating is an utter disregard of the approach taken by the Court in favor of his or her own approach, which is understandably enough not well supported in the Court's opinion. This kind of criticism is aimed at opinions employing structural argument as well.

Perhaps the most celebrated of Marshall's opinions is the one in *McCulloch* v. *Maryland* from which his famous phrase is drawn: "The power to tax is the power to destroy."[13] It also served as the stimulus for Justice Holmes's tart rejoinder, "Not while this Court sits."[14] For Holmes considered it absurd to claim that any tax, of no matter what magnitude, would destroy the federal structure. He thought that what was needed and what Marshall had failed to give us was a doctrine by which we could decide which impositions were so gross as to be impermissible. Viewing the issue from this vantage point, my students generally side with Holmes.

Consider, however, Marshall's argument as a structural one. The Constitution establishes the structure of federalism, within which the national body bears a certain relation to the states themselves by virtue of its structural composition as representing all states. If the national body were to tax the state, this tax must be weighed against the impact on the state, and a too heavy burden—one that crushed the state structure or deprived it of the ability to perform essential functions—must be struck down. But in the case of a state taxing the nation, *any* burden is impermissible because one body, whose very structure does not include representatives from the other states, is purporting to assume the generalized authority conferred only on the national government by virtue of its generalized representation. Waiving this argument momentarily, Marshall then asks whether a state may exercise taxing power over federal instrumentalities consistent with the nation's role as a supreme body (in contrast to the first argument which focused on the state's role). Why does a tax on one enterprise, it may be asked, amount to "a power to control the operations of" the federal government, as Marshall concludes? The answer given is a structural one: if a state could tax federal activities, *i.e.,* make certain Congressional allocative choices more expensive than others, it could manipulate which choices are ultimately made, and to some extent, exercise influence over all choices, a power clearly inconsistent with national supremacy.

These arguments do not, of course, "answer" Holmes, although they may quiet the discussion. They simply proceed from a different paradigm. And since the reconstruction I have proposed is mine and not Professor Black's, it supports the view that there has been a fundamental paradigm at work and not just a string of virtuoso performances.

At various times, Black has referred to several structural facts from the relationships among which one may infer certain constitutional rules. Some of these facts are: the electorate's assigned central role in the federal government; the existence of a federal court system as one of the agencies for redress of citizens' grievances; "the economic structure of nationhood"; the structure of "national unity"; the concept of "citizenship."[15] Let me show a couple of these facts in operation and then derive another.

Consider the problem posed by examining state statutes in the light of the First Amendment's guarantee of free speech. Preliminarily, we must decide what content, whether historically or textually guided, to give to the words "freedom of speech" in the First Amendment. Then we must somehow get over the fact that the First Amendment refers only to Congress and that the Fourteenth Amendment seems to forbid only those intrusions into our liberty—and restricting our speech is an intrusion—that come about without due process. To tackle that assignment we are currently confined either to discredited historical theories about the circumstances of the framing of the amendment or to fantastic doctrines that, although undoubtedly useful, seem to have no connection whatever with the text.

Black, by contrast, offers the following argument. He argues that "the nature of the federal government, and of the states' relations to it, compels the inference of some federal constitutional protection for free speech, and gives to a wide protection an inferential support quite as strong as the textual support . . ." Because the structure of our federal government is that of a representative democracy,

> discussion of all questions which are in the broadest sense relevant to Congress' work is, quite strictly, a part of the working of the national government. If it is not, what is our mechanism for accommodating national political action to the needs and desires of the people? And if it is, does it not reasonably follow that a state may not interfere with it?[16]

Notice that the structural approach, unlike much doctrinalism, is grounded in the actual text of the Constitution. But, unlike textualist arguments, the passages that are significant are not those of express grants of power or particular prohibitions but instead those which, by setting up structures of a certain kind, permit us to draw the requirements of the relationships among structures.

To Black's examples, one might add branch structure—the relation between the various branches of the federal government—and apply it in the following way. The text of the Constitution gives us three branches of government. Sticking strictly to the text, we may observe that different roles are allocated to different branches, their officers are each selected by different means, their procedures for decision are each different. From this we may infer a certain relationship. Questions are broken down into political and administrative decisions and these decisions are channeled to one or another of the branches at a particular time, depending upon the peculiar competencies and shortcomings of the branches. Thus in Article III Congress is given complete control over the scope of the jurisdiction of the lower federal courts and can thus determine which questions it does not wish to handle or does not wish the judiciary to handle. At the same time, the Supreme Court is given its own authority over cases in which a state is a party, thus removing this decision from Congress, whose representative makeup can jam against a particular state or states—while allowing the Court discretion as to the arena in which such controversies shall be fought out. And the Court's allocation is then subject to a subsequent review by Congress to protect the states generally, a role for which Congress composition is well suited. The congressional disposition of *Chisholm* v. *Georgia* [17] in proposing the Eleventh Amendment to erase the effect of a Supreme Court decision shows this process at work.

So we have these three structures whose relationship consists in part in passing on to each other questions whose features best fit them to be resolved by a particular kind of institutional decider. These features include the ease and complexity of fact finding, the need or desirability of an immediate resolution, the need for an ongoing supervision of remedies, the ability to reflect popular reaction to a decision, and doubtless many others. But it is a different picture than that offered by the doctrinal approach, captured in the misleading phrase "Separation of Powers." More importantly, this picture is derived from a different kind of argument regarding the Constitution, and the different results of this approach often seem to comport better not only with political realities but with the realities that form legal decision.

We can apply this approach to a current problem and test its usefulness. The question of the legislative veto is a contemporary constitutional question of considerable significance. We are told in a recent law review article by a United States Senator, that

> Congress has adopted the congressional veto procedure [by which it can] preclude implementation of proposed executive or administrative actions which have been advanced pursuant to statutory authority [as a means of controlling and limiting the exercise of . . . power by executive or administrative agencies.] . . . The congressional veto customarily takes effect in the following manner. Congress enacts a statute . . . requiring implementation by the executive or an administrative agency. Pursuant to a delegation of authority in the enabling statute, an affected agency must submit to Congress whatever executive orders, rules, regulations or directives it proposes to implement the stated congressional policy. If at the expiration of a specified time period, usually thirty or sixty days, no disapproval action is taken by the Congress, the proposed action becomes effective.[18]

The question is whether such congressional vetos are "an unconstitutional attempt by Congress to interfere with the execution of the laws" or, as Senator Abourezk framed it, "a permissible action which protects the legislative powers of Congress from encroachment by another branch of the government."[19]

If we approach the problem doctrinally we quickly reach an impasse. In this problem, as is so often the case, we have an interface between two powers, and doctrine gives us no basis for priority. This is why "balancing" tests are so prevalent in doctrinally oriented opinions. By the same token the text, viewed through a microscope as it were, is no help. The congressional veto in its variations is neither specifically sanctioned nor specifically disapproved by any single provision of the Constitution. If we abandon the text altogether, however, we are left with highly questionable political and prudential preferences in a controversial area. Thus I certainly do not agree with my colleague Professor Mendelson that "American government was conceived in fear"[20] and therefore also do not agree with the various prudential approaches that this premise counsels. Nor am I inclined to agree with *ad hoc* approaches coming from the other end of the political spectrum.

Finally, even a slight review of the historical literature would disenchant one from using that approach. Both Stewart, in the Harvard Journal of Legislation,[21] and Watson, in the California Law Review,[22] search the debates at the Constitutional Convention and the Federalist Papers to discover the correct "meaning" of the notions of separation of powers and the presidential veto. Stewart finds the congressional veto valid. Watson does not.

Structural argument is useful here. Given the structures and relationships of branch theory sketched above, we may fashion a constitutional rule. Congressional vetos requiring the act of less than both houses (since the text and history are decisively against substantive action by the whole of Congress that is not presented to the President for veto) to "turn on" executive action, i.e., to permit a proposed rule to come into force, are procedurally constitutional since they moot the presentment issue and avoid the unconstitutional example of positive action (rather than inaction) "turning off" previous executive authority (acting, that is, in a way the President ought to be able to review). Thus structural argument enables us to isolate features of the legislative veto that are constitutionally relevant: participation by the President, non-legislative action by Congressmen, the composition of the acting body, the timing and subject matter of the action (whether broad policy clarifying or ad hoc, specific to a single instance.) This allows us to discriminate among variations of the veto. At a period in which the destruction of the party system, among other events, has made Executive-Congressional collaboration almost impossible, such innovation enhances coalition building in the Congress and forces an up-or-down vote on Executive proposals. A structural approach enables reform that does not weaken an already greatly weakened Presidency. That the (to some) intuitively attractive view that the veto is constitutionally safest when both houses act, is clearly unconstitutional reminds us that the Constitution is attentive to the preservation of branch structure. Moreover, Congress, acting as a whole and subject to the President's veto, is unlikely to cede great power to a part.

Another example of branch structural argument at work is given by Justice Story. Despite the clear statement in The Federalist to the contrary,[23] it was determined early on that the consent of the Senate was not necessary for the removal of executive officials from office, even when such approval is necessary for appointments.[24] This decision was mutually agreed upon by Congress and the Executive. A Court decision to the contrary, undoing this arrangement, is absurd to contemplate. A similar, though less adroit, resolution was achieved in the recent intersession Pocket Veto Case in which the Attorney General quite wisely refrained from taking an appeal to the United States Supreme Court to determine whether a President could validly veto legislation during congressional recesses.[25]

Branch structural arguments are equally useful in treating questions such as whether a court should be able to review an impeachment conviction. Indeed, to test the structural approach, one might apply it to this question and see if the outcome is the same as that determined by someone else also using structural methods. I mention this experiment because it goes to the very heart of one of the two most forceful objections to structural argument. Structural arguments are sometimes accused of being indeterminate because while we can all agree on the presence of the various structures, we fall to bickering when called upon to decide whether a particular result is necessarily inferred from their relationships. For example, in an illuminating and thoughtful review of Black's *Structure and Relationship in Constitutional Law*,[26] Vince Blasi seems to suggest that structural methods are only useful in Charles Black's hands. Indeed, there has been little real commentary on Black's approach, though it is frequently cited and the term "structure" has even joined the litany with "history and text" in the clichès of respectable constitutional writers.[27] Why has this method been nominally accepted but so largely unassimilated? Is it because of its unpredictability? This objection is related to the observation that the structural arguments in Black's book all yield results precisely those rendered by the courts in the actual cases. Who cares, one may ask, how courts get there?[28]

I think I have shown that structural arguments may very well yield different results than other approaches. But to the cynical this may clinch the indeterminacy objection. The better answer to the objection is that Black's structural arguments yield results similar to those reached by courts employing other methods because those courts, without saying so, were aiming at results that were structurally satisfying. Thus, to take a famous example, it was intolerable to the Supreme Court that a state might, by standing aside, invite racially restrictive property sales—an entire de facto zoning system based on race—even if the Court was a little unsure what precedents and doctrines would lead them to that conclusion.

Indeed one good reason for adopting structural approaches is that they *are* more satisfying, being truer approximations of the interaction of actual reasons yielding actual results than are doctrinal or textual approaches. We share a constitutional sense and we use it. Why not, Black might ask, make that use explicit once we have determined the bases of the decision by taking a macroscopic view of the text. If we don't agree in hard cases, that is nothing new; and perhaps being forced to make the process explicit, we will sharpen our senses and eventually achieve a greater coherence.

Yet, think back to the Warren Court's controversial opinions and the defenses that Professor Black would year by year, after each term had passed, offer for them. Why were his more satisfying rationales always different from those of the Court? And if his reasons really were more satisfying why didn't the Court pick up the skill? If structural arguments can only be successfully employed by a very few then they are of little constitutional significance. Not only would we have a battery of district judges across the country trying to use an unfamiliar and unwieldy analytical tool, we would also sacrifice the plain understanding that is the Constitution's greatest asset in retaining the devotion of our people, and the lack of which is the principal shortcoming in the methods structural argument seeks to displace. This is the indeterminacy argument in a weaker form. I think it is too early to answer this worry. We are currently too much in the grip of a few conventions of argument that make it difficult to appreciate a novel approach, yet we must remember that even some of the accepted conventions were not always with us.

The second principal objection to structural approaches is that they can offer no firm basis for personal rights. Since under this approach personal rights are held to derive from the structure of citizenship, it is argued that the rights of citizens (to say nothing of aliens) are essentially statist and are therefore vulnerable to the state's desire for power and its ability to manipulate the relation between citizen and state.

Alexander Bickel's last book, *The Morality of Consent*,[29] published posthumously, advanced this objection. The original unamended text of the Constitution makes little mention or use of the word *citizen*. Even the Preamble speaks of "the People of the United States," although this terminology could perhaps be explained by saying that the citizen-state relation could only arise after the people had established a state structure. Nevertheless, it was natural enough that the Framers, who had just renounced one citizenship, were reluctant to make too much turn on the concept of "citizen."

Bickel argued that this all changed with the decision in *Dred Scott*,[30] which held that a Negro could not invoke the diversity jurisdiction of the federal courts since he had not been and could not be a citizen, diverse or otherwise. In this Bickel saw the fundamental flaw in a system of rights based on citizenship. What government may grant, it may take away. Rights of citizenship are therefore only rights in the sense that they express claims against the state which the state may, if it chooses, dishonor[31] by repealing the basis for such claims. Is this because Congress may withdraw particular rights, as, for example, it might withdraw from the federal courts the diversity jurisdiction? I think not, and therefore I think the *Dred Scott* case is a somewhat confusing example. It is rather because Congress, or the courts or the executive, may withdraw the status of citizen from someone and thus at a stroke obliterate that person's rights.

Accordingly the bulk of Bickel's chapter on the subject of citizenship is devoted to some of the past disabilities suffered by aliens and to the case law that has forbid government to strip citizens of their status. Bickel did not rejoice in the development of that case law, however. He objected because the rationale by which it proceeded—namely, that "Citizenship *is* man's basic right for it is nothing less than the right to have rights"[32]— yields the intolerable inferences of Taney, the author of *Dred Scott*, that non-citizens "[have] no rights . . . but such as those who held the power and the government might choose to grant them."[33] Bickel concluded,

> A relationship between government and the governed that turns
> on citizenship can always be dissolved or denied. Citizenship is
> a legal construct, an abstraction, a theory. No matter what the
> safeguards, it is at best something given, and given to some and
> not to others, and it can be taken away.[34]

In some ways this reminds one of Burke's attacks on Rousseau.
Indeed Bickel noted, warningly, that after the French Revolution the revolutionaries took to calling one another "citizen."
Bickel asks why this didn't happen here; and he answers by
asserting a relative unconcern on the part of the Framers with
the entire concept of citizenship.[35] I suspect a stronger reason
lay in the absence of a titled nobility in this country. The one
citizen we all recall from the French Revolution is, after all,
Citizen Capet. Free of a caste system, in all but one respect,
there was no occasion for the proud assertion of 'citizen' as a
name in itself. The exception was the status of the Negro, and
this exception suggests that Taney was perhaps tragically not
so far from wrong. If citizenship is really a set of strong rights
by which the people may make claims upon and put limitations
upon government, then surely the Framers did not mean to
include the Negro. Set aside for the moment what sometimes appears to be the point of attack in Bickel's assault on the
notion of citizenship as a constitutional basis for rights—that
the universal idea of personhood is better.[36] If there are *any*
rights which the Constitution confers on the basis of the citizen-
relation to government, it confers these rights without discrimination. Yet with respect to the most basic aspect of the citizen-
state structural relationship, namely representation, slaves were
from the start explicitly treated as something less than citizens.

Dred Scott[37] does not, then, support Bickel's attack, because
it does not present the spectre of a government withdrawing a
human or political right by withdrawing citizenship. In America, this simply was not conferred on the Negro slave.

The passages from the Warren Court opinion[38] that echo
Taney's notions of citizenship, to Bickel's disgust, also show a
quite different point. They stand for the proposition that because the relationship between citizen and government is a fundamental structural relationship, it cannot be altered in any
substantial way whatsoever except by the constitutionally established means of changing the structure itself by amendment.

In the paragraph preceding that which Bickel quoted, Chief Justice Warren wrote,

> This government was born of its citizens, it maintains a continuing relationship with them, and, in my judgment, it is without power to sever the relationship that gives rise to its existence.[39]

Bickel's objection to grounding rights in a structure of citizenship is not persuasive then if one holds that government does not have the power to unilaterally dissolve the bonds of citizenship. Indeed, I think that any structural theory that raises citizenship to such prominence must hold this axiomatically. It may even be this absolutism of structural argument that repels Bickel's prudentialism: knowing that absolutes are not the way of the political world, Bickel suspects that they will give way and, since they promise all, take all with them when they collapse, unlike more flexible barriers.

What of Bickel's second argument against reliance on the citizen-relation, that so doing deprives aliens of their rights?[40] This objection is also not a wholesale assault on structural argument, since it may be that with respect to a certain class of problems, other constitutional approaches may be superior while the structural approach is still to be preferred in other cases. Moreover, the objection depends on an antinomy between citizen and alien, a chiaroscuric relationship which may be found in Aristotle but is not a relationship established anywhere in the Constitution. It is simply not true that if a citizen derives his rights from his status as citizen then an alien may have no rights since he is not a citizen. If there is any relation between these structures, it is largely governed by the inference from the constitutional idea of national supremacy and its relationship to citizenship. Thus, at least as concerns state discrimination against aliens, Professor Black has argued,

> I should think that once the nation has decided that a man may live here, that decision implies by plain necessity a decision that he may live in some state, and that a state's putting him . . . on a different footing from its other residents amounts to diminution by a state of that which the nation, for its own purposes, has given—an action no more to be countenanced than would the discriminatory taxation by a state of foreign imports as such.[41]

Black even goes so far as to say that the rights of aliens are protected from national action because their position can be convincingly analogized to that of citizens for many purposes. Thus, Bickel's objection to inferences from the structure of citizenship respecting aliens can be blunted—perhaps even turned against its author—if one merely rejects the idea that "alien" and "citizen" are opposites sharing no characteristics, defined as negations of one another, and adopts instead the view that the resident alien is for constitutional purposes to be analogized to the citizen with only such exceptions—voting and office-holding—as the Constitution itself provides.[42]

May we conclude that structural argument is an effective all-round approach to constitutional matters? I think not. While structural approaches are very powerful for some kinds of questions, particularly intergovernmental issues, they are not adequate, as Bickel sensed, to the task of protecting human rights.

Citizenship may be the proper structure from whose relation to representative government we may infer the right to vote on equal terms,[43] to speak on political matters,[44] to hold office when duly chosen,[45] to associate for political purposes,[46] and even, as Black has argued, to be treated fairly when one is the object of action by government.[47] But these examples do not capture the personal values that animated both the American Revolution and Constitution making and that principally account for the phenomenon of limited government. I suppose you do have to be your own man to be truly capable of freely voting your choices in an election, but is that the *reason* why neither government nor a collection of individuals acting while government stands by ought to be able to deprive you of the various rights that are the exercise of independent choice? What, after all, do the choices of whom to marry,[48] whether to have children,[49] or whether to send your children to private school[50] what do these have to do with the "good *political* life"?[51]

Furthermore, isn't there a positive danger in relying on structural arguments in this area? Since such personal rights have no affirmative structure in the Constitution beyond the Bill of Rights, won't they always be sacrificed to those unchecked inferences which do plausibly flow from the citizen-state relation? For example: Might Congress legislate that each of us be required to listen to political debates or attend political discussions (assuming, of course, that these events were "unbiased")? Or might Congress plausibly decide, pursuant to its § 5 powers to enforce the guarantee of privileges and immunities of citizens, that the good political life includes the right to decent housing[52] and therefore require that those of us with sufficient space begin lodging those presently living in slums? "It is by such thinking," Bickel wrote at the end of the chapter I have discussed, "that the claims of liberty may be readily translated into the postulates of oppression."[53]

It is often said that man is a political animal. And we are a political people. But even a sensitive rendering of what this means in our society—that our politics depend on notions of individual autonomy and security of home and possessions and on the primacy of familial and intimate relations and that these personal matters contribute to our political attitudes—does not capture the fact that constitutional life in America is not just political life.

In fact it is not even clear that the notion of citizenship fully captures the political relationship between our people and our governmental structures.[54] For example, civil disobedience would probably never be countenanced from a purely structural perspective, since the relation between citizen and state implies an obedience to legitimately passed laws.

Structural argument has, as we have observed of other constitutional approaches, both its powers and its shortcomings. Like other approaches, structural argument also generates a particular attitude toward the basis for judicial review.

In 1978, in his Holmes Lectures, speaking from the podium at which Bickel, Hand, and Hart had stood, Black addressed the structural basis for judicial review. As might have been anticipated, he distinguished sharply between review by federal courts of state decisions and review of federal decisions. Obviously the relationships are altered where one structure or the other is in place.

> [T]he very nature of the case is that the national judicial power, interpreting the national Constitution, can be in relevant conflict—relevant, that is, to the problem of consonance with democratic assumptions—only with the national democratic branch.

> . . . [Legitimacy is] no more at hazard when Connecticut is subjected to national law than . . . when New Haven is subjected to Connecticut law.[55]

So Black focuses the question of legitimacy—*i.e.*, what justifies a court in reversing a democratically chosen rule—on the particular relationship between Congress and the federal courts, by drawing attention to the parallel national scope of the two structures.

With respect to this redefined question of legitimacy, the structural perspective is distinctive. Far from accepting the doctrinalist view expressed by Hart, which owing to his view of the source of the Court's legitimacy did not give Congress the complete control of the appellate jurisdiction of the Supreme Court that Article III seems to commit to it,[56] Black celebrates this control, finding in it and in Congress's acquiescence in the Court's decisions through the non-exercise of this power, that democratic legitimacy is conferred on the decisions of a body of appointed judges.

> Again we see how closely the question about the powers of Congress over jurisdiction, and the question about the suitability of the constitutional material for use as law in law courts, are intertwined. The effect of congressional acquiescence, amounting very nearly if not entirely to invitation, would approach zero, if it became a generally accepted belief that Congress has no choice but to acquiesce. One would have to ask then whether such material as goes into the making of constitutional judgment was suitably definite for interpretation and application by tenured judges, in the teeth of however bitter resentment by the recurrently elected branches, who under the Constitution could do nothing much about it.[57]

Structural arguments have not yet received the acceptance and attention they merit. This is perhaps partly a reflection of a narrow-minded formalism that persists in law schools and can be observed whenever one hears the clipped citation of a case which is, by its very mention, supposed to resolve a serious question. There are doubtless other reasons why *Structure and Relationship in Constitutional Law* is so much cited but so little applied. The future, however—once law professors have integrated the structural method into their own—will see more of structural approaches. As governments *qua* producers gain more importance in our lives, and hence as intergovernmental questions are brought to prominence, structural arguments will become more useful.

The great constitutional dialogue of the decade and a half that began in the late 1950s was silenced when Bickel died in New Haven in November 1974. My last conversation with him was about a book that had just been written by Black. Bickel's voice was strong and rapid even though he was largely paralyzed and blind and was dying that death whose agony is untellable.

There is a nobility in these lives devoted to the Constitution which is a reflection of the value that the Constitution presupposes in us. The memoriam for Bickel in the Yale Law Journal was written by Black.[58] It described an incident in which Bickel was asked by the then-current Administration in Washington to comment on the constitutionality of a particular antibusing proposal. After study, Bickel decided against the measure's constitutionality and so reported. It was said in many quarters at the time that this imprudent act cost Bickel the chance to be considered for an appointment to the Supreme Court, a post which he coveted.[59] Of course Bickel knew this when he reached his own decision, but his prudences were in the service of great institutions and were not merely personal expediencies.

Black's Holmes Lectures responded to his silenced colleague. They addressed the issue of legitimacy and how it is preserved by courts faithful to decision according to law. As if recognizing that questions of personal rights had not been successfully derived by previous methods of argument, Black devoted the largest part of his discussion to that issue. This effort—"a matter of reasoning from commitment" that is constitutional argument—I commend to the reader. As I sat in the wooden writing chairs of the Ames Courtroom I was anxious that Black attempt this task. It is to that same task, and the problem of personal rights, that I will turn next.

CHAPTER 7

ETHICAL ARGUMENT

Thus far, I have attempted to construct a typology of constitutional arguments whose existence I should think few would deny.[1] I have briefly discussed some of the powers and shortcomings of these arguments, arguments that are as much approaches to the Constitution as they are directions for its construction.

I now turn to one particular sort of argument whose very status as a coherent convention would be perhaps controversial. For reasons I will discuss later, I have called this approach "ethical" argument. For the moment I will only try to show that an ethical approach exists, that it is reflected in the U.S. Reports, and that it is often the animating argumentative factor in constitutional decisionmaking. I will leave for Book II a fuller treatment that shows the proper use of ethical arguments, examines the source of their legitimacy, and asks whether their proper use would help justify particularly difficult and otherwise troublesome decisions.

Thus far I have discussed the following types of constitutional arguments: historical, textual, structural, prudential, and doctrinal. If you were to take a set of colored pencils, assign a separate color to each of the kinds of arguments, and mark through passages in an opinion of the Supreme Court deciding a constitutional matter, you would probably have a multi-colored picture when you finished. Judges are the artists of our field, just as law professors are its critics, and we expect the creative judge to employ all the tools that are appropriate, often in combination, to achieve a satisfying result. Furthermore, in a multi-membered panel whose members may prefer different constitutional approaches, the negotiated document that wins a majority may, naturally, reflect many hues rather than the single bright splash one observes in dissents.

If you ever take up my suggestion and try this sport you will sometimes find (leaving aside the statement of facts and sometimes the jurisdictional statement) that there is nevertheless a patch of uncolored text. And you may also find that this patch contains expressions of considerable passion and conviction, not simply the idling of the judicial machinery that one sometimes finds in dictum. It is with those patches that I am concerned here.

The class of arguments that I will call ethical arguments reflects, like other constitutional arguments, a particular approach to constitutional adjudication. I will suggest that such arguments, like the others I have discussed, are especially suited to certain of the Supreme Court's functions (and those of other principal constitutional deciders) and reflect a particular commitment regarding the grounds for the legitimacy of judicial review. I hope that I shall be able to convince you not only that ethical argument shares these traits with other types of constitutional argument, but that it does so from a perspective sufficiently coherent and sufficiently distinct as to justify our counting it as a separate kind of argument.

By ethical argument I mean constitutional argument whose force relies on a characterization of American institutions and the role within them of the American people. It is the character, or *ethos*, of the American polity that is advanced in ethical argument as the source from which particular decisions derive.

Let me say at once that I am aware of some of the difficulties created by my choice of this particular name. As I shall use the term, ethical arguments are not *moral* arguments. Ethical constitutional arguments do not claim that a particular solution is right or wrong in any sense larger than that the solution comports with the sort of people we are and the means we have chosen to solve political and customary constitutional problems.

I might have chosen the word 'ethological' to describe such argument, but the cultural anthropologists have taken over that word; or I might have invented a word like 'ethetic' which bears a relationship to 'ethos' much like that borne by the word 'pathetic' to the word 'pathos.' I might have especially done this since 'pathetic' has to do with the idiosyncratic, personal traits and thus reflects one feature of illegitimate judicial opinions which is often confounded with the class of arguments I am interested in illuminating. In the end I decided on the term 'ethical' largely because of its etymological basis. Our word 'ethical' comes from the Greek ἠθικός (*ethikos*), which meant "expressive of character" when used by the tragedians. It derives from the term ἦθος (*ethos*) which once meant the *habits* and character of the individual, and is suggestive of the constitutional derivation of ethical arguments.

There is an almost utter absence of the discussion of ethical arguments *as arguments* in the teaching of constitutional law. Either they are instead regarded as disreputable reflections of the moral and political positions of the judge who lacks sufficient willpower to keep them properly cabined or they are indulged by both the cynical and the sentimental for being what "real" judging is all about, having little to do with the competition of arguments *per se*. Book II will provide a systematic basis from which to criticize these positions, but for now I am concerned with their general effect, which has been to encourage disregard for the treatment of ethical approaches as legal, constitutional arguments. With respect to students, the result of this has been profound. They know that the constitutional cases that most engage them are not decided on the basis, for example, of whether the Framers thought that contraception by pill could be banned or whether the word *'speech'* in the First Amendment means, among other things, wearing a shirt with a four-letter word on it. Because they know this Constitutional law may take on an unreal aspect for them or may simply dissolve into political science, a sphere from which civilized law has, I believe, long fled. Therefore I think that even the mere recognition of ethical arguments may have some salutary effect. To that task of observation—though of course no observation of this kind is not theory-laden—I shall devote the remainder of this chapter.

Let us begin with some recent examples of ethical argument. In *Moore* v. *City of East Cleveland*,[2] the Supreme Court confronted an Ohio zoning ordinance that limited occupancy of a dwelling unit to members of a single family. Inez Moore, who was 63 years of age, lived in her own home with her son and two grandsons. One grandson was the child of the son living at home. The other grandson was the son's nephew. She was convicted for the crime of having failed to remove the nephew as an "illegal occupant" as defined by the Ohio ordinance which did not permit collateral relations to share a home within a certain area prescribed by the zoning code.

Precedent in the form of previous cases sympathetic to the integrity of the family, had focused on the childbearing and childrearing functions of the *nuclear* family, as Justices Stewart and Rehnquist pointed out. At the same time, the recent case of *Village of Belle Terre* v. *Boraas*[3] had upheld a zoning ordinance that, in restricting land uses, had excluded groups of students, friends living together, and unmarried groups like the Moores that were not couples.

Nevertheless, a plurality of the Supreme Court struck down the Ohio statute. Justice Powell read the earlier decisions not in terms of their doctrinal consistency, that is in terms of the arguments and rationales they shared, but in terms of the ethical approach to constitutional questions that they embodied. Thus he wrote,

> Our decisions establish that the Constitution protects the sanctity of the family precisely because the institution of the family is deeply rooted in this Nation's history and tradition.[4]

Justice Powell placed the decision on an ethical ground—one based on the American ethos and not shared by all cultures— that values and utilizes extended kinship.

> Ours is by no means a tradition limited to respect for the bonds uniting the members of the nuclear family. The tradition of uncles, aunts, cousins, and especially grandparents sharing a

household along with parents and children has roots equally venerable and equally deserving of constitutional recognition. Over the years millions of our citizens have grown up in just such an environment, and most, surely, have profited from it. Even if conditions of modern society have brought about a decline in extended family households, they have not erased the accumulated wisdom of civilization, gained over the centuries and honored throughout our history, that supports a larger conception of the family.[5]

This is a clear and, to my mind, persuasive exposition of an ethical argument. As a distinct approach it not only enables us to deal with precedent in a way quite distinct from that taken by the dissenters, but it also establishes the opinion as a different precedent when understood in light of the approach. The value of this characterization may be appreciated when contrasted with more conventional analyses. Professor Tribe, for example, in his interesting and useful treatise, is forced to resort to extraordinary doctrinal pyrotechnics to rationalize *Moore* with *Belle Terre*. He notes that *Belle Terre* involved students who did not claim "an enduring relationship" with one another. Consequently, *Moore* should stand for the proposition that "governmental interference with *any* [enduring] relationship should be invalidated unless compellingly justified."[6] We are then told that *Belle Terre*, "the earlier case," cannot be said to foreclose this position.[7]

I fear that counsel who rely on this view are apt to be disillusioned. There is nothing clearly discernible in the American ethos that relies on the value of enduring relationships generally, except possibly magazine subscriptions and appeals from one's old college. I suggest that it is because he has elected a different constitutional approach than that taken by the Court that so able a reader as Professor Tribe is led to so profound a misconstruction.

Is ethical argument solely a feature of the current scene? Of course there will be fashions and preferences among styles, but if the Supreme Court term that saw *Moore* v. *City of East Cleveland* was the first whose decisions turned on ethical argument, I would be inclined to doubt that the approach I am describing is on a par with other constitutional approaches;

therefore I shall mention a few other cases that show the phenomenon of ethical argument.

The petitioner in *Meyer* v. *Nebraska*,[8] decided in 1923, was an instructor in a parochial school. Robert Meyer was convicted of violating a Nebraska statute that made it a crime to teach a foreign language to any child not yet in the eighth grade. Over the dissents of Holmes and Sutherland, whose doctrinal and historical perspectives were incompatible with his own decision, Justice McReynolds wrote for the Court invalidating the Nebraska law.

McReynolds defined the problem as involving the construction of the term 'liberty' in the Fourteenth Amendment,[9] but I think you will see that his approach was ethical and not textual. First, in his determination of what constitutes liberty, he presents us with a catalogue, largely derived from the otherwise constitutionally irrelevant institution of the common law, of various features of the American ethos.

> Without doubt, [liberty] denotes not merely freedom from bodily restraint but also the right of the individual to contract, to engage in any of the common occupations of life, to acquire useful knowledge, to marry, establish a home and bring up children, to worship God according to the dictates of his own conscience, and generally to enjoy those privileges long recognized at common law as essential to the orderly pursuit of happiness by free men.[10]

The text of the Fourteenth Amendment does not guarantee a right to liberty, however, but instead merely denies to states the power to abridge that liberty without due process. Even granting that the phrase "due process" means a procedure that yields a non-arbitrary result bearing a rational relationship to a permissible goal—a formulation, by the way, that the caselaw has achieved by ethical argumentative routes[11]—it seems plainly wrong to conclude that the Nebraska statute violated the Fourteenth Amendment's guarantee as textually or doctrinally construed. Many plausible goals, in the context of a large immigrant population unable to teach English adequately to their children at home and more than competent to teach their native German, are "rationally related" to such a statute. Even leaving aside such a context, there is ample latitude for states to specify certain curricula in preference to others. Had the legislature banned analytic geometry before the eighth grade, expressing a preference for algebra, one could hardly condemn such a decision as a deprivation brought about utterly without due process.

The same Court's subsequent use of *Meyer* in the consolidated cases of *Pierce* v. *Society of Sisters,* and *Pierce* v. *Hill Military Academy* [12] supports the view that ethical arguments were at work. There it was conceded that the state did not lack a purposeful statute, such as to fail even to be legislation on rational grounds (the Oregon law in question required all children to attend the public schools). Rather, the state had transgressed a general limitation of the means by which governments can effectuate their goals. Citing *Meyer,* a unanimous Court struck down the Oregon statute, saying:

> The fundamental theory of liberty upon which all governments in this Union repose excludes any general power of the State to standardize its children by forcing them to accept instruction from public teachers only. The child is not the mere creature of the State; those who nurture him and direct his destiny have the right, coupled with the high duty, to recognize and prepare him for additional obligations. [13]

It is sometimes said that *Pierce* could be better explained as involving statutes which abridged the First Amendment protection of the free exercise of religion. [14] As has been pointed out, however, this could hardly be the case with *Pierce* v. *Hill Military Academy.* [15] It is also sometimes said that First Amendment values of free association were at stake in these cases and that these would have provided a better ground for decision. [16] This is said by people who wish to avoid the notoriety of substantive due process—that is, giving the Fourteenth Amendment's guarantee of due process a scope far exceeding the procedural, common, and historical understanding of the term—but who nevertheless are quite unwilling to abandon the decisions in *Meyer* and *Pierce.* This puzzles me. First, because the First Amendment says nothing about the states one must assume that, unless some other constitutional clause is used, pinning the argument on the First Amendment is just another way of giving substantive content to the term 'due process.' Resorting to the First Amendment merely to define the term 'liberty' alone in that clause, is scarcely much protection for First Amendment values, and would not, as we have seen, yield the Court's results in either *Meyer* or *Pierce* or, I venture to say, in any significant First Amendment decision affecting the states.

Second, why is it thought more appropriate to say that freedom of association generally derives from a particular amendment (which does not mention association except to protect specific kinds) than to say that government may not employ methods fundamentally inconsistent with the nonspecific ethic of the whole Constitution? It may be that both assertions are improper. At this point all I wish to show is that such a disagreement reflects a conflict between the doctrinal and ethical approaches, neither of which can claim an explicit textual commitment specific to the restraint urged.

One may be tempted to conclude that ethical arguments are simply substantive due process by another name. This is not so, as a discussion of Chief Justice Marshall's work in the Cherokee cases will show. But in an interesting way it is almost so. At least as applied to the analysis of state actions, ethical constitutional arguments usually appear in the form of substantive due process because the due process clause is the textual vehicle by which the ethos of limited government is applied to the states. Of itself, this is hardly discrediting; the same form must be used in the application of the Bill of Rights. No matter how explicit its provisions may be, the Bill of Rights applies to national government and not to the states. We may not then dismiss the class of ethical arguments on such grounds as their embodiment in substantive due process modes unless one is also willing to dismiss the textual and doctrinal arguments that, to take two instances, constitute the entire main body of First and Fifth Amendment constitutional law. I will explore the relationship between ethical argument and the recurring phenomenon of substantive due process further in Book II. For now I will simply note that just as ethical arguments are not wholly of our time, so they are also not confined to those human and political rights associated with the modern phenomenon of substantive due process.

Indeed, one of the most interesting uses of ethical argument appeared (or perhaps I should say was effective and therefore failed to appear) in the *Pentagon Papers Case,* a classic First Amendment and not a substantive due process case.[17] In *Pentagon Papers,* no underlying congressional legislation was alleged to specifically authorize the President to prevent publication by the *New York Times* of various secret reports on the Vietnam War. Indeed, as Justice Marshall pointed out, "on at least two occasions Congress [had] refused to enact legislation that would have . . . given the President the power that he [sought] in [that] case."[18] And yet the Court applied conventional First Amendment analysis despite the clear terms of that Amendment limiting the powers of *Congress.* There is no discussion of this point, which is something of a triumph of avoidance since the case evoked nine opinions from the Justices. The reasons for the omission are twofold and relate to the nature of ethical argument.

The First Amendment, as the Framers repeatedly said of the entire Bill of Rights when it was proposed in Congress and campaigned for in the states, is merely a concrete application to a specific institution of larger notions of limited government and free political exchange. Presidents, for example, are not barred by the text of the First Amendment from establishing a national church by executive order. There are innumerable hypotheticals, perhaps not nearly so likely to happen as the specific situations anticipated by the Bill of Rights but sharing with them a common ground in the American constitutional ethic of limited government.[19] Relying on the main body of the Constitution to supply such an ethic, James Madison initially opposed the whole notion of a Bill of Rights on the grounds that it was unnecessary. It might even do harm, he said, by appearing to limit individual rights to those commemorated in the texts of the amendments. The Ninth Amendment itself exists as a rebuke to anyone who argues for such limitations.

It would be intolerable if a President could use means to restrict a free press that Congress plainly could not. But why would it be intolerable? Because it would be inconsistent with the ethic expressed by the First Amendment and by other passages in the Consitution as well.

Plainly, the text does not restrain the President. And as the various opinions of the Court made clear, the only congressional legislation on the matter—the Espionage Act—was highly relevant to the original theft of the materials but had no provision covering "holders in due course," if you will. Nor will it do to say that an injunction statute is the Congressional intervention required to bring the language of the Amendment into play. If this were so, then a jurisdictional statute might serve in this way and the element of Congressional action specified by the Amendment—a "law abridging the freedom of speech"—would be erased wholly in its substantive content. Yet no one contended that the injunction statute relied upon, any more than the Declaratory Judgment Act, could authorize a prior restraint by the Executive.

One might argue that the historical background of the First Amendment evidences a concern about governmental abuse of power generally; but this, I think, is really more an ethical approach. Historical argument, as narrowly used in these chapters, brings to bear on its construction concerns contemporary to the drafting of the text. There is little of specific relevance in the First Amendment or elsewhere that will serve as the scaffolding for such history. And there is no evidence that an analogous example of presidential abuse was foreseen in the debates proposing the First Amendment or arguing for its ratification.

It might be argued, from a prudential point of view, that a First Amendment barrier must be erected against the Executive in order to restrain Congress. After all, it would be a rather easy thing for Congress to evade the First Amendment if it could simply refrain from acting while a sympathetic President did its dirty work. But prudential arguments (there are two here) are also not persuasive. As to frustrating the general purpose of the First Amendment, such an assessment wholly begs the question. It assumes a general purpose the very nature of which the debate is about. As to the argument from collusion, there was no showing of this in the actual case, and—recalling Senator Gravel's reading of the classified papers at hearings of his subcommittee—there is, outside the record, much evidence to suggest that the opposite was true.

I am inclined to think that structural considerations, at least in their branch structural aspect, would argue for a result contrary to that reached by the Court. The President's ability to control information collected solely by and solely for Executive reflection and decisionmaking in an area, foreign affairs, largely committed to the President and taking as its subject past Executive action, would appear to frame a very strong case against using the First Amendment as a lever by which to alter the direction of such control and dissemination.

For the very reason that the case raises a novel point, doctrine is not much help here. Indeed, one suspects that the Court failed to explicitly consider the First Amendment's application to Executive action alone because it did not wish to make doctrine in this area.

In sum, an ethical tack was taken because others were unavailable and because it exerted its pull on the Court to move in the direction it provided. If as critics we come to see this particular mode of argument as more satisfying and therefore appropriate in some set of constitutional cases, we will have gone a long way to admitting the use of that sort of argument to the typology commonly recognized.

Consider, then, three famous cases, none of whose opinions purported to reach decision via an ethical approach. If the ethical pull was felt—if the decision is inexplicable otherwise—then an ethical argument ought to be available and ought to be more satisfying than other approaches including the ones overtly employed.

In *Trop* v. *Dulles* [20] a former private in the Second World War challenged the forfeiture of citizenship that had accompanied his conviction and dishonorable discharge for wartime desertion. This forfeiture was overturned by the Supreme Court on the grounds that it constituted cruel and unusual punishment in violation of the Eighth Amendment. It was a splintered decision, five to four for the result, with no opinion claiming a majority. And yet I suspect there are few students of the issue who think that military tribunals ought to be able to de-nationalize a citizen.

The difficulty, I suggest, is with the Eighth Amendment rationale. It is simply hard to swallow the argument that a collateral penalty for a constitutionally validated capital offense is unconstitutionally harsh. As Mr. Justice Frankfurter put it, ". . . can [it] be seriously urged that loss of citizenship is a fate worse than death?"[21] The collateral penalty was certainly not unusual in the sense of being novel or bizarre; the statute struck down was the lineal descendant of one adopted first in 1865.[22] The justification for our intuitive sense of the rightness of the holding in *Trop* v. *Dulles* lies elsewhere.

I would have thought a governmental agency could not unilaterally dissolve the bonds of citizenship of a natural-born citizen because the government was not responsible for joining those bonds in the first place. Since the relationship between citizen and state has constitutional status[23] and since so much of our political life is predicated upon it, I would assume it a principle of the American constitutional ethic that representative government, created by the People acting as a whole, could not begin slicing off parts of the Polity without the consent of the People. Now this ethical argument leads to some close questions. To what extent, for example, can a legislature disenfranchise citizens on some basis other than for a crime—say, mental incapacity—given the language of Section 2 of the Fourteenth Amendment that appears to assume such authority? But I think these questions are also best approached from the perspective of the constitutional ethic and not by asking whether they may be analogized to drawing and quartering.

In *Rochin* v. *California*,[24] a narcotics conviction was challenged by a defendant who, upon the arrival of police officers in his home, had swallowed two capsules that the police subsequently sought to extract from him, first by physical force alone and later at a hospital by forcing him to take an emetic. He vomited the capsules, which were found to contain morphine and were admitted in evidence against him at trial.

Urging an approach that has since been adopted by the Court, Justice Black wrote that the government's part in these events contravened the Fifth Amendment because the vomiting of the capsules amounted to self-incrimination without consent. "I think," wrote Justice Black, "a person is compelled to be a witness against himself not only when he is compelled to testify, but also when . . . incriminating evidence is forcibly taken from him by a contrivance of modern science."[25] Applying this standard twelve years later, the Court held that blood tests could be taken without consent from a conscious person after an auto accident, since it was thought that the results of a blood test are not evidence of a "testimonial" nature.[26]

There is something strange in these approaches. Could Rochin have been forced to vomit if a grant of prior immunity had made the Fifth Amendment inapplicable, or if the evidence had been sought for use against his wife (who was in fact present in the room at the time of the search and was therefore a potential defendant) and not against himself? We may disagree as to whether the forcible administration of blood tests or breath tests is permissible, but is whether or not the evidence produced is "testimonial" in nature the real issue? Isn't the issue, rather, whether or not a constitutional ethic applies—an ethic that finds partial expression in some of the passages of the Bill of Rights and that restrains the police from physically degrading an individual who is in custody in their efforts to enforce law?

Consider the notorious *Skinner* case.[27] An Oklahoma statute providing for the sterilization of habitual criminals was applied against a man convicted three times of theft and robbery (the first time for stealing chickens). Purporting—and I say this with humility and respect—to rest its decision on the ground that similar offenses (embezzlement, for example) were exempted from triggering the enhanced punishment, the Supreme Court held that the Oklahoma statute violated the Equal Protection clause. The challenged statute, Justice Douglas wrote for the Court, created an invidious discrimination[28] against a certain class of offenders and arbitrarily favored others. Despite this argument, I simply cannot believe that even if the measure had been extended to defendants convicted of larceny by trick, embezzlement, and so forth, that the statute would have or should have survived constitutional scrutiny. That is because I do not think American government may impose a system of eugenics no matter how egalitarian or, were it to adopt Chief Justice Stone's approach,[29] no matter how formal the hearing that preceded its implementation. I don't believe American government can do such a thing because among the *means* fairly inferred from the affirmative powers accorded the federal government—the limits of which means apply to the states, as I shall discuss in Book II—eugenic improvement is simply not present. Of course, it is not forbidden, but then the Framers may have thought better of us than to anticipate that it need be.

I do not disagree with the results in any of these decisions. My complaint, therefore, is not that the Court, in a few odd and famous cases, is wrongly deciding but that they are wrongly explaining. Since in law as in science explanation is prediction, my complaint is hardly an idle one.

If you believe that ethical arguments in these cases would have produced more candid opinions[30] or if you find ethical approaches in such cases more satisfying than the attenuated textual and doctrinal methods that the Court actually chose, then a case has been made for the use of ethical argument. If this approach is more satisfying, then I suggest that ethical arguments may actually be what is motivating the decision process. If this can be shown, then it will be established that ethical arguments do in fact function in constitutional law in the same way as other types of constitutional arguments.

For such a showing, I turn to the work of our most gifted and accomplished constitutional jurist, John Marshall, and to the Court which he served as chief. If we see ethical arguments functioning in this work it will have the collateral effect of showing that such arguments are not confined either to modern times or to cases relying on substantive due process.

Naturally enough I think first of the case of *Fletcher* against *Peck*[31] and Marshall's equivocal opinion for the Court. In *Fletcher* the Supreme Court confronted a more than ordinarily corrupt legislature that had enacted by statute a series of land grants giving away vast tracts of state lands to its patrons. When the legislature was turned out by an enraged electorate, its successor proceeded to revoke the land grants. The Court held the later, revoking statute invalid. Marshall's opinion offers both textual and ethical grounds. The statute was unconstitutional, he wrote, "either by general principles which are common to our free institutions, or by the particular provisions of the Constitution."[32] The "nature of society and government [may limit the] legislative power."[33]

This is a tepid example. The chief, or at least sole, reliance is not placed on an ethical argument, as the concurrence of Justice Johnson,[34] which would have done so, makes clear. And though one may ransack Cranch and Wallace and Peters—the court reporters whom Marshall inadvertently made immortal—there are few cases like *Fletcher* v. *Peck*.

In *Terrett* v. *Taylor*,[35] a Virginia statute that sought to reclaim lands previously granted to the Episcopal Church was held to be incompatible with the United States Constitution on grounds that would appear to be ethical in construction. Without resort—since these were unavailable—to a civil ex post facto provision or to the bar against the taking of property without compensation, the Court nevertheless applied to state action a principle that is correlative to both these ideas. The principle applied to decide the case was identified as "[t]he right of the citizens to the free enjoyment of their property legally acquired."[36] The source of this principle was simply inference from the very nature of republican government. Presumably, a government that could revoke its grants in the challenged way could not be republican, i.e., it could not be relied on to carry out its commitments and would be able to use its lawmaking authority to thwart that commitment-giving and carrying-out that a representative government requires. This principle and its constitutional status was reaffirmed by its author, Justice Story, in *Wilkinson* v. *Leland*[37] fourteen years later when he claimed, a bit diffidently, to know of no contrary legislative act which had ever been held a "constitutional exercise of legislative power in any state in the Union."[38]

But these are still very few cases. As Dr. Johnson said, it is no answer to a man who says "that orchard has no fruit" to reply that there are two or three apples in it. Since my task is to show the effective presence of ethical arguments, it seems damaging rather than helpful if only a few odd cases are brought out as evidence.

So I offer a particular series of cases which reflect not only that presence, but show the development of a legal strategy based on the role of ethical argument. That series is composed of the *Cherokee Cases,* beginning with the ill-fated writ of error in *Tassel's Case,* [39] followed by the holding in *Cherokee Nation* v. *Georgia,* [40] and culminating in the well-known opinion in *Worcester* v. *Georgia.* [41] To appreciate the various sorts of constitutional argument in the cases, one must know something of the context in which they operated.

Like *Fletcher* v. *Peck* [42] and *Chisholm* v. *Georgia,* [43] the *Cherokee Cases* arose in the financial maelstrom created by speculation in public lands in the early 1800s. The *Chisholm* case, discussed in Chapter 2, began as a suit seeking to enforce against Georgia the sale of twenty-five and one half million acres of public lands. The purchasers had tendered payment in South Carolina in Continental scrip that was practically worthless and had brought suit for specific performance when the tender was rebuffed by Georgia. The Eleventh Amendment resolved the ensuing crisis, and the land companies were thwarted, for a time.

Then in 1792 one event occurred that transformed the situation from one of mere profiteering to larceny of grand proportions. A Connecticut schoolteacher, having come to Georgia to take up a tutor's post and having found it unavailable, reluctantly decided to study law. This might be the history of many a current law student. Like students today, when the study of law palled he was tempted by distracting pursuits. During one of these diversions, he invented a simple device for removing the seeds from cotton balls. The invention of the cotton gin—a machine so simple and efficient in design that a model of it was stolen and freely duplicated throughout the South—changed the state lands of Georgia into a vast, valuable white El Dorado. Beveridge notes, for example, that in 1791, the year preceding the invention, only 189,500 pounds of cotton were exported from the entire United States; ten years later, Georgia alone exported more than three million pounds. [44]

It was to seize the finest cotton fields in the world, now that cotton had become a much more valuable crop than before, that a conspiracy of land speculators and politicians, led by a United States Senator from Georgia who possessed secret information that a new treaty with Spain would remove the cloud that currently existed on Georgia titles in its western areas, combined to pass legislation that within a single week disposed of thirty-five million acres of fertile Georgia land at less than 1.5¢ per acre.

In time the extent of this monstrous theft became known, as did the fact that every member of the legislature who had voted for the land sale, save one, had owned shares of stock in the land companies. A wave of public outrage swept a new legislature into office, most of whose members were pledged to undo the fraud that had been perpetrated by their predecessors. This was attempted by the statute declared void in *Fletcher* v. *Peck*.[45] Justice Johnson concurred in the result ratifying the earlier sale, but he dissented with respect to the question of the validity of Indian titles to the land. To the land developers of that era, which is to say much of the white population of the state, it must have appeared that, after *Fletcher* v. *Peck,* only these Indian claims stood in their way.

Two decades earlier, in 1790, a treaty had been negotiated between the federal government and the Creek Indians, one feature of which was the provision of a federal guarantee to the Creek Nation for all lands not ceded by the Creeks. The history of the subsequent forty-eight years, beginning almost immediately with the adoption by the Georgia legislature of a resolution condemning this provision of the treaty, is a history of constant agitation by Georgia to seize the entire corpus of Creek lands. The efforts of President John Quincy Adams to limit Georgia's aggrandizement while at the same time trying to negotiate further cessions from the Creeks foundered in the fall of 1827 when Congress, through a committee of the Senate, refused to support the President, claiming that federal authorities could not interfere with the state's rights of Georgia, whose surveyors were already at work mapping the boundaries of the state's newest claims, to the consternation of the Creeks.[46]

The Senate Committee cited the majority in *Fletcher* v. *Peck* to the effect that Indian title was not inconsistent with title in fee to the state.

It was against this background, and the recent election to the presidency of Andrew Jackson whose opinions were known to be hostile to Indian claims, that Georgia determined to move against the Cherokee Nation. In December 1828 the legislature adopted a resolution appropriating all Cherokee lands[47] and extending state criminal jurisdiction over land occupied by Indians. Two months later a Cherokee delegation to Washington was informed by President Jackson that their only remedy was emigration to the West. The Cherokee, whose gifted Sequoia had devised an alphabet and written language, whose constitution provided for representative institutions and was modeled on the United States Constitution, regarded the western plains as barren and their inhabitants as savages. They refused to leave. Then in July gold was discovered on Cherokee land and the fate of the Cherokee, if ever in doubt, was sealed.

In his first Annual Message President Jackson dismissed Indian claims as "visionary" and urged Congress to provide western lands to which the Indians must move. Emboldened by this statement from the federal government, which by virtue of treaty commitments was the Indians' sole protector, the Georgia legislature eleven days later passed a complex statute adding the Cherokee lands to seven Georgia counties; making any act hindering cession a crime; and declaring that no Cherokee could testify in court. Jackson relayed word through his Secretary of War to the Georgia governor that federal troops in the area, sent to protect the Indians from intrusion, would not interfere with state officials. Despite all this, the Cherokees still refused to cede their land. In his second Annual Message, President Jackson noted that, historically, savage tribes had been exterminated to make way for victorious peoples and called the present policy "a continuation of the same progressive change by a milder course."[48] He then renewed his endorsement of coerced emigration.

In December 1830, the Georgia legislature passed even harsher measures. The Cherokees were forbidden to act as a government except for the sole purpose of ceding land. White men were forbidden to reside on Indian lands without a license from the state (this owing to the widespread conviction, often heard since in other contexts, that agitators were the true cause of the group's otherwise inexplicable obstinacy). "With the United States government no longer protecting them," one historian noted, "the Cherokees were subjected to harsh treatment. Roving bands of whites looted Indian homes and the Cherokees, unable to testify in court, could do little to defend their property."[49]

Then, in the same month, the first of the *Cherokee Cases* arose. Historians and contemporaries disagree as to whether the Indian's correct name was George Tassel or, as some reports have it, Corn Tassels. He was convicted of murder by a state court and sentenced to death. The Cherokees had retained William Wirt, the distinguished former Attorney General, and Wirt obtained from Chief Justice Marshall a writ of error calling on the governor to show cause why Tassel should not be released. Ten days later the Georgia governor denied the authority of the Court and appealed to the state legislature for support. That body responded with a resolution declaring Marshall's order an "interference" and directing the governor to disregard "any and every mandate and process" from the Supreme Court and to order the sheriff of Hall County, where Tassel was being held, to execute the prisoner. Five days later, before the January term of the Court began, Tassel was hanged.

A second case reached the Court. In *Cherokee Nation* v. *Georgia*,[50] Wirt sought an injunction for the Indians to restrain enforcement of the various measures by which Georgia had asserted control over the Cherokee. Marshall wrote an opinion for the majority which came down only four days later. No counsel appeared for the state of Georgia. I shall discuss this opinion in more detail when, having seen its use in the later and final Cherokee case, we can better understand its purpose. For now, I shall simply summarize the holding.

The Cherokee Nation was not, Marshall decided, a "foreign nation" within the meaning of those words as they are used in Article III to grant original jurisdiction to the Supreme Court. Granting that the Cherokee had been the subject of treaties, that they were not states, and that each of their members was an alien, yet they were not truly a *foreign nation* either. Marshall supported this view in part by a textual argument from the phrase in the Commerce Clause empowering Congress to "regulate commerce with foreign nations, and among the several states, *and* with the Indian tribes" (emphasis added).[51] Additionally, he argued that the Indian tribes depended on the United States for protection; this was not a characteristic of a truly foreign state. Furthermore, their negotiation with a foreign state without United States auspices would have been regarded as an invasion of U.S. national prerogatives. From all this Marshall concluded that the Indians were a sort of domestic nation, *sui generis* in their relation to the United States. The Court was therefore without original jurisdiction to hear the Indians' claims.

On the very day after oral arguments in *Cherokee Nation*,[52] the Georgia Guard arrested Samuel Worcester and several other white men for violating the recently passed statute prohibiting whites from living in Indian territory without state licenses. Worcester was at first released by a Georgia court which ruled, perhaps trying to avoid an appeal to the Supreme Court, that as federal employees (Worcester was the Postmaster for the Indians) the missionaries were specifically exempted by the statute's provisions.[53] In May, however, after the opinion in *Cherokee Nation* had come down, the Georgia governor, encouraged by what appeared to be the self-asserted impotence of federal judicial authority, wrote Worcester and advised him to remove himself from the state to avoid arrest.[54] Worcester, an eighth generation Congregationalist minister from Vermont who was then living among the Cherokees as a missionary, refused. Accordingly, the Georgia militia rounded up and arrested as many of these white men as they could find in Cherokee territory. But the Guard leader, reasoning that Worcester and the ten others arrested might be considered government agents, ordered their release. It was only when the still cautious Georgia governor wrote the War Department, which replied by expressing approval of the arrests,[55] and when the President removed Worcester as Postmaster, that the missionaries were rearrested. They were placed in chains and taken before a Georgia court, which convicted them and sentenced them to four years confinement at hard labor. Nine of the prisoners, on promising to leave the Cherokee territory, were pardoned. Only Worcester and Elizur Butler refused, intending, it was reported, to test their case before the United States Supreme Court.

Wirt asked for and received a writ of error from the Court. Georgia again refused to appear, this time announcing in advance that it would disregard any order of the Court. In March 1832, Marshall delivered the opinion of the majority.[56] That opinion, and the constitutional arguments that form it, are important to the analysis I am proposing; we shall return to them at the conclusion of this narrative. At present, I shall outline the holding and outcome of this case.

The Court struck down Georgia's statute as repugnant to the Indian treaties which, as with all treaties, Article VI declares to be the supreme law of the land. The statutes, because they sought to impose control over the Indians, could not coexist with the Indians' status as a *nation*, (implicit in the very existence of a treaty), even if they were a peculiar kind of nation. Following the decision, the Clerk of the Court sent a mandate to the judge of the Georgia court reversing the convictions of Worcester and Butler. On a motion from Worcester's local counsel that the prisoner be discharged, the Georgia judge refused to receive the mandate, declaring that the United States Supreme Court had had no jurisdiction to hear the case.[57] Worcester's counsel requested that the judge record his refusal so that it could be appealed and, presumably, the mandate enlarged, but the judge refused even to have his own decision officially recorded.[58] The next legislature repealed the provisions of the statute struck down by the Court, but the missionaries remained at hard labor in the penitentiary, and Georgia continued to assert jurisdiction over the Indian territory.[59] Jackson wrote his friend John Coffee that "the decision of the Supreme Court has fell stillborn."[60] And it was of *Worcester* v. *Georgia* that Horace Greeley reported the probably apocryphal remark attributed to Jackson that "John Marshall has made his decision. Let *him* enforce it."[61]

Finally, in 1833, after instructing their counsel to inform the Georgia attorney general that they would no longer prosecute their case in the Supreme Court, Worcester and Butler were pardoned and released.[62] The next year the final episode in the *Cherokee Cases* occurred when the Supreme Court issued a writ of error in the *Graves* case, summoning Georgia to show cause why the error alleged in the trial and conviction of an Indian for murder should not be corrected. The governor and legislature responded with bombastic refusals, and before the case could be heard John Graves, like George Tassel before him, was executed.[63] That same year divisions developed within the Cherokee nation and the Jackson Administration finally found some chiefs in favor of emigration, who, as they stated in their memorial to Congress, had come to see the futility of opposition.[64] A new treaty was proposed and ratified in Washington. On May 10, 1838 General Scott issued a proclamation in Georgia that every Cherokee man, woman, and child must be en route West within a month. The emigration was delayed, but on December 4 the last party of Cherokees left their homelands and headed west.[65]

Knowing this tragic narrative, we can better discern the roles of different kinds of constitutional arguments in the legal decisions that comprised the development and conclusion of this history. First, there was the decision to issue the writ of error in *Tassel's Case.* We don't know much of the constitutional argument involved because the appeal was aborted by Tassel's execution. We do have, however, the almost contemporaneous opinions in *Cherokee Nation,* and I shall begin with these.

Recall Marshall's holding in *Cherokee Nation* that the Supreme Court was without jurisdiction since the Indian nation was not a *foreign* state. Beveridge praises this holding as reflecting Marshall's supreme moral force because, though sympathetic to the Indians, he rose above his sympathy and chose the law above "emotion."[66] Similarly, an excellent discussion of the *Cherokee Cases* in the Stanford Law Review by Professor Burke tells us that "Chief Justice Marshall resisted the political and moral pleas of the Cherokees because he believed that the Constitution would not allow the court to accept jurisdiction."[67] I think there was nothing moral about it, and I see instead an artful example of prudential constitutional decision.

Carefully consider Marshall's holding. If he had accepted jurisdiction on the basis urged and had been willing to regard the Cherokee as a foreign nation, the Court would have been unable to oversee a decree and would have had to abandon the issue as a constitutional matter. This follows from our Constitution's commitment of foreign relations largely to the Executive. Had the Indians been truly a "foreign state" the Constitution and the Court could have offered them no protection.

Furthermore, prudential arguments are often waiting arguments, assessments that the time and the context aren't quite right for judicial resolution. They don't end the matter. Marshall here used a prudential approach because he anticipated the ethical coup to be delivered in a later case. Only a holding which both denied current jurisdiction and at the same time would serve as a precedent to leave the door open for future cases would do.

It is interesting that jurisdiction is so useful a prudential tool. This is in part because it may precede arguments on the merits and thereby allow the Court to remain silent on issues to which it does not wish to commit itself. But it is mainly so because jurisdiction is a matter, in an instant case, almost wholly within the judgment of the judiciary. With respect to the Court's original jurisdiction, as was the case in *Cherokee Nation,* it is always within the Court's control and does not depend on coordinate action by other branches of government.

Not only does Marshall rely on the jurisdictional holding to accomplish prudential goals, but he combines it, as modern prudentialists have often done, with expressions about relative institutional competence. Thus he writes that even if jurisdiction could be had, it might be that the judicial department would not be the appropriate actor to resolve the dispute. This issue is left open by the holding.

Marshall intended *Cherokee Nation* to be but the opening play in a constitutional sequence culminating in an ethical holding, a sequence for which the prudential play had to first be made. We may gather this sequential strategy and its design for ethical argumentative use from several facts.

First, there are important hints in the opinion. In establishing that the Indians are a domestic, dependent nation, Marshall relies on an examination of the constitutional ethos which has emerged between the American nation and the people it displaced. "Their relation to the United States," he writes, "resembles that of a ward to his guardian. They look to our government for protection, rely upon its kindness and its power; appeal to it for relief to their wants; and address the President as their great father."[68] And later he writes, "In considering this subject, the habits and usages of the Indians, in their intercourse with their white neighbors, might not be entirely disregarded."[69] It was to precisely this sort of consideration that Marshall was preparing to turn later, as we can see in the cases that followed.

Second, Marshall went to unusual lengths to insure that there would be another case, and he did so in a way that set up the later case as one primed for the use of ethical argument.

Despite its holding and the qualms expressed about institutional competence, the opinion in *Cherokee Nation* notes that "the mere question of right might perhaps be decided by [the Court] in a proper case with proper parties." It even goes so far as to suggest that a title dispute would serve. But the most important steps Marshall took were outside the opinion. We now know that Marshall arranged the dissent from his own opinion. Story, writing a few weeks later to Peters, the Court reporter, said that "neither Judge [Thompson] nor myself contemplated delivering a dissenting opinion, until the Chief Justice suggested to us the propriety of it, and his own desire that we should do it."[70]

That dissent reached the merits left largely untouched by the Marshall opinion. "The laws of Georgia set out in the bill," it read, ". . . go the length of abrogating all the laws of the Cherokees, abolishing their government and entirely subverting their national character."[71] The dissent concluded that when concrete future cases were presented to the Court, in which a particular personal or property right had been invaded, an injunction should issue.

The next step taken by Marshall was to encourage Peters to publish a separate report, to be sold to the public, that would include not only all the opinions in the case—the dissents had not been read the day decision was announced—but would also include the arguments of Wirt and his co-counsel for the Cherokee, the various treaties, and James Kent's favorable opinion on the status of Cherokee claims. Story knew precisely what effect was being aimed at. He wrote,

> The publication will do a great deal of good—the subject unites the *moral* sense of all New England—It comes home to the religious feelings of our people. It touches their sensibilities and sinks to the very bottom of their sense of Justice—Depend on it there is a depth of degradation in our national conduct which will irresistibly lead to better things.[72]

The hoped-for and prepared-for opportunity came the next term in *Worcester* v. *Georgia.* It is important to see precisely what Marshall did to see how ethical argument works. It is easy to mistake the holding and its doctrinal rationale for the arguments by which the rationale itself was chosen. Thus one is tempted to say that the opinion in *Worcester* reflects the view that the Cherokee Nation is accorded status as a nation by virtue of its treaties with the United States; that because these treaties are accorded supreme legal status by the Constitution, any state acts inconsistent with such status are repugnant to the Constitution; and that, Georgia's statute being inconsistent, it was struck down.

But this account, which is more description than analysis, does not tell us how we know that the Cherokees' role as signatory to treaties, a role which was insufficient in the *Cherokee Nation* case to establish them as a "foreign state," here entitles them to status as a nation. Marshall does not argue that simply being a treaty signatory is sufficient. Nor does he argue that the provisions of the treaties—without more—are inconsistent with the Georgia statute. Instead, Marshall's argument is that the treaties reflect, not establish, a relationship between the Indians and the American government. This can also be detected, he tells us, in a study of the history of the Indian tribes and their previous relations with other regimes. The importance of the treaties is that they give this relationship constitutional significance. The bulk of Marshall's opinion is thus devoted not to particular contradictions between the Georgia statute and specific Cherokee treaty provisions, but instead to a review of political relationships between the Indian tribes generally and

American governments. Marshall was well aware that this relation had ethical importance for both parties. Indeed, it is this realization rather than mere sympathy that is reflected in Marshall's letter to Story several years before on this subject. In it we can see the expression of ethical, *constitutional* argument, an argument that our particular character as a people has certain constitutional implications once the people have brought the Constitution into being.

> It was not until after the adoption of our present government that respect for our own safety permitted us to give full indulgence to those principles of humanity and justice which ought always to govern our conduct towards the aborigines when this course can be pursued without exposing ourselves to the most afflicting calamities. This time however is unquestionably arrived; and every oppression now exercised on a helpless people depending on our magnanimity and justice for the preservation of their existence, impresses a deep stain on the American character. I often think with indignation of our disreputable conduct—as I think it—in the affair of the Creeks of Georgia.[73]

As a general matter, how is ethical, constitutional argument to be given shape? I will discuss this issue in detail in Book II, but one method is relevant here. The federal government is limited in its powers by the general conception, nowhere made textually explicit, that the government may not do what it is not empowered to do. Thus, the Bill of Rights is to some extent, as Madison said, a superfluity. We know that government may not do certain things because the fundamental constitutional ethos embodies this notion of limited powers. What is of great interest in *Worcester* is this application of ethical argument. By removing the Cherokee completely from the laws of Georgia and holding that the whole intercourse between the United States and the Cherokee Nation is, by the Constitution, vested in the government of the United States, Marshall superimposed the model of limited government on the treatment given the Indians. At a stroke Marshall accomplished what the Fourteenth Amendment was not able to do until our own day: extend the Bill of Rights (and more rights than are there enumerated) to a class of persons that had been at the mercy of state law unrestrained by those restrictions. This, as we shall see by analogy in Book II, was a wholly *ethical* tactic and provides the paradigm, perceived in retrospect, for the most important ethical arguments of our own era.

We shall have an opportunity, in Book III, to consider the expressive function of the Court by which certain values are given institutional statement. For now I should like simply to consider who was the ultimate victor in the Cherokee cases? Not the Cherokee, obviously enough; but not the reckless legislature of Georgia either.

In 1830 Marshall had written about the possibility that the Indians would be forced to emigrate from their treaty lands:

> The subject has always appeared to me to effect deeply the honor, the faith and the character of our country. The cause of these oppressed people has been most ably though unsuccessfully sustained. 'Defeat in such a cause is far above the triumphs of unrighteous power.'[74]

II

CONSTITUTIONAL ETHICS

INTRODUCTION

The principles of constitutional law are patterns of choice between kinds of constitutional argument. From each of these patterns one may derive a particular justification for judicial review. It is an error virtually endemic to most constitutional commentary, however, to do this in reverse, deciding first on what seems to be a convincing basis for judicial review and thereafter being persuaded by those arguments appropriate to that particular judicial role. This is a profound error, because it assumes that the commentator comes to the question of judicial review from a fresh perspective, one outside, as it were, the process of legal argument.[1]

But in choosing which justification of judicial review to adopt, we are following a rule. Indeed, insofar as we are persuaded by the arguments for a particular justification, we are not really "choosing" anything, since we cannot choose to be persuaded. By the same token, when within the context of a particular constitutional case we apply a particular rule, we are also in fact following a rule. In Book I, I asked, "What is *that* rule, the deeper, predeterminate rule?" These rules were examined as various approaches to the construction of the Constitution.[2] In Book II, I intend to focus on the approach that I have called "ethical."

As we have seen of other approaches, ethical argument has various strengths and weaknesses. I would emphasize that no sane judge or law professor can be committed solely to one approach. Because there are many facets to any single constitutional problem and, as I shall discuss in Book III, many functions performed by a single opinion, the jurist or commentator uses different approaches as a carpenter uses different tools and often many tools in a single project. What makes the *style* of a particular person, as I endeavored to show in Book I, is the preference for one particular mode over others.

CHAPTER 8

ETHICAL PERSPECTIVE

I have devoted Book II to the ethical approach to the Constitution because this approach has not been well-defined by scholars. (I do not mean, of course, that ethical discussions or particular moral frameworks have not been put forward in the commentary on constitutional law. Rather, I mean that as a type of constitutional argument, ethical argument has not been established.) Like the other approaches, ethical argument is a function of the kind of Constitution we have. Indeed, I will spend part of this discussion showing that ethical argument is inescapable precisely because of specific features of our Constitution. Yet ethical approaches are thought to be disreputable and are usually treated disparagingly. Our initial discussion was devoted to determining whether such an approach exists, entirely apart from its merits, so that we might then evaluate it as we have the other sorts of constitutional argument.

Because of the wariness with which ethical approaches are treated, however, it is not easy to find direct evidence of their use in constitutional law. There is the often mentioned opinion by Justice Chase in *Calder* v. *Bull*.[1] In that opinion the Justice argued that the Court should strike down state statutes—the one in question was challenged as an ex post facto law, and actually upheld—even when the Constitution does not expressly forbid the statutory action, if they are inimical to "republican principles." For example, a law that made a man a judge in his own cause must be struck down on such grounds. One may assume from the opinion that, even if there were no ex post facto provision, as there was no due process provision applicable to the states in 1798, a law punishing a citizen for an act that was not criminal when committed would also be struck down for offending the "republican" ethic.[2]

To take up another opinion, every law student is familiar with Justice Bradley's eloquent plea for a broad construction of the Privileges and Immunities Clause of the Fourteenth Amendment[3] in the *Slaughter House Cases*. It was his view, as it is mine, that the Fourteenth Amendment was adopted "to provide National security against violation by the State" of various rights.[4] But how do we determine what these rights are? And, to take the case that confronted Justice Bradley, how do we determine whether a monopoly imposed by a corrupt Reconstruction legislature that gave black butchers the sole right to slaughter and render in New Orleans infringes such rights? Bradley would determine this by an appeal to an ethic of personal liberty that is only partially expressed in the text of the Constitution, and which, as Bradley points out, long antedates it.[5] In a dissent in the same case, Justice Field would have construed the clause to protect those rights that "belong to the citizens of all free governments," rights which require no Bill of Rights for their assertion.[6]

Plainly, these are not textual arguments, although their aim is the construction of a text. They are ethical arguments, appeals to an ethos from which rules may be derived, whether they are embodied in the text or not.

In our own period, a case recently arose in New Jersey in which an elderly man, whose gangrenous legs would have led to his certain death in a few weeks, asserted a constitutional right not to have them amputated.[7] A major hospital had petitioned for the appointment of a guardian to authorize the operation against the will of the patient. The patient was gamely described as a "conscientious objector to medical therapy." He indicated a desire—"plebian," as he described it—to return to the trailer in which he had lived. It was there that, though suffering arteriosclerosis, he had chosen to sleep upright so that he might give the only bed in the trailer to an 82-year-old companion. Owing to these circumstances he had contracted the gangrene which had destroyed both his legs. The trial court determined that the amputation would save his life; that the probability of recovery from the operation was good and the risks involved limited. Despite a recognition of the state's interest in the preservation of life, however, the Court held that this interest must yield in these circumstances to a constitutional right not to be forced to have a major operation. An extraordinary case.

In 1979 the Supreme Court granted certiorari to determine whether "safety" and "effectiveness" requirements for new drugs under the federal Food, Drug, and Cosmetic Act had any application to the drug laetrile when it is desired by terminally ill cancer patients.[8] The District Court had granted an injunction to permit such patients to receive Laetrile injections,[9] a holding that relied in part on a determination that a patient has a constitutional right to exercise control over his own health care and that the FDA, by denying cancer patients the right to use a nontoxic substance, had violated the Constitution.[10] This issue was wisely avoided by the Circuit Court[11] and ultimately avoided also in the Supreme Court's disposition.

Such prudence masks the pervasive influence of ethical approaches in Constitutional law. Indeed, it may even contribute to questionable analyses of the sort offered by the District Court in the amputation case since such courts are offered little guidance in the pages of the Federal Reporter 2d. or the U.S. Reports, because the distrust of ethical arguments among constitutional actors keeps such approaches out of appellate opinions. And yet these approaches are enormously significant as arguments, since they often guide a decision that is only then reconstructed by building an avenue from a different approach. For this reason, one may profitably examine oral arguments before appeals panels and questions from the bench to observe the uses of ethical argument.

One might expect that for a number of reasons there would be few examples of ethical approaches in the oral arguments before the United States Supreme Court. The Justices control the emphasis and direction of oral argument before them, and they have numerous incentives to discourage ethical approaches. In the first place, appellate judges are seldom persuaded in the few minutes allocated to oral argument. As a member of a panel as large as the Supreme Court, a justice would be wise to reserve to himself and his colleagues at the Friday conference the powerful ethical approaches, rather than have their force dissipated and their form mangled beforehand. Moreover, there is little reason for the Justices to rely on counsel for such arguments. The constitutional sense on which these arguments are based is probably more highly refined and sensitive among the Court than among any other nine persons in the country. It is more profitable to use counsel in oral argument to inform the Court about the underlying facts, to treat jurisdictional points overlooked in the briefs, and to respond to inconvenient precedents. But most important, the notoriety of ethical argument fostered by our narrow view of the legitimate conventions makes it an approach that an advocate would only attempt at his or her peril. It seems almost a concession that the "law" is against you if you resort to nontextual, nondoctrinal appeals. Of course, the sophisticated advocate realizes that the Justices do it; he may even hint that they should do "it" in the present case by mentioning an earlier example of such use of judicial authority. But this is probably as far as the shrewd advocate will go. So, for example, after repeating the true but scarcely helpful cliché that the duty to say "what the law is" rests with the judicial branch, Leon Jaworski happened to refer to *Gravel* v. *United States* [12] in arguing against executive privilege in the *Tapes Case*.[13] He noted in passing that even though the Speech and Debate Clause[14] provided grounds for the assertion of privilege there, "the Court . . . looked into the alleged wrongdoing of those who were seeking to invoke the privilege."[15] This is about as far as an effective and sophisticated advocate is likely to go in oral argument, at least in our current era. The addresses of Webster and Wirt were not so inhibited,[16] but they belong to another age.

Occasionally, also, the powerful advocate may let drop an ethical argument in the guise of a sort of double entendre, to get the force of his argument across while giving it the appearance of a conventional approach. Thus, for example, Thurgood Marshall, when Solicitor General, presented the Court with an argument that close inspection reveals to be an ethical one. The case was *Harper* v. *Virginia State Board of Elections,*[17] in which the Court faced the question whether a state poll tax in nonfederal elections was constitutionally permissible. Marshall appeared as amicus curiae; he began by stressing the urgency of striking down the poll tax because of its effect on Negro voting in the South.[18] But in response to a question, he urged that any tax of any amount was unconstitutional. He appealed to the constitutional ethos of free elections by adverting to the then recent subway strike in New York, saying, "While a city can charge 15 cents to ride on a subway, people wouldn't want to put a dime in a turnstile to get into the voting booths. Or buy a $1.50 ticket [the amount of the Virginia poll tax] to get into them."[19]

Then Marshall offered the phrase that was to serve as the constitutional basis for this assertion.

> How does this get into the Constitution? [the Solicitor General asked himself]. Very simple. The Framers of the Constitution proclaimed a government of the people. They proclaimed a republican form of government.[20]

This sounds like both an argument from the constitutional ethos of free government as well as an invocation of the text's guaranty of a republican form of government.[21] But the Court hearing the argument knew well enough what it was. They knew that the Solicitor General was not going to ask them to overrule the century-old doctrine of *Luther* v. *Borden,*[22] in which the Court had pronounced itself powerless to enforce the Guaranty Clause (thereby rejecting one of Webster's most eloquent ethical oral arguments). To confirm this, we need only turn to the Solicitor General's brief in *Harper,* where we find not a single citation either to the Guaranty Clause or to the cases that have construed it. We do find, however, repeated reliance on the assertion that the Constitution demands a government "of the people."[23]

For another vignette that depicts a celebrated Supreme Court advocate using ethical approaches before the Court, we may turn to Archibald Cox's successful argument in *Shapiro* v. *Thompson*.[24] There and in consolidated cases, Cox challenged, and the Supreme Court struck down, a one-year welfare residency requirement in two states and the District of Columbia.

The first ethical argument Cox offered was that a law may not condition the exercise of one constitutional right (here, equality of treatment) on the abdication of another (travel).[25] This is a most interesting argument. It is sometimes said that rights are not the limiting boundaries of powers, not the interface I shall describe in a few pages, but are instead "trumps,"[26] that is, authority of a different kind. On this view one might say that the commerce power is sufficient to permit Congress to pass a law prohibiting the interstate transportation of contraceptives, but that such a law would be unconstitutional by virtue of its offending the "right to privacy." The other view, which I shall argue is crucial to ethical approaches, is that Congress' power does not extend so far as, in the example, to permit Congress to use commercial regulation as a means of regulating private sexual behavior. It is my view that although these two characterizations of rights are incompatible, neither is wholly sufficient. Which characterization is to be used depends on which convention or approach is being employed and, in turn, on which function is sought.

Cox's ethical argument is suited to the interface perspective. For how do we know that a statute may not constitutionally condition the exercise of one constitutional right upon the abdication of another? If rights are trumps, one may play them as one pleases. But if rights are the limits of government, then governmental powers cannot extend to imposing substantive conditions on the exercise of rights, much less to conditioning the enjoyment of one on the abandonment of another.

Cox made a second, also highly interesting, ethical argument. Continuing oral argument the next day, he asserted "that under our laws no state should be allowed to keep newcomers in a condition of alienage" as the parishes of England did with the Elizabethan Poor Laws.[27] But what do welfare residency requirements have to do with alienage? The English poor laws Professor Cox had in mind—mainly an extension of Tudor poor laws after the English Civil War[28]—did, it is true, create a state of alienage. By amending the Poor Law—first in 1685 so that the forty days necessary residency in the settlement would only toll after written notice and then in 1693 adding that the tolling only began when this notice was read at services in the parish church—the statute offered a stranger little opportunity of gaining a settlement without the general consent of the taxpayers.[29] The stranger was kept an alien; by denying him a settlement the community was able to manage the number of those eligible for poor relief.

This example shows what is constitutionally wrong with the American residency requirements. The English laws were very much like the American scheme in that, while doubtless motivated by the sentiment that the provision of relief is a local one owed to persons with ties to the community, the scheme became a device whereby the relationship to the community was manipulated to serve as a regulator on community relief costs. The District of Columbia statute denied benefits to any baby less than one year old, since such a child could not meet the residency requirement. Cox's historical analogy gives us another variation of the subtle, almost indirect use of ethical approaches at oral argument.[30]

It is no coincidence, I suspect, that one hears ethical approaches more often in the oral arguments of experienced and sophisticated Supreme Court advocates. Professor Cox was Justice Marshall's predecessor as Solicitor General, the government's lawyer before the Supreme Court. Yet it is the justices who most often give us ethical approaches during oral argument.

In *Kennedy* v. *Mendoza-Martinez*,[31] the Supreme Court was asked to strike down a statute that stripped American citizens of their citizenship for various reasons, including, as was the case with Mendoza-Martinez, having fled the country to avoid the draft. The relevant ethical constitutional approach is the "limit" argument, the argument predicated on a constitutional ethos of government limited in its powers to those granted by the People. And so, early in oral argument we hear Justice Stewart asking for the basis of the power over citizenship[32] and Justice Brennan answering the government's reply by observing that "[n]othing in the Constitution says Congress can take citizenship away."[33] A few minutes later, Justice Black makes the same observation, adding that the federal government possesses only those powers expressly granted by the Constitution or necessary to the exercise of those powers.[34] The attorney for the government parried these remarks, as he did in his brief, by asserting that "a government which cannot exert force to compel a citizen to perform his lawful duty is, to that extent, not sovereign as to him."[35] But that is precisely the ethical point. The ethical approach is bottomed on the notion that to some extent in every matter, and wholly in some matters, government is just not "sovereign" as to its people.

The same point is evident in the transcript of the oral argument in *Reid* v. *Covert*,[36] a case involving the jurisdiction of a military tribunal over civilian dependents overseas. Mr. Rankin, the Solicitor General, had argued for this jurisdiction as deriving from the "extension" of constitutional power by the Necessary and Proper Clause.[37] After a sharp exchange with Justice Black, Rankin finally conceded that it was one purpose of the Constitution to limit the influence and authority of the Army. "But," he said, "[the Framers] did not want to leave the country without any defenses."[38] Except for the available ethical argument—the limit argument which defines rights—this lame reply might have passed unnoticed. Instead it became the occasion for Justice Black's rejoinder as to the Framer's plans: "They did not want to leave *civilians* without any defense *against the Army*."[39]

We may hear the special timbre of ethical argument in the sincere question as well as in the lightning riposte. The final examples I have chosen are all of this questioning kind, and they have this character because they show an earnest, questing man trying to find the approach that will yield a just result. He is troubled and at the same time frustrated because ethical argument does not appear to be available to him. So he breaks through to it by asking whether the nonethical rules will yield justice.

The following exchange at oral argument occurred in 1961 in the case of *Poe* v. *Ullman*,[40] an attack on a Connecticut statute that made it a crime to use contraceptives. An assistant state attorney general, Mr. Cannon, is defending the statute. The Chief Justice, Earl Warren, asks Cannon:

> If this diagnosis of Mrs. Doe is accurate and if her life is to be endangered unless she has medical advice and medical treatment, do you believe that the State has sufficient interest in enacting this type of legislation to prevent her from getting this type of advice?[41]

And Cannon answers,

> It is our view that it is the problem for the Legislature to determine what is the greatest good. There are few statutes under the police power that do not do someone some harm.[42]

The Chief Justice presses the point,

> So your position is that, even if this woman would die if she had another child, the State can enact a statute to prevent her from getting this medical care.[43]

Cannon answers,

> Yes, but the doctor can advise against pregnancy. . . . [He merely] cannot tell her or advise her to use artificial contraceptives.[44]

And then he continues:

> There is substantial medical authority, that there are natural ways to prevent conception. It may be that these are not the best methods, but it is not for this Court to determine what is the best way.[45]

Then Cannon referred the Court to statistics in his brief, showing that there were only seventy-five maternal deaths in Connecticut for the five-year period from 1951 to 1955.[46] Finally Warren breaks in again and repeats his question, still looking for an approach to make the matter less strange, but still obviously aware of the statute's horror. The Chief Justice:

> Do you know of any comparable situation in the law of medicine where a doctor has a patient whose life is in danger and who, according to the best medical opinion, needs specific medical advice and the doctor is prevented from giving it?[47]

Cannon:

> No, your Honor, I do not think I can think of any such case.

And then, as if it settled the matter:

> But I cannot find any case holding these statutes unconstitutional.[48]

It would be four more years before the Court finally dealt with the Connecticut statute challenged in *Poe*.[49] One can hear in the questioning from the Justices at oral argument all the various approaches, including the one used in *Poe* and ultimately in *Griswold*, which struck down the statute. But the answer to Warren's question—how can a statute seem so clearly unconstitutional without a conventional approach for so establishing it—is not heard.

We can hear the same question in the oral arguments in *Reina* v. *United States*.[50] At issue was the *Murdock*[51] rule that a threat of state prosecution would not support assertion of the privilege against self-incrimination in a federal investigation. Reina, the witness, was already serving a five-year sentence for a federal narcotics offense when he had been summoned before a federal grand jury. When he asserted his Fifth Amendment privilege, the United States Attorney obtained immunity for him and an order from the court directing him to testify. Reina refused, was judged in contempt, and was sentenced to two years imprisonment. The conviction was unanimously affirmed on this ground: a grant of immunity from federal prosecution is coextensive with the Fifth Amendment privilege against self-incrimination because that privilege only protects against incrimination under federal, not state, law.

Since the United States Attorney wished to question Reina about the very activities that had sent him to prison in the first place, Reina faced a difficult choice. If he remained silent, his first prison term, still in progress, would be lengthened even though he had already been sentenced once for the crime. If he talked, the state authorities could prosecute him for various crimes not covered by the federal Narcotics Control Act prosecution. In either case he could be compelled to serve time in prison solely on the basis of his assertion or waiver of the priv-

ilege of self-incrimination, in either situation he would be forced
to send himself to prison. The Chief Justice asked the Assistant
U.S. Attorney:[52]

> —Do you make any distinction between questions involving
> narcotics but in no sense involved in the crime of which he was
> convicted and questions involving his offense?

> —No, Your Honor.

> —In other words, after a man is convicted and serves his full
> term, then he can be compelled to give this testimony that may
> cause his death or put him back in prison?

The Chief Justice continued:

> —That is what bothers me. Of course, a man is not immune
> just because he is an ex-convict. But, if he is convicted and sen-
> tenced and serves his term, should society then be able to bring
> him into court and force him to reveal his whole crime or send
> him back to the penitentiary?[53]

To this the Assistant replied that it was very difficult to find
cases on this subject. "This is a problem," he said, "not alluded
to by the courts."[54]

Conventional argumentative approaches are not very helpful with such questions. We have Mr. Justice Brennan's testimony that Warren fought in conference for the "summary re-
versal of a state criminal contempt conviction of a black woman
who refused to answer questions from the witness stand until
counsel stopped addressing her by her first name 'Mary' and
addressed her as 'Miss Hamilton.' "[55] There were probably not
many cases on that point either.

Chief Justice Warren has also given us the most famous
question from the bench during our era, the celebrated "Yes,
Counsel, but is it fair?"[56] It is a source of some puzzlement that
efforts to verify this question in transcripts have been fruitless.
But we have the testimony of a former Solicitor General on the
matter, quoting Warren. Archibald Cox writes that with increasing frequency in the fifteen years after Earl Warren took
his seat as the fourteenth Chief Justice,

. . . lawyers at the [Supreme Court] bar found that arguments based upon precedent, accepted legal doctrine, and long range institutional concepts concerning the proper role of the judiciary and the distribution of power in a federal system foundered upon Chief Justice Warren's persistent questions, "Is that fair?" or "Is that what America stands for?"[57]

These are expressions of an ethical constitutional perspective. They ask for an ethical approach. But a question cannot by itself provide such an approach. The balance of Book II is devoted to the derivation of ethical arguments.

CHAPTER 9

GOOD AND BAD / GOOD AND EVIL

I hope the examples given in the previous chapters reaffirm the very existence of ethical arguments in constitutional law. Their absence from discussions in law school classrooms has, I believe, yielded the cynical conclusion that mere expediency governs constitutional decisionmaking. Even the most gullible student is reluctant to accept the doctrinal justification in, say, *Shapiro* v. *Thompson*[1] that welfare residency requirements are unconstitutional because they interfere with the equal protection to be afforded *travel*. Ignoring the existence of ethical arguments has had other costs as well: not only candor, but simplicity too is sacrificed. Most importantly, the exile of ethical argument from the domain of legitimate constitutional discussion has denied an important resource to the creative judge who exploits all the various approaches from time to time and case to case.

Ethical argument has been neglected because it is feared. We are unwilling to use constitutional institutions as a supreme moral arbiter, and therefore many would like to remove moral argument from constitutional law altogether.

Why are we unwilling to view ethical argument as appropriate to constitutional decisionmaking? There have obviously been many societies (indeed, we may soon see the emergence of one in Iran) which have wholly integrated ethical and constitutional functions. There are two reasons, I think; one is widely accepted in various forms, and the other is correct.

The first view is roughly analogous to the empiricist's hostility to moral observations generally. One reason we are disinclined to admit moral statements into a calculus of truth functions about the world, and are not opposed to admit scientific hypotheses, is that the latter are verifiable by observation evidence. If I observe a vapor trail in an electron chamber, I am inclined to count this as evidence of an electron. If, on the other hand, I feel moral indignation at the government's decision to suspend food stamps, this scarcely establishes the wrongness of the government's act. It only counts as evidence of my feelings.[2] Conventional constitutional arguments appear to have the same epistemological basis as statements of scientific observation. There are independent phenomena—the text, or historical events, or the political structure, or the calculus of costs and benefits, or previous caselaw—that stand for a state of affairs independent of our feelings. True, you and I may put different interpretations on a piece of historical evidence, but this is no different than our trying out different scientific hypotheses for fit. There is an objective fact. But when I say that a statute is unconstitutional because it violates the ethic to which our government ought to cleave, am I not simply saying something about my perception, a conclusion perhaps, but not anything about the Constitution *per se*?

This view of things is, I think, quite probably wrong about science and the role of observation evidence,[3] but I am certain it is wrong about the process of constitutional law. In both cases this view treats an object—the constitutional rule or the electron—as severable both from our apprehension of it and from our use of it with other concepts. This is an error with respect to the Constitution since the choice of a particular mode of approach and argument is not the product of an "objective" fact. There is not only nothing in the Constitution which dictates, for example, the use of historical argument, but even if there were, our application of such a provision would be made in light of how we apply textual provisions generally. I am not saying that there were an infinite number of kinds of constitutional argument available, "logically" as it were, to the authors of the Federalist or to the first litigants before the Supreme Court. Of course, the Constitution was written by men with certain kinds of institutions and arguments integrated into their very debates. In those debates one finds the full range of arguments I have discussed, and I derive from them the principle of constitutional construction that none of these modes can be shown to be necessarily illegitimate.

The second objection to ethical argument is more telling. It admits that we see our Constitution through various legal conventions, that the Constitution is inseparable from the organizing framework of these conventions, and that the Constitution we are to apply will appear differently depending on which convention is chosen. But it is observed that competing moral conventions generally do not themselves provide the methods for resolution which are provided by competing legal approaches. Thus, for example, a change in a statute may cause some things to cease being illegal, while they may well still be immoral. Since ours is a society of considerable moral pluralism, to admit ethical arguments in the constitutional arena is to sacrifice the ameliorative, assimilative power of constitutional law, to take advantage of which, political questions, as Tocqueville observed, are in America so often transmuted into legal questions.[4] One fears the result would be the kind of intractable ideological conflict so notable on the European scene. The conventions of a legal language are then exchanged for ideologies, in the face of which no event, much less an argument grounded in a differing approach, can but confirm to each side the rightness of their principles and their desires. (Writing recently of Professor Noam Chomsky's radical political views and the naive historical analysis which the reviewer thinks those views compel, a book reviewer has said,

> Unfortunately, one can't argue with Chomsky on this matter because he insists that any claim about the need for professional competence in the analysis of historical events is part of the prevailing liberal ideology, whose main objective is to con-

ceal and distort reality. The situation is analogous to arguing with a Freudian about psychoanalytic theory, where the Freudian contends that your objections are really resistances.[5])

This is a substantial and highly important shortcoming of ethical argument in constitutional law. When the authoritative decider is the Supreme Court, this shortcoming is greatly worsened, since the finality of a constitutional decision by that Court often freezes the situation, limiting action by other constitutional institutions. Indeed, given the federal structure of law in our society, a good argument might be made that moral arguments should generally be excluded from the constitutional discourse.

I believe that this argument justifies, for example, the phenomenon of federal habeas corpus, for which it is otherwise difficult to give good grounds. Habeas corpus severs the constitutional decision from the moral question of guilt or innocence, so that the former can be dispassionately weighed as one suspects it seldom can be in the context of a trial. At the same time federal habeas corpus gives the matter to a group of deciders whose customary business is, by comparison to state courts, largely amoral. It is the state courts that must confront questions of moral blame, broken promises, negligent or intentional harm, marital collapse, and virtually all crime. The federal courts, on the other hand, except for their diversity jurisdiction, are largely given over to matters of government regulation, intergovernmental conflict, and national commerce. Federal habeas corpus enables the constitutional questions to be given the priority they can seldom achieve when held in the balance with a moral conviction widely enough shared to have found its way into a state's criminal code.

But doesn't such a distinction between moral argument and moral deciders on the one hand, and constitutional argument and federal judges on the other, actually reflect a way of compensating for the principal shortcoming of ethical argument, that is, its lack of a nonethical referent? Aren't the values of the Fourth and Fifth Amendments, which habeas corpus has protected to the extent of turning many guilty men free, also "ethical"? If so, then we may be able to identify a class of ethical arguments that originate in a specifically *constitutional* ethos and hence avoid the difficulties of ethical and moral arguments generally.

This is precisely what Chief Justice Marshall accomplished in the *Cherokee Cases* discussed in Book I. Well aware of the distinction between moral arguments generally and arguments arising from a constitutional ethos, Marshall wrote in a private letter[6] that the questions presented by the *Cherokee Cases* were easy for the moralist but difficult for the jurist. For the balance of Book II I shall explore this difficulty and examine the uses of this narrower class of ethical arguments, ones with a claim to be derived from constitutional rather than moral conventions.

CHAPTER 10

DERIVING ETHICAL ARGUMENTS

Arguments are most clearly and easily derived from the constitutional ethos when that ethos may be identified from some specific text in back of which, so to speak, it may be said to stand. For example, Charles Black has suggested that it would be unconstitutional for government to require a landlord to rent to a specific party—as by a statutory extension of open housing laws—since to do so would be to exercise a power analogous to that proscribed by the Third Amendment's provision against the quartering of soldiers in private dwellings.[1] Notice that this is an ethical rather than a textual argument, despite the fact that it depends for its force on an analogy to the text. The argument is ethical because it assumes a constitutional ethos which is manifested textually in one instance by the words of the Third Amendment. Only by such a tacit assumption may a relation be said to hold which permits the analogy establishing the nontextual right.

The same kind of move is made by Marshall in the *Cherokee Cases* discussed earlier. There a text was used, not for its own force, but rather as evidence of a more general principle from which a nontextual argument was derived. By contrast, the classic *textual* argument applied to the open housing case would

142

be that since the language of the Third Amendment is specifically limited to military occupation, any constitutional applicability to civilian rules is insupportable, at least by that text.

If we could neatly limit constitutional ethical arguments to those which have textual cousins, so to speak, relatives whose characteristics identify for us the common ancestor, then perhaps we would be able to clearly demark such arguments from moral arguments generally. For example: Assume we confront the practice of a state mental hospital to sterilize some of its patients without their consent. One way to resolve this would be to characterize such confinement as "punishment" and find that the practice of sterilization within such confinement offends the Eighth Amendment.[2] This is a textual argument (one that is somewhat strained). Remember that we still have to make another textual transformation to fit the text of the Eighth Amendment into the Fourteenth Amendment, in order to apply the words of the former to the states.

Yet the Eighth Amendment might nevertheless be of help here. Suppose we think that the textual provision of the Eighth Amendment which forbids cruel and unusual punishment is evidence of a more general constitutional ethos, one principle of which is that government must not physically degrade the persons for whose benefit it is created. If we have this principle, or something like it, we may then make the ethical argument against sterilization *per se*. We would be able to take advantage of the resolving power of legal conventions—the teaching of which I have come to believe is the principal duty of law schools—while not pretending that only nonethical arguments are truly constitutional, are truly "legal."

To take another example: Justice Jackson is surely right in refusing to rely on the Free Exercise Clause to strike down a statute that compelled a Jehovah's Witness to salute the flag.

> While religion supplies appellees' motive for enduring the discomforts of making the issue in this case, many citizens who do not share these religious views hold such a compulsory rite to infringe constitutional liberty of the individual. It is not necessary to inquire whether nonconformist beliefs will exempt from the duty to salute unless we first find power to make the salute a legal duty.[3]

Just as surely such a statutory compulsion to conformity is unconstitutional. Is it unconstitutional because "Congress shall make no law . . . abridging the freedom of speech" (here, presumably, the freedom not to speak)? Or is it unconstitutional because that rule, like the related rule applied in the flag salute case, proceeds from the constitutional ethos of a government limited in its powers to make orthodoxy a legal duty, whether by the various means specifically proscribed by the First Amendment or by other means? The latter position may appear to be supported by one specific text—the Ninth Amendment[4]—which makes quite clear that the Bill of Rights and the body of the Constitution do not exhaustively enumerate the specific rights of persons.

But this nice position is not really available to us. In the first place, it is not sufficient to use the Ninth Amendment as the linkage by which these analogies are made because there is simply nothing in that amendment or elsewhere to suggest that only the enumerated rights can lead us to the unenumerated ones. Given the limited nature of the government that the body of the Constitution describes, the retained rights of persons—even if there were no Ninth Amendment—would necessarily constitute an infinite list. Both the unspecified rights and the enumerated prohibitions derive from the general constitutional ground of enumerated and implied powers. Many puzzles in constitutional law and history have been caused by a failure to appreciate this.

In Book I, I observed that the initial opposition of James Madison and others to the Bill of Rights arose from their view that such specific protections were unnecessary since the power to achieve the objects which the various amendments would prohibit had not been delegated to the federal government. The Constitution establishes a government of limited powers. Those means not fairly implied from affirmative grants of authority are inferentially denied the government. Thus, Madison held, in effect, "Why need we prohibit government from pursuing objects that are not assigned to its attention in the first place?"

As Hamilton wrote in *Federalist No. 84*, "Why for instance, should it be said that the liberty of the press shall not be restrained when no power is given, by which such restrictions may be imposed?"[5] The Bill of Rights, therefore, is, on this view, an incomplete list of those objects as to which government has no power to act. Of course, without such a partial list, the body of the original unamended Constitution is, in Hamilton's words, "itself, in every rational sense, and to every useful purpose, a Bill of Rights."[6] Indeed there was concern lest this partial, arguably superfluous list obscure the indefinite, generative function of the unamended text. In presenting the draft of the proposed bill of rights to the House, Madison said, "It has been objected also against a bill of rights, that, by enumerating particular exceptions to the grant of power it would disparage those rights which were not placed in the enumeration; and it might follow, by implication, that those rights which were not singled out were intended to be assigned into the hands of the General Government, and were consequently insecure."[7] This difficulty was resolved as Madison proposed, by the adoption of what became the Ninth Amendment.

The Constitution does not say that the government may not create a nationwide police force to enforce the common law of crimes; nor does it say that Congress may not pass a law establishing domestic relations jurisdiction in the federal courts or adopt a uniform probate code governing testate succession to real property. Nor does the Constitution prohibit the government from bribing legislatures into ratifying amendments to the Constitution proposed by Congress. Nor does it prohibit Congress from drafting whole groups of the population so that they may be resettled in other parts of the country or put to work in useful trades or in depressed areas. The Constitution, though it charges the President to faithfully execute the laws, does not forbid him from exercising an absolute veto by issuing executive orders at cross-purposes with congressional legislation or by refusing to appoint judicial officers. Nor does the Constitution prohibit the use of torture to acquire evidence or the passage of a statute blacklisting a person from work or exiling him from the country.

The Constitution—indeed the body of the Constitution standing unamended—need not declare these prohibitions because the affirmative power to accomplish such acts does not exist. In this way, we may in part account for the fact that there are virtually no human rights cases as such in which a federal statute is challenged, before the twentieth century brought an increase in the exercise and recognition of the affirmative grants of national authority.

So one way we may understand the Bill of Rights is as a collection of those examples of power denied the federal government which simply happened to occur to Madison and others as requiring reinforcement, perhaps on account of the historical experience with respect to unlimited government.

I don't think one has to say whether the limitation of governmental power defines rights or whether rights override powers, although it is wrong to accuse the Framers of a Rylean "category mistake"[8] in treating the two, rights and powers, as a silhouette. Indeed I would note that if rights are not treated in Madison's way—that is, as negatively defined by the limitation on power—then in some situations anomalies will be derived. If this photo-negative model is unavailable, then a federal court's extension of Sixth Amendment rights to a grand jury indictment, for example, to persons *vis a vis* the states would amount to an incursion into rights; namely an incursion into the right to be indicted by information or to have one's dangerous peers indicted this way, rights reserved to the people by the Ninth Amendment.

Or one can generate the sort of absurd impasse reached by a recent Court of Appeals asked to hold that an antitrust case was of such complexity that it was inappropriate for jury decision. The court concluded that the Seventh Amendment required a jury decision but that the Fifth Amendment's due process clause forbade a jury.[9]

This has more than theoretical significance, as we shall see, in contexts in which we do not wish to allow persons to bargain away their rights to the government. If a right is that which is beyond governmental power, then government-induced waiver does not augment governmental power. This is not so if a right is categorically separate. In a mixed economy such as ours, in which persons occupy very different positions of relative wealth, we should be wary of a single formulation of rights that allows such bargains.

Constitutional ethical argument cannot be generated solely

by analogies to the Bill of Rights.[10] To do so would be to treat the Bill of Rights as the generative constitutional mechanism (a role it does have, of course, with respect to doctrine) and would ignore the fact that it has no greater claim as a limit on power than have all the other rights that can also be generated by the ethos of limited government.

To understand this is to understand, by way of our constitutional grammar, the notion of substantive due process. However much doctrines of substantive due process may be despised, they are a *necessary* occurrence, given the necessarily partial list of rights which is the Bill of Rights. Regardless of how many politicians, jurists or professors rail against substantive due process doctrines, they cannot be avoided without doing violence to the constitutional ethos that every lawyer and judge has internalized.

Substantive due process is not a function of politically aggressive judges who have lost their heads and are acting as would-be legislators, abandoning any sense of judicial self-restraint. Rather, the doctrine is the necessary product of the superimposition onto a state system of *plenary* authority, of a federal court system committed to preserving those individual liberties that animated the *limited* federal Constitution. It is the inevitable by-product of the constitutional events of the 1860s and 1870s, events that far transcend the customary meaning of the few phrases in the first sentence of the first part of the Fourteenth Amendment. How constitutional development has responded to these events can be better understood by bearing in mind that the theoretical constitutional dilemma they brought about had its origin in the interface between limited powers and personal rights.

The Civil War amendments affected a revolution in the constitutional arrangement by deploying the federal courts to enforce limitations on state power with respect to citizens and other persons in the states. In casting about for a theoretical structure that would accomplish this the courts first tried what may be called the "federal closed-set model." The doctrines of substantive due process are the result of applying the *federal* mapping that a limited grant of power, by its very limitation, implies a personal right, to a *state* context. In other words, the federal courts chose to overlay on state power the federal model of limited power defined by affirmative grants. Something like this was inevitable since there was no definitive list—and could be no definitive list—of all the activities denied the states. This theoretical move by the federal courts was the source of the notion of the "police power" as a kind of limited grant of authority to the states, authorizing them to take those measures which, by means that did not deny equal protection or procedural due process, advanced the health, safety, morals and welfare of society.[11] By inventing this new use of the old concept of the police power, the federal courts drafted a sort of uniform state constitution of limited grants of power.

In many ways this was a promising dialectical move. It sidestepped the principal shortcoming of applying federal constitutional doctrine to state-citizen relations, that all federal precedent concerned the general political interest of the nation and not "the regulation of every species of personal and private concern."[12] Indeed, the federal judge who looked solely to the affirmative federal grants of power as a substantive model of the limits to impose on the states would have seen that much of what was forbidden the federal government by its absence from the enumerated powers was precisely what was allowed the states.

And yet treating the police power as a sort of enumeration of authority for the states could not succeed. All constitutional students are familiar with the havoc this approach brought about.[13] There is no point in recounting it here. We live in its aftermath. Like the generation of American strategic planners who were traumatized by Pearl Harbor, a generation of constitutional experts has advanced doctrines to prevent a recurrence of a crisis now forty years past. The most significant aspect of this crisis was the constitutional limitation of state authority by the use of the Fourteenth Amendment. It was accomplished by the remarkable development of the Due Process Clause in response to the same phenomena to which the idea of the closed-set model of state power had responded.

This can be seen in a case such as *Pierce* v. *Society of Sisters*,[14] the seminal case for contemporary substantive due process, personal rights decisions. In retrospect it appears that *Pierce* was the transition case from limited power theories to reliance on the affirmative aspects of the Fourteenth Amendment itself. The former method was fundamentally unsound because it depended on an unreal depiction of the states' constitutional authority. First, it represented the states as creatures of limited authority when they were in fact organs of plenary authority, antedating the Constitution and deriving no powers from it. Second, this view demanded a very difficult judicial task, namely that legislative motivation be used by federal courts as an object of analysis since only by determining the purpose of legislation could it be decided whether a measure had exceeded the states' limits.

For a number of reasons it was only a very few years before the Court virtually abandoned the method of determining what the object of challenged legislation was. This abandonment had two consequences. It meant that the explicit guarantees of human rights would have to shoulder the responsibility heretofore borne by those negative regions defined by the limits of affirmative grants of power. This in turn meant that some explicit phrase, like "due process" or other phrases applied through due process as their conduit, would have to be made open-ended, because it was impossible that any finite collection of specific prohibitions could cover all instances of unwarranted power. The greatest strength of the closed-set theory on the federal level had been its internalization by Congress.

There may be a few detached statesmen who would forebear employing substantive due process no matter how outrageous the exercise of state power. But insofar as this forbearance dwells in coexistence with doctrines of incorporation, which in turn may encompass nonexplicit rights and immunities tangential or merely related to the explicit prohibitions, one is left with the same riddle. How do we give specific content to the unavoidable command of unspecified rights? How do we generate correct and decisive ethical arguments?

Owing to the theoretical morphology I have described, it is to be expected that we should see ethical argument used most often in cases nowadays thought of as involving substantive due process. There they find their greatest use, and also their greatest difficulty since treating such an approach with an irrelevant textual talisman such as "due process" and all the redundant doctrine of "fundamental rights" is hardly a promising beginning in developing the distinction between Constitutional ethical arguments and moral arguments generally. Only such a distinction will permit us to use the resolving power of constitutional argument and avoid introducing a competition of moral conventions. Thus we stand troubled by guilt-ridden memories of the twenties and thirties when ethical argument was used as a trump by a particular political faction, and yet unshakeably convinced that current proposals to ignore unspecified personal rights would do violence to the Constitution. The result is that virtually no judge is, in practice, willing to confine himself to arguments honestly derived from non-ethical sources. The commentary on such cases is full of scolding,[15] and the resulting opinions either lack argument or desperately contrive farfetched textual and doctrinal approaches.[16]

This need not be so. What is needed in a judge's chambers is the same reasoning from the constitutional ethos that produced the first Bill of Rights. The limited nature of federal governmental power suggests a means of generating that ethical perspective. First, a rule is suggested by the limited powers of the federal government. This must be the initial step if we are to avoid slipping into a competing moral convention which is all the more dangerous if it is widely shared. The limited powers of the federal government may indicate the constitutional ethos either by the direct means of a specific provision in the Constitution's original text or in the amendments—as the Fifth Amendment points to the larger principle that government may not force defendants to assist in their own condemnation in a criminal trial, and the Fourth Amendment points to the larger principle that privacy may only be infringed by government on a showing of necessity—or by inference from the limited nature of the express powers. With respect to the states, who are not creatures of limited, delegated purposes, one may say as a general matter that those means denied the federal government are also limitations of the states, by virtue of the integration of federal constitutional norms into the contours of state authority produced by the Civil War. That is to say that states, in the pursuit of their quite different ends, are denied those means which are not necessary and proper to the achievement of federal ends. We can *say* this was accomplished by the Civil War amendments, but this is deeply misleading since those amendments are, like the Bill of Rights, mere reflections of the Constitutional change which generated them. Like most Southerners, I am acutely aware that the Civil War, or the War Between the States as we were taught to call it, was a constitutional war. The questions of constitutional authority and human rights were not, as the opposing sides thought, two alternative questions. Then, as now, they were really one question, as I have argued by putting forward the photo-negative paradigm. The textual necessity for stating the constitutional change wrought by the war was deeply felt; but I can hardly believe, for example, that black disenfranchisement could have been constitutionally continued after the War regardless of whether the Fifteenth Amendment had been adopted.[17]

Furthermore, there is a provision appended to the Civil War amendments, as the Ninth Amendment is appended to the Bill of Rights, to remind us that the list of prohibitions against involuntary servitude, denial of equal protection, and so forth is not exhaustive. I am referring to the Privileges and Immunities Clause of the Fourteenth Amendment. When that clause is construed in light of the ethical approaches sketched in these pages, its analogous role will appear.

It has been thought that there were two principal difficulties with using the Privileges and Immunities Clause as the vehicle by which human rights can be enforced against the states. I leave aside the doctrinal roadblocks which derive from precedent, since these are merely reflections of the Supreme Court's appreciation of these difficulties.

First, it is said that we are unsure of just what the "privileges and immunities" referred to actually consist in. The catalogues of these rights we have been offered sound like nothing more than lists of rights the speaker considers important. In this they resemble the "fundamental rights" of contemporary due process analysis, and therefore to rely on them scarcely improves the situation. Second, it has been thought that the protection the Privileges and Immunities Clause offers would shield only citizens. In this respect, the Due Process Clause, which speaks of "persons," would seem more promising.

Thus we have been tempted to ignore the plain meaning of the Due Process Clause—that life, liberty, and property can be taken so long as it is done in a procedurally correct way—and responding to the theoretical demands that arose from the Civil War's rearrangement of constitutional limits on state authority, we have constructed the doctrines of substantive due process.

The following alternative will better serve these theoretical demands, however. An ethical view of federal constitutional human rights describes them as beyond the boundary limned by enumerated powers and implied means. The federal government may not employ any means not necessary and proper, not fairly inferable, from its enumerated powers. One might say that this is a sort of "immunity" as respects the federal government: one is immune from such means, or to put it another way, one is privileged with respect to national government, to be treated only in those ways that are constitutionally mandated. The Ninth Amendment emphasizes that this fundamental relationship is the privilege and immunity of *citizens of the United States,* because it is the very foundation of national authority. (It thus has nothing to do with the privileges and immunities of state citizens mentioned in Article IV.)

If, as I argued a few pages ago, the application of the ethic of limited constitutional government to the states yields the rule that states may not, in pursuit of their unenumerated and plenary ends, employ those means denied the federal government, we may now see textual support for this assertion. Moreover, we will now have a generative rule for determining what are the privileges and immunities of citizens of the United States. We need only ask: is this legislative means (whether federal or state) one that is fairly inferable from one of the federal enumerated powers? Finally, this formulation enables us to deal with the citizen/person problem. It shows us that the problem was a false one. Because we were mesmerized by the model of rights as trumps we treated "privileges and immunities" as rights which belonged *to* someone, *i.e.,* citizens. But the text does not say that no state shall deprive "any citizen" of privileges and immunities, a construction that would be parallel to that of the due process and equal protection provisions that forbid states to deny to "any person" those protections. Instead the text reads: "no state shall make or enforce any law which shall abridge the privileges or immunities of citizens of the United States." If we give the meaning I have suggested to the entire clause—privileges and immunities of citizens of the United States—we have a general limit on state government, not a specific right held by any specified group. States may not abridge the right to be the subject of only that governmental action that is within the constitutional means of the United States government, regardless of who is affected by the abridgement.

I offer this account of the Privileges and Immunities Clause hopefully. It makes useful what has been, up to now, a barren provision and does so within a relatively spare theoretical construction that simultaneously explains the historical development of the police power and substantive due process doctrines as post-Civil War constitutional limits on state authority. But suppose there were no Privileges and Immunities Clause. If it were a mere text we required—and not the morphogenesis the text records—we could make use of the Tenth Amendment's equivocal but clear statement that some powers not prohibited the states are nevertheless reserved to the people. The Tenth Amendment reads,

> The powers not delegated to the United States by the Constitution nor prohibited by it to the states are reserved to the states respectively, or to the people.[18]

Strictly speaking, this means that unless the last phrase is surplusage there must be some unspecified, unenumerated rights which belong to the people against the states. That is, there are some powers which, while not delegated to the United States nor explicitly prohibited to the states, are nevertheless in the hands of the people and not the states.

Such explicit texts as the Tenth and Ninth amendments, and the Privileges and Immunities Clause of the Fourteenth Amendment, confirm the constitutional grammar from which the ethical approach can be derived. These texts are not the basis for such an approach, any more than structural argument can be assimilated into textual argument because the relationships on which it depends exist between textually affirmed structures. The real test of ethical arguments, however, is in their application to concrete cases. Therefore I will devote the rest of Book II to a discussion of three cases that could have, or perhaps I really mean should have, been resolved by an ethical approach.

Before doing so I should like to anticipate one objection to the method of ethical approaches as applied to the states. Any analysis that depends on the usefulness of the notion of "means" (and therefore also of the notion of "ends") is relying on concepts that are notoriously unreliable and have caused constitutional trouble in the past. Just when is a "means" a "means" and not an "end"? And when is an "end" simply an "end" in itself and not a "means" to some other "end"? This problem so bedeviled the Supreme Court that after twenty years of trying to make these concepts useful—in the course of which, for example, the Court struck down a tax in *Carter* v. *Carter Coal* [19] despite the clear grant in Article I, § 8 to Congress of the power to tax for the general welfare, because the taxing power was used only as a "means" to effectuate an "end" held to be beyond the commerce power—the Supreme Court simply abandoned the effort altogether and announced it was going out of the means–end analysis business, at least as applied to the enumerated powers of the federal government. The grounding of the 1964 Civil Rights Act [20] in the Commerce Clause suggests how far we have come since *Carter Coal.*

Ethical arguments as applied to the states present difficulties arising from the fluidity of means and ends and the continuum this fluidity creates. How do we know precisely where to put our brackets in the continuum so that, granting that a means is often an end of some other means and that the end it serves is often a means to yet another end, we may nevertheless choose the appropriate pairs? Let me give examples to illustrate the difficulty. The rule we are applying, the application of which distinguishes constitutional ethical argument from moral argument generally, is: A state may not, in pursuit of its powers, employ a means denied the federal government in pursuit of *its* powers, a means that is not plainly adapted to the various ends enumerated in the Constitution. Such a rule is impossible to apply if it either leads us to an overly restrictive view of state power or is so broad as to have no force whatsoever beyond the specific prohibitions of the Bill of Rights (since it was to go beyond these specifications that we were led to the rule in the first place).

If we assume that Congress is not able to pass a nationwide murder statute pursuant to its commerce power—this being a means poorly adapted either to stopping trafficking in murder (which is relatively rare) or to closing the channels of interstate commerce to murderers, since they are unlikely to be transported as such across state lines—does this imply that a particular means (making murder unlawful) is beyond the *states'* powers? For that is absurd. Congress could surely pass a statute making it a crime to murder the President. Is this necessary to show that a state may pass a criminal statute against murder generally, that is, protecting persons other than state officials, subject to the various specific prohibitions of the Constitution?

What is needed is a principle that will direct us to choose a particular pair of means–ends, to cut into the chain at a particular place. I propose that in applying the ethical approach against state action we may not limit the inferred means merely to a restatement of the federal end, since the ends of state power are by definition largely different from those of national government and such a limitation would amount to the imposition of a test for federal ends, *i.e.*, a reimposition of the closed-set model. Thus we may ask whether, at least on the basis of ethical approaches, a state statute making robbery a criminal offense is constitutional by looking at the specific method used— the trial of the offender and his imprisonment for stealing another's possessions—that does not embody a federal objective. We may then test this means against a similar federal means for constitutionality—for example, the federal bank robbery statutes.

Of course, even within this parenthesis of generality there are many methods employed in a means. One might have analyzed the statute above as coercing persons into leaving the possessions of others alone or as restricting persons in the way in which they may acquire property, and so on. But each of these methods has an analogue in either actual or plausible federal legislation whose constitutionality almost all of us would concede. None of these methods contains within its statement a uniquely federal objective.

Naturally, this rule works better in a society like ours, that is no longer young and that has both a good many statutes and a well-developed constitutional sense. We are inclined to forget that the White House and the Capitol are older in use than Buckingham Palace and the Houses of Parliament. As a practical matter, the rule of selection among means is not necessary to select the appropriate analogue within state and federal systems to determine what is both beyond federal power and not reserved to the states but to the people. Conceptually, however, it is helpful to explain our bearings along the means–end continuum as well as to help find them.

I do not mean to suggest that the mere existence of a federal statute validates a similar state means, but, rather, that from the vantage point of ethical argument what is denied one is denied the other. For example, I take it as a constitutional, ethical principle that government may not mutilate persons save in self-defense, which means the defense of itself, its communities and their inhabitants. This could of course happen incidentally, as when a postal truck runs down a pedestrian, but I do not think government has the power to use this means—the actual destruction of its people—as an instrument to further any end whatsoever. For this reason, one may argue that both federal statutes which provide for capital punishment and state statutes with similar provisions are unconstitutional. This is a close question that may be tested as a principle in the way I have suggested: Is, for example, the state acting in the sort of self-defense experienced by a policeman facing an armed robber when it orders capital punishment, given the option of mortal confinement of the offender? The direction of ethical argument in such a matter is plainly different from our asking whether capital punishment is "cruel and unusual" as envisaged by the Eighth Amendment prohibition (although here, as elsewhere, the language of the Amendment may be taken as an objective correlative, as it were, of the underlying ethos).

CHAPTER 11

APPLYING ETHICAL ARGUMENTS

Roe v. *Wade*[1] is perhaps the most important and certainly the most controversial constitutional decision of the previous decade. The decision in *Roe,* which struck down the Texas abortion law,[2] has done almost as much to shape current attitudes about ourselves and our society as have the social and technological changes that did so much to bring the decision about. And yet one rarely encounters a law professor or judge willing to defend the decision. I think the universal disillusionment with *Roe* v. *Wade*[3] can be traced to the unpersuasive opinion in that case, and I will propose an ethical rationale that may be more satisfying than the doctrinal and textual approaches taken by Justice Blackmun. Let us begin by simply recounting his approaches.

The opinion of the Court may be parsed in the following way. First, the Court asserts the doctrinal argument that the constitutional right of privacy has been established by case law.[4] Second, without explication of the development of that right in precedent, the opinion asserts that this right "is broad enough to encompass a woman's decision whether or not to terminate her pregnancy."[5] Third, largely nonprivacy cases are cited to support the proposition that only a compelling state interest will permit the state's regulation of the personal right, whose exercise is the woman's decision.[6] Fourth, with respect to the state's interest in protecting the fetus, the Court concludes that "the 'compelling' point is at viability." We are told, "This is so because the fetus then presumably has the capability of meaningful life outside the mother's womb."[7] Accordingly, a woman's constitutional right to privacy guarantees her absolute discretion with respect to the abortion decision until the moment of viability permits state intervention. Fifth, the Court decides that for constitutional purposes a fetus is not a "person" within the meaning of the Fourteenth Amendment's use of that term,[8] and the Court says it does not decide at what point life begins.[9]

Thus the Court determines that the state, having no viable fetal life in which to take a "compelling interest" in the first trimester, may not regulate abortion at all during that period. In the second trimester the state may not forbid abortion. Only in the third trimester, after quickening, can the state outlaw abortion of the fetus. The approach of the Court is wholly doctrinal, applying the due process algorithm of fundamental rights weighed against compelling state interests.

Several features of this rationale command attention. No reason is given why the right-to-privacy cases establish a right to that less than private experience, an abortion (certainly the privacy of the bedroom and of sexual practice, so important in *Griswold*,[10] has been left far behind by the time a woman checks into an abortion clinic). Surely a technology which allowed a fully clothed woman to abort by passing through an X-ray gate would not make that woman's right less fundamental than the right of a woman electing an operating room procedure. Even assuming that the right to procure an abortion is "fundamental" in the way in which other privacy-derived rights have been held constitutionally significant, there is no reason to suppose, and none is offered by the opinion, that the protection of an embryo or fetus is an insufficiently "compelling interest" to permit the state to infringe such a fundamental right. For the case law which establishes privacy as a fundamental right also relies on a compelling state interest analysis to determine the scope of that right. The latter determination is a part of the doctrine of fundamental rights.

The opinion in *Roe* tells us that only when the fetus is viable does the state's interest become compelling. No reason is given why viability should be the measure of the significance of the state's interest. This metaphysical assessment of worth is scarcely inferable from the Constitution or from the record in the case. Moreover, it would appear to rely on the unacknowledged and plainly incorrect premise that only self-sufficient living entities may serve as objects of a state's compelling interests. Furthermore, it would plausibly follow that if a state may have a compelling interest in the life of a viable fetus sufficient to forbid its destruction—as the Court holds—a necessary step in this protection would seem to be protecting against anyone who would prevent the fetus from reaching viability. Finally, the Court's estimate of the constitutional status of a fetus—the determination that a fetus is not a "person"—resolved a matter not before the Court. No fetus was a party to the action, and it was never claimed that the state statute in question infringed any rights a fetus might have.

As such, this opinion is a doctrinal fiasco. The two principal propositions on which it rests are neither derived from precedent nor elaborated from larger policies that may be thought to underly such precedent. And the precedent it establishes is broader than the questions before the Court, while at the same time disclaiming having decided issues that appear logically necessary to its holding.

Yet I doubt that the members of the Court, any more than the rest of us, were actually persuaded by such arguments. Rather the Court was engrossed by one convention of constitutional argument.

To try a different approach, we may begin by asserting a rule which would decide *Roe* v. *Wade* and then testing that rule in the way suggested a few pages ago.

I propose this rule: Government may not coerce intimate acts. There may be no cases formally establishing this rule by holdings, but that scarcely counts against its constitutional status, since legislators may so take it for granted that they simply do not pass laws that are offensive to the rule. And the constitutional text needn't confirm the rule either, saying as it does merely that there are unspecified prohibitions. So the next step is to try out our constitutional sense of the matter by testing the rule in various situations that might implicate it.

For example, it would seem clear that a teacher in the public schools may not order students to perform sex acts as part of a sex education class. To take another case, does anyone think that a state might be able to order marriages as a remedy in paternity suits? Or, from another angle, could a state order conception between individuals thought to have desirable characteristics or among classes—say state workers—thought to be reproducing too little? Does anyone reading this page even entertain the possibility that the state might be able to order errant husbands or wives to rejoin the families they have abandoned? Certainly the state may order parents to pay support to the families they have abandoned; why not order them back into the home, where they could provide a fuller kind of support?

If we don't think for a moment that states could order these practices, why don't we think so? The barriers must be constitutional it would seem, to account for our sense of absolute prohibition. And while I confidently expect the barriers to be enforced by legislatures, I cannot imagine that this empirical fact implies that a federal court may not enforce such barriers if a single legislature failed to enforce them. In the absence of some explicit textual or structural command, what reason is there to say that legislators may enforce rights reserved to persons, but federal courts may not?

The limitation on government which our method has tested was stated as the rule: Government may not coerce intimate acts. Stated generally, does anyone really doubt this? We may disagree as to what are truly intimate acts, and some will think that there could be overriding governmental interests which would justify striking a balance in extreme cases. I shall take up these two matters. But for now I simply wish to argue that there is a plain principle which few will dispute that a state may be restricted by courts from coercing intimate acts by persons within its power.

Whatever else may be an intimate act, carrying a child within one's body and giving birth must be a profoundly intimate act.

It is suggestive in this regard to consider the word *intimate*. It derives from the Latin word *intimus*, which means in-most, the intensified derivative of the old Latin *interus*. I can conceive of no other relation as intimate as that between woman and developing embryo, a relation so intermingling that all other acts that seem intimate to us are by contrast momentary and detached. If the state cannot coerce women into conceiving in its behalf, how can it be claimed that the state can coerce a woman into carrying an embryonic form until she is forced to give it birth?

Yet perhaps government is not in every case delimited from coercing a woman to carry a child to term because in many cases the woman has waived her right to object to coercion. To take polar examples, few would probably argue that nine months after a voluntary and knowing conception—if such a thing is to be had in current technological epistemology—a woman could assert a claim to be unencumbered by carrying a child. On the other hand, one could hardly demand that the victim of a forceable rape be denied an immediate abortion on the ground that she has consented to a waiver of her rights. We may disagree as to time period and circumstances appropriate to a conclusion that waiver has occurred, but in resolving this question we have familiar legal concepts as guides. It is not unreasonable to suggest that a woman who voluntarily consents not merely to sexual intercourse (since intercourse is relatively unlikely to lead to pregnancy, and the woman can therefore hardly be said to have knowingly consented to giving birth) but also to carrying a child for a period long enough so that she can both be presumed to be aware of her condition and to have had the time to reflect on it, has by her acquiescence waived any claim against the state's coercion. Moreover, this perspective justifies the intuitive notion given expression by the state legislatures that a woman who is raped or is the object of incest is different from one who consents to sexual relations, despite the fact that the fetuses in both situations are in the same condition.

Such a basis for determining under what circumstances government may intervene might be given effect in statutes that reflected a conclusive presumption of waiver after some period and in particular circumstances. Or such a statute might provide instead for some initial showing by the state, as part of the enforcement of the statute, that the woman had by her own acts waived her right.

It will be observed that the ethical analysis augmented by waiver would yield the same outcome—the trimester rule—as that achieved by the Court (with the wholesome modification that not all regulation need be forbidden in the first trimester and therefore that sterile surroundings and competent physicians and therapists may be required, so long as these rules do not coerce the woman into carrying to term). I am inclined to believe that this similarity of outcome reflects the actual pull of unacknowledged ethical argument on the members of the *Roe* majority. Or it may be that I am simply writing in the tradition of law professors who employ a certain facility to rationalize what the Court will in fact do.

The Court's result is not, however, available to us by this route. Ethical analysis cannot be augmented by waiver. To ask, for example, whether there are "overriding government interests which will justify striking a balance, in extreme cases, in favor of coercion" is to ignore the entire argument of Book I and all of Book II so far. Because the mode in which the *Roe* argument I have given is ethical, as I have used the term, it cannot yield to waiver. Ethical arguments arise from the ethos of limited government and the seam where powers end and rights begin. No "waiver" on the part of a woman can augment the government's authority. Indeed, she has such a right because government has no power to begin with.

The ethical argument I have proposed in *Roe* v. *Wade* differs from a similar one that may be recognized as a moral argument *simpliciter* in my scheme of arguments. That argument is that a state may not require a person to risk her life for the purpose of benefiting another. The common law rule has long been that one has no duty to intervene in behalf of one stricken or in peril,[11] and the Good Samaritan statutes[12] adopted by some states scarcely go so far as to require significant risk. A variant of this argument has been put forth with her usual eloquence and clarity by Judith Jarvis Thomson in *Philosophy and Public Affairs*.[13]

This argument seems to treat the embryonic child as a stranger who merely happens to be inconveniently placed proximate to the mother. There is much law, however, for the proposition that one owes a duty of care to one's child. This puts us back in the position of deciding when a child's life begins, a position the *Roe* Court was doctrinally forced to take in its argument despite its disclaimers and one which sound constitutional decision ought to avoid completely. The ethical argument I have given avoids the necessity for this determination.

As far as my own rationale for *Roe* v. *Wade* is concerned, it must be painfully apparent that constitutional, ethical decision—decision arising from a constitutional ethos—cannot only be distinguished from moral argument but can lead, as many will feel it does here, to a clearly immoral end. It may be that a similar consequence occurs when the constitutional ethos of unrestrained communication prohibits the eradication of pornography.[14]

The complementary features of ethical argument, applied in the way I have described, are that while it confines government in few respects it provides an absolute bar as to the rights it does protect. This can provide an easily replicated decision procedure. Is it more practical to say government may not force a woman to carry to term under any circumstances than to say that fact determinations of the viability of the fetus (which will vary with technology and circumstances), legal holdings as to the scope or intensity of government's interests, and philosophical speculations about what constitutes "life," and so forth, shall settle the question?

Thus, although the *Roe* opinion has been criticized for being far too specific in its remedies,[15] it has not given us a system of rules to resolve related cases. Doubtless the court was so explicit because it held the view that it might stem future court challenges by simply anticipating various applications of its judgment. This is poor form indeed for the doctrinalist, but it is virtually forced on a court that is unwilling to make explicit the constitutional rules by which it arrives at a decision. It must try to prevent future cases, knowing that if it does not, it will face future dilemmas. So *Roe* was handed down, and a complete guide came with it; even the hostile commentators,[16] themselves ideologically committed to a doctrinal view, thought this was the end of the matter.

How wrong this proved to be. The first unanticipated challenge concerned government financing of abortions.[17] The *Roe* rationale, constructed as a pretext—that is, only to please the conventional standards of judgment—could not serve to guide the later case. We will look at some of these later cases further in Book III.

That the proferred opinion was a pretext, though not of course merely pretext, and that some argument like the one above in fact moved the Court in *Roe* is suggested by several facts. Within the ethical argument I have outlined, Jane Roe's standing is of principal importance. She is the one actor who would have been coerced, but she is by no means the only one who could have been charged with a crime. It is significant, therefore, that the court accorded Jane Roe this primacy while dismissing the physician, Hallford, who had joined in the suit, despite the fact that Roe had terminated her pregnancy by the time the Supreme Court decision was handed down and the Court was thereby presented with a difficult standing issue.

The more recent Supreme Court decision in *Colautti* v. *Franklin*[18] also lends support to the view that ethical argument played a decisive but unexpressed role in *Roe*. In *Colautti* the Court struck down a Pennsylvania abortion law that required physicians to try to preserve the life of a fetus if there "were sufficient reason to believe" the fetus might be viable. In contrast to *Roe,* which was fundamentally concerned with the coercion of the Mother, the opinion in *Colautti* reaches its decision on the grounds of the statute's vagueness and its chilling effect on the rights of physicians. These were grounds studiously ignored in *Roe,* though they were as relevant there as in *Colautti* if the Court's opinion were what had truly led it to decision. Indeed, the grounds used in *Colautti* had been relied on by the lower court in *Roe,*[19] which makes their absence from the Supreme Court opinion in that case, and their reemergence in the later case, all the more telling.

Who was Jane Roe? Perhaps a fuller record would have strengthened the case for the ethical approach I have advocated and would have made the ethical aspects of coercion and intimacy all the more forceful. A more complete record would have revealed that "Jane Roe" was an unskilled, young white woman. She was also a lesbian. She had become pregnant through rape. By the time of the United States Supreme Court argument, she had already terminated her pregnancy. In *Roe* v. *Wade,* no fetus was left to protect. It is an extreme claim to hold that the state should have prosecuted her and sent her to prison because she had refused to wholly and forever choose the most intimate of human experiences.

Finally, consider one more case by which to test the use of ethical arguments, the case of *O'Connor* v. *Donaldson.*[20] In 1957, Kenneth Donaldson was committed to confinement as a mental patient at the instigation of his father, who thought his son was suffering "delusions." Donaldson remained in a Florida state asylum for fifteen years despite his frequent demands for release and the state's failure to provide any psychiatric treatment. His requests for occupational therapy and even consultation with hospital authorities were repeatedly refused. In 1971, Donaldson sued Dr. J. B. O'Connor, the hospital superintendent, for damages. His relatively modest award was ultimately affirmed by the U.S. Supreme Court in a decision which held that the confinement without treatment of a nondangerous patient capable of surviving safely in freedom violated the patient's constitutional rights.

I suspect that few reading this page will doubt the rightness of this decision. In contrast to *Roe* v. *Wade,* the decision in *O'Connor* v. *Donaldson* was not met by a storm of disapproval but was greeted instead by the gentle rain of praise.

The Court's presentation of its rationale was, however, elliptical. Confinement in a mental hospital is a denial of liberty, true. And the Fourteenth Amendment protects persons from such denials, but only when these occur without due process. I will not lay out the series of doctrinal leaps by which this qualification—the permission of due process—is wished away, and the deprivation of liberty in these circumstances is counted as a deprivation of due process itself. But, even accepting this transformation, is it the *process* by which Donaldson was committed that unites us in thinking that there is something fundamentally intolerable in his situation? If so, why didn't the Court focus on Donaldson's assertions that his initial commitment was procedurally defective, or on the fact that court-appointed counsel had been denied to him by the state even though he was indigent and adjudged incompetent, or on his claim that he had been unable to even obtain review of the hospital's decision to retain him, a decision which conceded that he required only cursory treatment? The Court discussed none of these issues, understandably enough perhaps, since on four separate occasions over a ten-year span it had itself denied Donaldson's petitions for certiorari and habeas corpus.[21]

I suggest that the common source of our attitude about the state's treatment of this man arises from a general constitutional ethos of limited government, one rule of which is that states may not, for whatever benign reasons, confine a person dangerous neither to himself nor to others. This is a means beyond constitutionally implied methods, even though there is no specific prohibition against it. I am as deeply skeptical that the Due Process Clause of the Fifth Amendment would have barred this when it was adopted as I am that its Framers would, therefore, have thought the state's behavior in this instance really "all right" since they had neglected to specifically prohibit it. But the true test is not my guess of history but a legal sense of what is fitting. This sense seems to have been held unanimously by the Court.

There is virtually no argument—of any kind—in the Court's opinion in *O'Connor* v. *Donaldson.* When direction is so sure and argument so absent, it is because we have made the arguments that gave us direction somehow unnameable. But they continue to exert their force on us. I do not mean that the process of constitutional decision consists in judges first making up their minds and then casting about for a suitable doctrinal argument. That is often the accusation, indeed, most often when, as with *Roe* v. *Wade,* the doctrinal opinion is unconvincing.

This is wrong, and it is defamatory. Rather, judges in such circumstances find a particular doctrinal argument persuasive precisely because they are being pulled by the unacknowledged force of constitutional, ethical argument. This alone can excuse the unconvincing rationales actually offered by the Court.

We shall need to improve the structure of such arguments as we approach the third century of our constitutional life. Whether a state may offer chromosome "corrections" which are said to enhance the "intelligence" of offspring, or whether a state may forbid the marketing of such products; whether a state may, as Singapore continues to do, read someone out of the welfare state because that person refuses to voluntarily make certain life choices (such as a particular family size), or whether a state is required to guarantee a certain amount of government product to all (based perhaps on family size); whether the federal government or states may engage in drug experimentation with prisoners or employees who have waived their objections; or whether a government has a right of free speech and may spend money on political propaganda; whether parents will have a right to be allowed to choose the gender of their child when this is technologically feasible, or whether the state may regulate such choices—these are, or soon will be, live *constitutional* questions. Even the answer that the Constitution has nothing to do with these situations is a constitutional answer. We will need ethical argument in these contexts; other forms of constitutional argument will be disfigured if they are corrupted to perform tasks for which they are poorly suited, and the tasks done will be done poorly.

CHAPTER 12

CONSTITUTIONAL CONSCIENCE

Although I think that ethical arguments are best understood in the process of applying them, some general observations about them remain to be made.

Are ethical arguments simply substantive due process by another name? The answer is that substantive due process is ethical argument by another name. That is, the attempt to require of states a process that yields fair legislation is in part a reflection of the constitutional ethos of limited government. So, for that matter, is the case law by which the First Amendment was applied to the states; this, too, is ethical argument by another name. And so are the binary, on–off tests of strict scrutiny which the multi-tier equal protection analysis promises to replace. And so also are the underpinnings of the right of association and the right to travel. None of these examples, at least in the contexts of the cases in which they were developed, have much to do with the texts of the various guarantees of the Fourteenth Amendment that we have chosen to do the work once assigned to the misconceived police power doctrine, which was *also* the theoretical result of the pull of constitutional ethical argument.

This is one reason why it is important to identify and study ethical argument. Only then will we be able to discern its constitutional basis and the limitations this basis imposes. Only then

can we identify characteristics by which constitutional ethical
arguments can be distinguished from moral and ethical arguments generally.

Otherwise, since these are by definition rights which are
largely unspecified, we will be led into textual and doctrinal
constructions so strained as to realize the fears of trackless decision which drove us to textual approaches, for example, in
the first place. The alternative is to ignore the pull of ethical
argument by pretending we have a different Constitution than
we do. It was, after all, the textualist Hugo Black who simply
refused to give effect to the words of the Ninth Amendment.
Conceding that the Ninth Amendment was passed "to assure
the people that the Constitution . . . was intended to limit the
Federal Government to the powers granted expressly or by
necessary implication," Justice Black chose to treat this guarantee merely as one "enacted to protect state powers against
federal invasion,"[1] even though the language of the Amendment gives no warrant for such a limitation. Insofar as the Ninth
Amendment was adopted to quiet fears arising from the fini-
tude of the Bill of Rights, I should think there would be much
more justification in asserting that persons, rather than states—
which are scarcely mentioned in the Bill of Rights— are its objects.

To refuse to take notice of ethical argument is to render
incomprehensible some of the most significant of our Constitutional decisions. Thus generations of commentators have
professed to be puzzled as to whether *Erie Railroad* v. *Tompkins*[2]
is a constitutional case, which it plainly is, since the rationale
results in a derivation of rights (the otherwise inexplicable reference to "equal protection of the laws") from the limited nature of federal power. Brandeis's argument is a straightforward
one: Congress has no power to declare substantive rules of
common law applicable in a state and no clause in the Constitution purports to confer such a power upon the federal courts;
what is not given is denied.

To recognize ethical argument is to confine judges and lawyers to the legal grammar. To ignore it is to compromise the
other approaches which must perforce do its work. The important case of *Griswold* v. *Connecticut*[3] is instructive in this regard.
In *Griswold* various sorts of arguments are encountered among

the opinions, providing a way to test which approach is satisfying.

Griswold was Executive Director of the Planned Parent-
hood League of Connecticut. He was arrested, along with a
physician, for giving information to married persons about
contraception. Both were convicted as abettors of those persons
who would violate a Connecticut statute which made it a crime
to use any drug, medicinal article, or instrument for the purpose of preventing conception. Justice Douglas wrote the opinion for the Court, holding the Connecticut statute unconstitutional. It is a largely prudential, instrumental opinion that
proceeds in three steps.

First, a feint is made toward doctrine. *Pierce* v. *Society of Sisters*[4] and *Meyer* v. *Nebraska*,[5] cases I have discussed in earlier
chapters, are said to stand for the proposition that "the State
may not, consistently with the spirit of the First Amendment,
contract the spectrum of available knowledge."[6] But doctrinal
argument is scarcely of help here. For one thing, neither *Pierce*
nor *Meyer* even mention the First Amendment. For another,
neither the retrospective principle regarding "the spectrum of
knowledge," nor the right of association established in various
First Amendment cases to which the Justice then turns,[7] has
much to do with the actual use of a contraceptive. To forbid it
is not to forbid knowledge of it or learning about it. Under the
state statute, one might even lawfully have been fitted with such
a device, so long as this was not done for the purpose of preventing conception. And the use of a contraceptive can hardly
be claimed crucial to those political associations, even taking
this phrase in a broad sense, protected by the cases cited.[8]

Turning from these doctrinal beginnings, which were
doomed by the very fact that *Griswold* was to be an innovation
in the development of the law, the Justice feints toward the
text. The Constitution, he says, creates various zones of privacy. Thus, the Third Amendment's prohibition against quartering soldiers "in any house," the Fourth's protection of the
"person, houses, papers and effects" of the people, and the
Fifth's "self-incrimination clause"—which Douglas says gives "the
citizen . . . a zone of privacy which government may not force
him to surrender to his detriment,"[9]—are all taken as textual
evidence of private constitutional refuges. But a textual ap-

proach must also be unavailing. If the texts of the Third, Fourth, and Fifth amendments do actually create zones of privacy, they are zones which extend, as the texts direct, to the quartering of soldiers, unreasonable searches and seizure by authorities, and compelled confessions.

And so the opinion, in its last paragraph after a hint or two of what is to come,[10] chooses to exploit a prudential approach. The opinion now concedes that the texts and their construction in caselaw do not really establish a right to privacy which inheres in the marriage relationship *per se*. But, it argues, such a right must exist if these explicit guarantees are to be fully protected. This is what is meant by Douglas's famous reference to the "penumbras" and "emanations" from the texts of the Bill of Rights. These implicit guarantees are not penumbral in the sense that they follow from the explicit guarantees. Nor are they emanations that can be deduced from the texts. Rather, as a practical matter, they must be given force if the specific guarantees are to have "life and substance."[11]

The last step in the argument is as instrumental as the argument itself. "Would we," the opinion asks, "allow the police to search the sacred precincts of marital bedrooms for telltale signs of the use of contraceptives?"[12] If the statute is inimical to the privacy of the marriage relationship, which Justice Douglas here calls for obvious reasons an "association," then it is likewise inimical to the Constitution, some parts of which are only made "fully meaningful"[13] when such associations are protected.

A tour de force, if one performed with a jaded deference to form. What is ultimately unsatisfactory about this approach, though, is that the resolution it so cleverly fought its way to is not where we really wanted to go. I suspect any argument that strays so far from the argument which actually persuaded its author is unsatisfying in this way. Thus we have the interesting phenomenon that *Griswold* holds, as it must from the argument given, that only the *use* of contraceptives may be banned. And yet it is universally understood by judges and lawyers to also prevent the banning of the manufacture and sale of contraceptives. Such a paradox is a grave criticism of an opinion.

Justice Black dissents in *Griswold,* as one might have guessed, and his approach is textual. Of the majority opinion, he writes

> The Court talks about a constitutional "right of privacy" as
> though there is some constitutional provision or provisions for-
> bidding any law ever to be passed which might abridge the
> "privacy" of individuals. But there is not.[14]

And yet Black's solution, too, is far from satisfactory. "I like my
privacy as well as the next one," Justice Black writes, "but I am
nevertheless compelled to admit that government has a right to
invade it unless prohibited by some specific constitutional provision."[15] Moreover, Justice Black warns us that a provision's
application must be restricted to the precise words of the text.[16]
In a society whose government has the technological capacity
to electronically monitor the movements of every single one of
its citizens, to gather dossiers of tedious but frightening thor-
oughness, such judicial stoicism is hardly reassuring. If it is correct, it is correct because the other approaches are wrong and
there is nothing the courts can do about it.

The *Griswold* case also gave us two more opinions—there
were six in all—which reflected differing approaches. Both, in-
terestingly, employed ethical argument, one quite studiedly and
quite unfortunately and the other successfully and unobtru-
sively.

Justice Goldberg joined the judgment and the opinion but
offered a concurring opinion in addition.[17] His ethical argument ran roughly as follows. The Fourteenth Amendment's
protection of "liberty" includes all fundamental rights; the Ninth
Amendment is evidence that the Bill of Rights does not exhaust
such fundamental rights; the purposes which underly the explicit fundamental rights "demonstrate that the rights to marital privacy . . . are of similar order and magnitude as the fundamental rights specifically protected."[18] I hope that no one
reading a summary of this approach will conclude that the arguments represent the ethical approach I endorsed in *Roe*. On
inspection, the Goldberg opinion is really no more than a statement of rather bland moral preferences which bears only a superficial similarity to argument from a constitutional ethic. Just
as one may learn much about a particular artist or school by
studying forgeries, it is precisely this superficial similarity that
makes the opinion valuable to our immediate enterprise. Let us
take the premises summarized, one by one.

Although Justice Goldberg emphatically eschews the incorporation doctrine,[19] his redefinition of the Fourteenth Amendment's "liberty" includes all "fundamental" rights. These rights turn out to be, among others, the rights specified by the Amendment which other judges "incorporate." Plainly, Justice Goldberg does not mean that such liberties can, as the constitutional text suggests, be denied when this is done by due process; nor do confessed "incorporators" always confine substantive due process to the explicit guarantees of the first eight Amendments. The first premise of his argument is therefore not really ethical but rather conventional doctrinal argument dressed a little differently.

The second premise draws the conclusion from the Ninth Amendment that the Bill of Rights is not exhaustive.[20] But what is done with this promising beginning? The Ninth Amendment obviously cannot be "incorporated" as a prohibition against the states. Perhaps this awkward fact is the source of the Justice's mistaken decision to conclude, a little defensively, that the Ninth Amendment has no respectable role here.

> I do not mean to imply that the Ninth Amendment is applied against the States by the Fourteenth. Nor do I mean to state that the Ninth Amendment constitutes an independent source of rights protected from infringement by either the States or the Federal Government. . . . Nor am I turning somersaults with history in arguing that the Ninth Amendment is relevant in a case dealing with a State's infringement of a fundamental right.[21]

There is no analysis to suggest that the Ninth Amendment is evidence of the exact interface in a system of limited government between enumerated powers and implied means, on the one hand, and personal rights and prohibited means, on the other. As a result, the third premise is really no more than an analogy. Whatever the Framers had in mind when they chose the Bill of Rights, it is suggested, would as well support a right to privacy in marriage. To support this argument we are given Justice Brandeis's eloquent statement of the purposes of the Fourth and Fifth amendments.[22] Brandeis being as close to the Framers as our century is likely to achieve, it is perhaps natural that Justice Goldberg should take this passage so wholly out of context and advertise it as a comprehensive summary of the "principles underlying the Constitution's guarantees of privacy."[23] It is odd, still, since if it were the summary Goldberg claims it to be, then presumably only the Fourth and Fifth amendments, to whose protection the passage from Brandeis explicitly limits itself, would be the concrete expression of these principles.

Odd, I say, but not daunting, since Justice Goldberg augments this characterization with his own assertion that the protection of marital privacy is at least as central to the Constitution as the specific guarantees. He does this in two steps. First, he cites a dissent for the view that the sanctity of the home is so "fundamental that it has been found to draw to its protection the principles of more than one explicitly granted Constitutional right."[24] Then, ignoring this excellent insight, he announces

> Although the Constitution does not speak in so many words of the right of privacy in marriage, I cannot believe that it offers these fundamental rights *no* protection.[25]

This is the end of the argument.

We may ask of this, as of the opinion for the Court, whether such a resolution will yield a holding that a proponent of the right to privacy and an opponent of the Connecticut statute would strive for. We really can't know this, of course, without knowing the arguments, and therefore the approaches, which first convinced them. But I am inclined to doubt that a holding which lifts a ban on contraception only to the extent that it is used by married persons with their spouses is much of a victory against governmental intrusion and oppression. Yet only this holding can be reached via Goldberg's approach.

The dissenting opinion from which the quoted insight, that the explicit guarantees are often successfully invoked to protect the marriage relation, is drawn is by Justice Harlan in *Poe* v. *Ullman*, a previous case[26] considering the same Connecticut statute. It is necessary to recall that opinion now because Justice Harlan's brief concurrence in *Griswold* refers the reader to it[27] and, by this reference and by its brevity, reasserts in *Griswold* the view taken in *Poe*.

There one finds an elegant example of constitutional ethical argument. The opinion begins with a recognition of the plenary power of the state. Granting this recognition, Justice Harlan explicitly also recognizes that "the *choice of means* [his emphasis] becomes relevant to any Constitutional judgment on what is done"[28] in pursuit of these powers. Then the opinion considers several hypothetical instances of various means, testing them to see if a rule may be drawn.

> The moral presupposition on which appellants ask us to pass judgment could form the basis of a variety of legal rules and administrative choices, each presenting a different issue for adjudication. For example, one practical expression of the moral view propounded here might be the rule that a marriage in which only contraceptive relations had taken place had never been consummated and could be annulled. Compare, *e.g.*, 2 Bouscaren, Canon Law Digest, 307–313. Again, the use of contraceptives might be made a ground for divorce, or perhaps tax benefits and subsidies could be provided for large families. Other examples also readily suggest themselves.[29]

This examination of alternatives is undertaken in much the same way as we tested the constitutional rule proposed in *Roe* in the previous chapter. It is done in a highly stylized way by listing the intuitively clear violations of the Constitution's limits on state methods and deriving a rule from these comparisons. The rule achieved is that the state may not "enquire into, prove and punish married people for the private use of their marital intimacy."

I am neither adopting the view of Justice Harlan's dissent *in toto* nor am I saying that it can be fairly summarized as employing but one approach to constitutional decision. I offer this judicial vignette to show contrasts between the various modes of argument. There is much in Justice Harlan's opinions in *Poe* and *Griswold* which is, if not antithetical to, at least not wholly in harmony with the ethical argument as I believe it will develop. This is as it must be, because new arguments will evolve as the ongoing relationship between the Constitution and our people works out its history. It is to this evolution that Book III is directed.

CONCLUSION

If my assertion is correct that the constitutional ethos of limiting the means available to government can serve as the basis for asserting personal rights and that the specific prohibitions of various means in the Bill of Rights are necessarily and acknowledgedly only a partial list, why do we need a Bill of Rights at all? Their formalization in specific texts has hardly made the prohibitions inviolable. Congress, after all, has made laws that abridge the freedom of speech, and these laws are customarily upheld by the United States Supreme Court.[1] Moreover, when Congress had made no law, in the *Pentagon Papers Case*,[2] this absence was so trivial a bar to Court action that it wasn't even discussed.

Indeed, to some extent the fears of Madison and others that the enumeration of specific rights would inevitably lead to the disparagement of others have been fulfilled. Insofar as we treat the Bill of Rights as the sole source, by enumeration or analogy, of constitutional rights, we are contributing to the realization of the Framer's misgivings. If the function of the Bill of Rights were to generate a grammar of constitutional arguments—as it does on a very small scale, for example, with each new precedent—then it might be that we should not have had a Bill of Rights. But making constitutional doctrine, and deciding cases by means of those doctrines that make possible the adjudication of rights among parties, is not the only function of a court or of a constitution.

Another function of constitutional decision is an expressive one. The Bill of Rights certainly performs that function: the freedom of speech; the right of the people to be secure in their persons; the right of an accused to be informed of the nature and cause of the accusation; the absolute bar against compelling him to be a witness against himself. These phrases were plucked out of many by the First Congress. Their wording is more economical and more poetic than that first proposed by Madison. They read quite unlike the other amendments of the Constitution, save the Fourteenth Amendment, with its graceful litany of immunities, liberty and equality, of privileges process and protection. The other amendments are largely mechanical, often longer in text.

The particular Bill of Rights we have serves, and seems chosen to serve, as more than a text for exegesis. It acts to give us a constitutional motif, a cadence of our rights, so that once heard we can supply the rest on our own.

III

CONSTITUTIONAL EXPRESSIONISM

INTRODUCTION

The working of the arguments maintains legitimacy. These arguments are predicated on the operation of judicial review; that is how they arise. Therefore a legitimate judiciary, in the American constitutional context, must review.

This review takes place in several functions. These functions are exercised through the means of the various arguments. Thus the functions are disconnected from legitimacy (the mere exercise of a proper function not assuring legitimacy). The conventions of argument and the related functions are therefore alternative overlays, taken out for use depending on whether one is interested in the legitimacy or the justification of judicial review. Book II focused largely on one sort of argument. In Book III are presented some of the functions of judicial review.

CHAPTER 13

CONSTITUTIONAL REVIEW

If tort law may be said to be a system of allocating the costs of accidents,[1] and contract law a system of allocating the transaction costs of market decisions,[2] then constitutional law may be thought of as the allocation of roles—who is to have the authority to make what sort of decision. On this view, one test for failure of a constitutional system would be whether or not its allocation of power was stable and functioned in a way that minimized conflict. To take an extreme example, civil war, I should think, is an indictment of a particular constitutional arrangement, just as the worst architecture, I have heard it said, is that of a building that collapses. The most successful constitutional order is one that encourages collaboration and harmony among the various constitutional institutions and actors, and thereby enhances its own stability.

From this perspective, we could conceive of the constitutional problem as a sort of n–person Prisoners' Game,[3] a version of the familiar two-person Prisoners' Dilemma. "The Prisoner's Dilemma" is a parable whose features parallel some kinds of decisionmaking under conditions of uncertainty. Two persons have jointly committed a crime for which they are both arrested and isolated in separate cells. Each is then approached by the prosecutor with the following deal: If the prisoner will turn state's evidence and implicate the accomplice, the informing prisoner will be set free and given a reward. If the prisoner refuses to speak, however, and his accomplice confesses, then the tables will be turned. The accomplice will be rewarded while the first prisoner will receive a harsh sentence, since his guilt is compounded by his refusal to aid the authorities. Both prisoners know, of course, that if each will only stay silent then both will go free; the prosecutor's anxious proposals tell them that much. But they also know that if they both confess, their testimony will become of little value to the prosecutor and neither will be set free and rewarded, though the sentence of each will not be as harsh as if he had been the one not to confess.

The dilemma is twofold. First, how can one prisoner be sure that the other won't betray him, so that each can hold steadfast to the best outcome for both? Second, even if each can be induced to trust the other, that is, to expect silence, how can each be further induced to forego the best individual payoff which that silence makes possible—a choice which exploits the other prisoner's trust. Without some such inducement, neither prisoner could rationally remain silent, both would be condemned to the least attractive mutual outcome, and their total sentence would be the worst possible. To leave the story and generalize to the heuristic aspects of the game, "the dilemma lies in the conflict between what is rational action for oneself as an individual and what is rational action . . . as a member of a two-person collective. By attending to their individual payoffs, prisoners will be led to an outcome that is at best suboptional for themselves and at worst a collective disaster."[4]

If we expand this notion to a game for n–persons, we may have some basis from which to evaluate constitutional rules. Do constitutional rules encourage collaboration among citizens for a common good? Do they maximize the availability of information so that the possibilities of collaboration are recognized? Do they permit shifting coalitions so that the opportunity costs for cooperation are minimized? And so forth.

Indeed, one very ingenious defense of *Roe* v. *Wade*—that it represents a particular allocation of the role of decisionmaker to the pregnant woman—may be supported on the ground that the holding thereby puts the right of decision in the hands of the one constitutional actor who has the most control as well as the most information and the highest payoffs and costs.[5]

The important thing to recognize about this view is that it is only that—a *view*. It is an overlay—a simple analytical mode which cannot fully capture all the significant features of constitutional decision. It is therefore in this one way an approach, as the arguments discussed in Book I are approaches.

Like those arguments it also has particular shortcomings, principally the following two. It relies on too narrow a concept of the game itself, and it assumes some general external good that a third party observer can discern. The features of constitutional law which are responsible for these particular shortcomings are the richness of functions served by constitutional decision (by the game) and the actual ways in which direction and change in constitutional development take place, ways that are not extricable from participation or even discernible without participation. These two topics—functions and participation—are the subjects of Book III.

In 1974, Grant Gilmore delivered the Storrs Lectures at the Yale Law School. At the end of the final lecture he spoke the lines that have become so famous since.

> Law reflects but in no sense determines the moral worth of a society. The values of a reasonably just society will reflect themselves in a reasonably just law. The better the society, the less law there will be. In Heaven, there will be no law, and the lion will lie down with the lamb. The values of an unjust society will reflect themselves in an unjust law. The worse the society, the more law there will be. In Hell, there will be nothing but law, and due process will be meticulously observed.[6]

This unforgettable passage, written with that elegant irony that distinguishes Gilmore's prose, quite overstates a general thesis. For the process we use does itself determine what sort of people we are, and therefore there is a reflexiveness, a kinaesthetic, mutually affecting reaction between a society and its law.

We may observe this in the construction of the important procedural idea of due process. This idea operates in a given context according to the valences of the various values of accuracy, efficiency, federalism, and fair play. And yet, what is fair play?

As an expression *fair play* is relatively new to our language, having arrived in common usage it seems not much before the time of Shakespeare. Its early uses[7] leave no doubt that the term was a conjunction of ideas parallel to expressions like "fair maid" in the phrase "Fair maid, send forth thine eye"[8] or "fair day" as in "a fair day in summer, wondrous fair."[9] What then is fair play? It is play—a serious game, if you will—that is fair, that is beautiful to us. And foul play is that which revolts us. Because I do not believe we are born with a taste for jury trials or the Australian ballot, I must assume that our institutions play some role in establishing our aesthetic principles in these matters. The Constitution is first among such institutions. And yet we must apply to it, in its construction, the very standards it teaches us, knowing that even as we do so we are creating a changed institution which will, in turn, change us.

Constitutional decisionmaking has, therefore, an expressive function. Of course it is a commonplace to observe that this is true of law generally. The triteness of the more general observation may account for the lack of appreciation of the precise operation of this expressivity in constitutional decisionmaking. Perhaps it is true for all societies that constitutional operations as well as forms play an expressive role. It is truer still for ours. The Constitution is our Mona Lisa, our Eiffel Tower, our Marseillaise.

All constitutional actors participate in creating constitutional decisions of principally expressive significance. For example, Lincoln's First Inaugural Address[10] may be taken as nothing more or less than a constitutional decision—announced through a different medium than a court's opinion—that secession was not permitted by the Constitution.[11] The address, so moving in its efforts to persuade and so melancholy when set against subsequent events, is a series of constitutional arguments, largely from text and structure but also from history and ethic, doctrine and prudence. For our purposes, it is most important to note that since the address decides no concrete case between two supplicant parties, its arguments can exercise, as a Court can never quite do, a wholly expressive function. Lincoln calls on the South to think of itself in terms of its constitutional identity. His decision that the Constitution does not permit secession and that various national functions will continue to be maintained is not of course without legal and political importance. But no one can read those pages and miss the point of the arguments. It is not simply to persuade but, by persuading, to recast the conflict.

I think it is important to be reminded of the absolute requirement of our system that each significant constitutional decider must exercise his or her own judgment and not simply assume that all constitutional questions are matters for the judiciary. In the present essay, however, I have drawn my focus on judicial matters, and it is to a consideration of the Court, rather than the President or Congress, and its role in performing the expressive constitutional function to which the balance of this book is devoted.

First it should be observed how well suited our Supreme Court is to fulfill an expressive role. For most of the life of the Court, there has been a tradition of unanimity. This is crucial if the Court is to be perceived with clarity and with an undivided force. The strenuous efforts of the Court to achieve unanimity in the *Brown* desegregation opinion[12] are evidence that the Court itself is not unmindful of this fact, although the recent proliferation of opinions suggests that such virtues are not always decisive. For a very long period of our history the Court spoke either through one opinion for the entire Court or through a single opinion not joined in by dissenters.[13] The splintering of the Court and particularly the fractionization of a majority renders an expressive role more difficult. A second distinctive feature of the Court is the provision for lifetime tenure. It has been shown that the average length of years served on the Supreme Court is no greater than that served by the average senior Congressman in Congress, who, far from having a lifetime appointment, must begin a new race soon after the old one is over. It is not simply the length of service of Supreme Court justices that is significant; two Republican presidential terms were enough to obtain a majority on the current Supreme Court. Rather it is the security the Justices are seen to have while they are on the bench that is important. Lifetime tenure does not remove them from the political process so much as change their role within that process. They are secure so that they need not be expedient and so that what they say can be believed to reflect their motives. In a political system like ours, which requires a healthy and pervading skepticism about political motives, this effect is indispensable.

The most interesting features, and the most illuminating, are those in which we differ from the English practice because these have been deliberately chosen. It is largely to John Marshall that, as with so much else, we owe a debt for halting the English practice of seriatim opinions delivered orally and summarily reported and for replacing them with a single written opinion. Only once in Jay's tenure was this done, and this, in the important jurisdictional case arising from the Neutrality Proclamation,[14] seems to have been done in part to evade giving reasons for the decision rather than to account for it. Jay's successor, Ellsworth, tried to eliminate the seriatim practice, but his absence on a mission to France in 1800 provided an opportunity for backsliding, so that when Marshall was sworn in the following year the practice of delivering seriatim opinions was still in some use.

Marshall at once began urging their abandonment and replacement by a single written opinion.[15] This, for two reasons, was a crucial step in permitting the Court to exercise an expressive function. First, it allowed the Court to speak with a single voice, so that its message was both unqualified and the prestige of that message thereby enhanced. Second, the effort to achieve agreement on a single opinion increased the importance of bargaining and persuasion among the Justices.[16] This meant that the statement finally agreed to would reflect more than the attitudes of a single person, and it increased considerably the proximity an opinion was likely to have to the views shared by the larger polity (by a sort of regression to the mean, I would surmise).

The expressive function was also enhanced by a second departure from English practice. This was the assumption from the beginning of our constitutional life that the Court could overrule precedent.[17] This assumption permits the Court to shift from supporting one view to a contrary one when the latter appears more compelling; this prevents the Court from being locked into a single view. Without this flexibility, no Court could wisely undertake an expressive function, since conflicting truths will from time to time require reinforcement at each other's expense.[18] This feature of the Court's operation is most important because it permits the Court to be an agent and conduit of change.

Alasdair MacIntyre has given us an account of the development of the ethical views of the English generation that came to maturity in the period between the wars.[19] That generation's intellectual direction came in great measure from G. E. Moore's *Principia Ethica.* Keynes was so influenced by this work that he could write almost 50 years later, "I see no reason to shift from the fundamental intuitions of *Principia Ethica . . .* they furnish a justification of experience wholly independent of outside events." The view expressed in *Principia Ethica* is that a right action is valuable only as a means to what is good. And what is good are "certain states of consciousness which may be roughly described as the pleasures of human intercourse and the enjoyment of beautiful objects." This view—of the supremacy of personal relationships and of the beautiful—would guide us to right actions only, of course, if we could know what was beautiful and what human relations were pleasurable. Indeed, the argument which determined that these were the good depended on general assent to what Moore took to be the non-subjective reality of the good.

He described "goodness" as a nonnatural property. It was a fallacy, he thought, to treat ethical predicates as though they were statements about things or objects. But this did not mean that a statement about goodness was merely a statement about the speaker's sensibility. It was, rather, like a statement about a color. When I say something is yellow I don't say anything the truth of which can be reduced to a description of the physical arrangement of particles. On the other hand, I *am* saying something about the world and not just about my sensibility. Thus, everyone who has learned the word need only have an example pointed out to immediately "see" the quality. So it was, Moore held, with the good.

"In an extremely homogenous group," MacIntyre writes, "like that of Moore's immediate disciples," such agreement was easily achieved, even likely. "But the arrival of D. H. Lawrence on the scene, who reacted against [this] attitude [passionately] might have made them aware that if challenged on their valuations, their own position allowed them no use for argument, but only for reinspection and reassertion."[20]

Much the same might be said of the role of the Court and its expressive function in constitutional law. Those cases which principally serve an expressive function depend on a high congruity between what different persons see as fundamentally right. This congruity is made possible by the use of the various conventions and by our historical experience of knowing the Constitution through time, gaining a sense of what it is, what we are, an experience that has come to us in part from expressive decisions of the past. At the same time, the existence of various constitutional conventions allows differing parties each to claim the Constitution as their own. That is why, over time, it is the ability to *overrule* precedent that gives the Court such vast importance in the expression of values. To paraphrase Lawrence's remark about the novel, it can inform and lead into new places the flow of our sympathetic consciousness and can lead our sympathy away in recoil from things that are dead.[21]

CHAPTER 14

FUNCTIONS OF REVIEW

In 1959, Charles Black wrote, "Judicial review has two prime functions—that of imprinting governmental action with the stamp of legitimacy, and that of checking the political branches of government when these encroach on ground forbidden to them by the Constitution as interpreted by the Court." [1]

This account reflects Black's structural perspective. You will recall that I said in Book I that each of the different kinds of constitutional argument implied a particular justification for judicial review. For example, historical argument suggests a sort of social contract between government and the people, the original intention of both parties being held to determine the construction of that instrument, the written Constitution, that is the memorialization of the agreement. Courts, on this view, examine legislation to see if it comports with the original understanding of the parties.

Structural argument also implies a justification for judicial review, the outlines of which follow from the passage I have quoted. A court exercises a legitimating force with respect to legislation that it necessarily if inadvertently validates in the process of applying it; and of course there could be no real legitimation without the power to *in*validate. Judicial review is justified as a robust exercise, rather than a denial, of the democratic principle that the people choose; here the people have chosen to place limits on the institutions by which their wishes are carried out.[2] This is in contrast to the customary view of judicial review as an imposed, antidemocratic institution. It is the difference between self-restraint, as Professor Black says, and coercion. It yields what he calls "the noble paradox . . . that the State itself must set up this limit on itself, and submit to the organ of its enforcement."[3]

One's view of the functions of the Supreme Court is as much a product of the approach one adopts to the Constitution as are one's convictions as to the proper foundation of judicial review. Philip Kurland has written that he doubts whether any such legitimating function is really exercised.[4] Alexander Bickel took up the legitimating idea so thoroughly that he would have added yet another function to describe the Supreme Court's role when it wishes neither to check nor to legitimate; I need hardly add that a prudentialist approach would be most useful to this function.[5] For my own part I should like to draw attention to still other functions of the Court, though I expect that other students of constitutional decisionmaking may not see these functions.

To break the spell of believing that there are only one or two functions of judicial review, I should like to discuss briefly what I have called elsewhere[6] the "cueing function" in constitutional law. I will do this in the context of a single exemplary case to suggest the difference it makes whether a decision is attributed to one function or another.

On June 24, 1976, the Supreme Court handed down *National League of Cities* v. *Usery*.[7] At issue were the 1974 amendments to the Fair Labor Standards Act by which the Act's minimum wage and maximum hours provisions were extended to state employees. The Court determined that these amendments would displace the states' freedom to structure operations in areas of traditional authority by vastly increasing the expense of and limiting the choices by which police protection, sanitation, fire prevention, and the like were to be provided. The constitutional system of federalism was held to impose implicit limits on the otherwise plenary commerce power. As observed in Book I, the argument is largely structural, although a passing nod is made to the Tenth Amendment's reservation of powers to the states. To remove from the states those choices which are essential to the functions which they perform is to simply make the states into geographic regions of the federal government. There is no text saying this can't be done; it is simply incompatible with the constitutional relationships of the federal structure.

The opinion in *National League of Cities* was met by considerable adverse commentary.[8] Many persons, including four members of the Court,[9] felt that this decision was a step back to the pre–New Seal era in which the Court routinely found reasons to limit the exercise of Congress' commerce power. Some said that *National League of Cities* cast doubt on the landmark *Darby* case[10] which had virtually ended the invalidation by the courts of social legislation enacted by Congress pursuant to its commerce power.

The case is indeed troubling if one assumes that it represents a new point at which the checking function is to be exercised. And how can one not see it this way? Legislation is struck down; that is surely the result of a check. And it does constitute a new checkpoint, as the overruling in *National League of Cities*[11] of *Maryland* v. *Wirtz*,[12] reaffirmed only the preceding term,[13] makes clear. Furthermore, this can't be an example of the referring function since the Court did, after all, strike down a congressional statute.

But assume for a moment that this decision serves a different function, that of a cue to some other, coordinate constitutional actor. Begin with the view that the three branches of the federal government[14] have the burden under the Constitution of judging their own actions to see if they conform to the limits and restraints placed on them by the Constitution. Their oaths of office demand as much. Furthermore, the presumption of constitutionality which is given legislation validly passed and signed into law, as well as the custom of avoiding inquiry into legislative motivation, necessitates some kind of constitutional review by each of the nonjudicial branches. Indeed, it was the holding in *Darby* that stated the rule of review that "whatever their motive and purpose, regulations of commerce which do not infringe some constitutional prohibition are within the plenary power conferred on Congress by the Commerce Clause."[15] Unless we are willing to assume that Congress simply will never act in pursuit of an unconstitutional purpose, such a rule demands congressional scrutiny of its own purposes. Of course, even though Congress has this responsibility and must determine the constitutional basis of its acts, this does not always mean that Congress' determination is final when other actors are called upon to exercise their constitutional functions. In such a situation these branches must also apply constitutional standards to their own acts.

Congress is not insensitive to its responsibility, despite some unfortunate and widely repeated remarks that constitutionality is really a matter for the courts. In fact there are absences from judicial case law so vast that one can only conclude that Congress has so internalized constitutional standards that many adventures are not even thought reasonable and never find their way into legislation. Furthermore, the Congressional Record reveals a good deal of reference to Court decisions as a guide to the constitutionality of a particular statute. This is in part an example of Congress proceeding analogically, much as a lower court might, given the relative rarity of Supreme Court decisions, although it is also a matter of legislative efficiency for the Congress to try to craft legislation that will be upheld in the courts and not overturned.

These general responsibilities of constitutional care are greatly enhanced with respect to one particular subject, the protection of federalism. Herbert Wechsler has drawn attention to the important part played by the states in the selection and composition of Congress.[16] More than the obvious facts that the Senate is drawn wholly from a constituency of states and that the state legislatures decide districting for the House are involved here. The perception of common interests, the background and associations of elected officials, the influence of local business and political groups are but a few of the factors that, as Madison foresaw,[17] so aptly fit Congress to exercise the restraint of the local against the centripetal force of the national. In this regard, it may prove useful to remember the prime purpose envisaged for judicial review in relation to federalism, namely, to maintain national supremacy and to protect individual rights.[18]

If we assume with Wechsler that the protection of the states' sovereignty is primarily the work of Congress, we need not conclude, with the dissent that cites Wechsler,[19] that the majority in *National League of Cities* is wrong. Instead we may come to think that the case is not a major doctrinal turn but a cue to a fellow constitutional actor, an incitement to Congress to renew its traditional role as protector of the states. It's not the threat of invalidating legislation *per se* so much as the argument for a different construction of the Constitution, particularly for a sturdier Federalism. There are several reasons why Congress' role as protector of Federalism has been less filled lately, not the least of which, as the Congressional Record and various committee reports confirm, is the popular conception of the Court's work in *Wickard* v. *Filburn*.[20] The frequency and looseness with which the "Wheat Case" has come to be mentioned and interpreted in Congress as meaning that there are no limitations on the commerce power (beyond the specific prohibitions of the Bill of Rights) has undermined this role. *National League of Cities* changed this facile characterization, and with immediate effect, as the Social Security controversy contemporaneous with the decision shows. Before *National League of Cities* was handed down, an amendment to the Social Security Act to include state workers was widely expected to pass Congress. Since the Court decided *National League of Cities*, H.B. 13040 has never emerged from committee.[21] So it would seem the cue was taken. But how do we know it was just a cue? And what difference does it make?

My thesis is, unlike so many others, testable. If the Court were exercising a cueing function in *National League of Cities* then we would expect to see the Court not granting certiorari in cases which present a development of the doctrine announced in *National League of Cities*. We would expect to see little development of the doctrine in the cases taken on appeal. Indeed, citation of *National League of Cities* would be virtually absent except for dicta. Finally, if we were lucky, we might even encounter a case presenting a substantial *National League of Cit-*

ies issue which the Court chose wholly to ignore. When the Court did rely on *National League of Cities* it would only be in cases in which lower courts, misled by the erroneous checking assumption, had actually struck down legislation on that basis.

What do we find? We find virtually no development of this potentially major doctrinal change. The Court has not once relied on *National League of Cities* to invalidate a Statute or regulation.[22] And in the case of *City of LaFayette* v. *Louisiana Power & Light*,[23] which applied the federal antitrust laws to state municipalities, there is scarcely a reference to *National League of Cities* even though it was discussed in both briefs and at oral argument and is clearly enough germane to the decision which followed.[24] Much of the commentary on *National League of Cities*, then, if my view is correct, is irrelevant, and it makes a great difference which function the Court is exercising.

The purpose of this excursion has been to provide an example of a different function than the ones commonly thought of, one that makes something other than a doctrinal artifact of a judicial opinion. One can perhaps only appreciate this, recognizing it as a truly distinct function, if one accepts my general mapping of the various constitutional approaches and the family of functions they serve. Otherwise one might be inclined to reduce this analysis to an example of mere speculation about motivation and assimilate it into a more general function which nicely comports with a single approach. A similar misapprehension often occurs with cases serving another function of Court constitutional decision, the expressive function.

Before turning to a discussion of this function, however, I caution that my enumeration of the various functions is not exhaustive; I do not purport to give a complete list. Each function appears to us only in contrast with the others, as Bickel's referral function appears only once one accepts Black's legitimating function and as one can only see certain colors when they are next to others. When I have described certain functions, others will perhaps occur to those readers who see the ones I now present. Let us then turn to an examination of the expressive function at work in several well-known, much-analyzed constitutional cases.

CHAPTER 15

EXPRESSIVE FUNCTION

The School Prayer case—*Abington Township* v. *Schempp*[1]—was, with the *Miranda* decision, perhaps, the most controversial Supreme Court case of the 1960s. Unlike *Miranda,* however, *Abington Township* is widely disobeyed.[2] Perhaps this means that it is an example of poor constitutional deciding, like collapsing architecture, and, if so, it may be related to an erroneous choice of function by the Court analogous to the erroneous choice made by commentators interpreting the *National League of Cities* opinion.

On February 14, 1958, three students in the public schools of Abington Township, Pennsylvania and their parents filed a complaint alleging that the school district and its employees were violating the students' religious consciences and liberties by causing the Bible to be read in the classrooms of the Township as required by a Pennsylvania statute. This statute read:

> Section 1516. Bible To Be Read in Public Schools.—At least ten verses from the Holy Bible shall be read or caused to be read, without comment, at the opening of each public school on each school day, by the teacher in charge: Provided, That where any teacher has other teachers under and subject to direction, then the teacher exercising such authority shall read the Holy Bible, or cause it to be read, as herein directed.

> If any school teacher, whose duty it shall be to read the Holy Bible, or cause it to be read, shall fail or omit so to do, said school teacher shall, upon charges preferred for such failure or omission, and proof of the same, before the board of school directors of the school district, be discharged.[3]

The three children were from the Schempp family. Edward Louis Schempp, an electrical engineer, and his wife Sidney had moved to Abington in 1948. By the time of the complaint their three children, Ellory, Roger, and Donna, were in the local senior high school, the junior high school, and the elementary school respectively. (This was a family uniquely suited for litigation: Donna Schempp was twelve years old at the time of the initial trial and was in her final months as a graduating senior in high school by the time the United States Supreme Court heard the case.) The Schempp family were Unitarians. The trial record reveals that Ellory, eighteen at the time, had tried for some months to interest A.C.L.U. attorneys in filing the complaint. Certainly his testimony is remarkably fluent and careful, giving the impression of rehearsal and close attention to what seemed likely to be relevant legal detail.

The three children all testified at the trial. They said it was the practice in the various schools of the Township which they had attended to begin the first period of each school day with a brief ceremony consisting of the reading of ten verses of the King James Version of the Bible, followed by a standing recitation in unison of the Lord's Prayer, usually followed by the Pledge of Allegiance to the Flag, and rounded out by routine school announcements. There were some variations in the execution of these ceremonies in the various schools. Two of the children said that the Bible reading and the recitation of the prayer were conducted by the individual homeroom teacher, who either chose a text and read the ten verses herself or delegated both choice of text and reading to the students. Ellory testified that his building was equipped with a public address system and that the Bible was read over the loudspeaker, after which the voice on the loudspeaker directed the children to rise and repeat the Lord's Prayer.

Ellory and Donna testified that it seemed to them that a "particularly high standard of physical deportment and attention" was exacted during the Bible reading, and Donna noted that such deportment was not always required when other works were being read. The three Schempp children and their father also testified about various doctrinal positions reflected in the King James Version of the Bible that were at odds with their own beliefs: among other things, Christ's divinity and the concepts of the Trinity and of God as a Being were mentioned. In fact, much of the testimony at the trial was devoted to theological expressions by the children, their father, or various "expert" witnesses. Dr. Solomon Grayzel, editor of the Jewish Publication Society, testified that there were marked differences in the Jewish Holy Scriptures and the Christian Bible: "the most obvious of which," he said, "was the absence of the New Testament in the Jewish Holy Scriptures."

The Township countered with its own witness, Dr. Luther Wegile, Dean of the Yale Divinity School. Dr. Wegile testified lengthily as to his experience with theological matters. In his opinion the King James Version was not a "sectarian" work; cross-examination revealed this opinion to mean "non-sectarian among the various Christian bodies." Dr. Wegile further testified that he thought there was educational value in reading the King James Version, both because of its moral teachings and literary value and, finally, because it is "the Word of God to man."

Edward Schempp testified that he had not requested that his children be excused from the morning devotions although the family felt the reading of the King James Version was "against our particular family religious beliefs," because his children would have been labelled "oddballs" and their classmates would have tended to assign immoral, un-American, and atheistic connotations to the children's absence. Mr. Schempp pointed out that reciting the Pledge of Allegiance to the Flag followed directly upon the recitation of the Lord's Prayer. Noting that in Abington High School a common form of punishment was exclusion from the classroom to stand in the hall, Mr. Schempp testified he felt that simply permitting his children to leave the room during the exercises would "be very detrimental to the psychological well-being of the children."

William Young, an English teacher at the high school, was at that time in charge of the school's radio and television workshop. Approximately thirty of the workshop students did the actual reading of the Bible and led the rest of the school in saying the Lord's Prayer. Because he hoped to impart to them technical skills of microphone address, Mr. Young had his students practice reading in advance whatever material was to be read the following day. He had adopted a practice of having the students study with their own Bibles, out of which they would select a section. Consequently, on occasion Jewish and Catholic students read from their Bibles. Mr. Young did not say what the Jewish students did about the Lord's Prayer.

Dr. Eugene Stull, principal of the Abington Senior High School, testified that the Township school authorities provided a roll book for the teacher to use in keeping attendance. In the front of this book were suggested texts for Bible reading. Whether or not these suggestions were followed was apparently up to the teacher. The book was not an official publication of the school district or the state but was procured from a private publisher.

Only Ellory Schempp testified that he was "compelled" to attend Bible reading.

On September 16, 1959, a three-judge court declared the Pennsylvania statute unconstitutional. The conclusion of the court was predicated on its factual finding that attendance by all pupils and participation by the teachers were compulsory. On the same day the three-judge court enjoined the Township from causing the Bible to be read in public schools.

On December 17, 1959, in an effort to eliminate the compulsory features of the statute, the legislature of Pennsylvania amended Section 1516 of the Public School Code to read as follows:

> Bible Reading in Public Schools.—At least ten verses from the Holy Bible shall be read, without comment, at the opening of each public school on each school day.

> Any child shall be excused from such Bible reading, or attending such Bible reading, upon the written request of his parent or guardian.[4]

Following the passage of this amendment, the Abington Township School District altered its practice and excused any child who wished to be excused from Bible Reading.

On December 23, 1959, the Township filed a rule 60(b) Motion for Relief from Judgment with the three-judge court. This motion asked that the final decree be vacated on the ground that the passage of the amendment and its effects had eliminated the controversy. On June 9, 1960, the three-judge court denied this motion for want of jurisdiction to entertain or decide the question, since jurisdiction had passed to and been vested in the United States Supreme Court. On August 5, 1960, the Supreme Court issued an opinion per curiam, vacating the judgment and remanding for consideration in light of the Pennsylvania amendment.

A very brief second trial was held at which Edward Schempp and one son, Roger, testified as to the possibly coercive effect of excusals. Since none of the Schempp children had asked for such excusals, this testimony was largely speculative. In the main, the Schempps relied on the testimony of the former trial. On February 1, 1962, the three-judge court issued an opinion declaring the amended statute unconstitutional on the ground that it violated the "establishment of religion" clause of the First Amendment, made applicable to the Commonwealth of Pennsylvania by the Fourteenth Amendment. The court held that the reading without comment of ten verses of the Holy Bible each morning at an exercise from which any or all students could be excused constituted an obligatory religious observance (an Establishment claim). The first case had held that the Schempp children could not exercise their freedom not to repeat doctrines that were distasteful to them (a Free Exercise claim). The court evidently thought it could avoid the effect of the statutory change, by which the legislature had sought to remove the common element of compulsion which tied the establishment and free exercise claims together, by limiting the grounds of the decision to the establishment clause. Therefore the second case held that regardless of the lack of compulsion the simple reading of the Bible *per se* constituted an establishment of religion. While an appeal to the United States Supreme Court was pending, *Engel* v. *Vitale* [5] was decided on June 25, 1962.

The United States Supreme Court's majority opinion in *Schempp* is difficult to understand outside of the context created by two facts. First, the three-judge panel below had removed the finding of compulsion from its second-round finding of facts. The result of this was the elimination of a Free Exercise rationale for the opinion. Second, the controversial holding in *Engel* v. *Vitale* had become the dominant caselaw in the area. *Schempp* came to be seen by all concerned through the matrix of the *Engel* precedent. This was decisive. Not only did it mean that *Schempp* would be used to answer the critics of *Engel* and to construct a new rule of Establishment Clause precedent, but it also structured the views of the Court so that they saw the important facts of *Schempp* as those that coincided with *Engel*. Actually, the two were only superficially similar (viewing *Engel*, of course, in the absence of its subsequent role as precedent for *Schempp*), and the key fact that gave *Engel* its character was wholly absent in *Schempp*.

In *Engel*, parents of children in New York public schools sought to enjoin classroom recitation of a prayer composed under the auspices of the New York Board of Regents. The prayer was recommended but not required, and read,

> Almighty God we acknowledge our dependence upon Thee, and we beg Thy blessings upon us, our parents, our teachers and our country.

A divided New York Court of Appeals refused to issue an injunction halting the practice. On certiorari the United States Supreme Court, however, concluded that the prayer amounted to an establishment of religion by the state. The majority opinion by Justice Black pointedly does not rely on the *McCollum*[6] case which had invalidated a program of religious instruction on school premises during school hours. Instead Justice Black wrote,

> The Establishment Clause, unlike the Free Exercise Clause, does not depend upon any showing of indirect governmental compulsion and is violated by the enactment of laws which establish an official religion whether those laws operate directly to coerce nonobserving individuals or not. . . . The purposes of the Establishment Clause go much further than that. Its first and most immediate purpose rested on the belief that a union of government and religion tends to destroy government and to degrade religion.[7]

Justice Douglas's concurring opinion is more explicit.

> There is no element of compulsion or coercion in New York's regulation . . . [A] child is free to stand or not to stand, to recite or not to recite, without fear of reprisal or even comment by the teacher or any other school official . . . *McCollum* v. *Board of Education* does not decide this case.[8]

A state prayer: that is, I believe, the significant fact in *Engel*. For a state legislature to compose a prayer for distribution in the schools seems almost the paradigmatic establishment of an official religion. That it occurred in a context in which no recognized religion seemed to be favored, that it was recited in a public school, and that compulsion to conform was not proved— these facts were inessential. The Regent's prayer might just as well have been the Welfare Board's Prayer, engraved on the back of all welfare checks with the suggestion, but not the requirement, that caseworkers have their clients recite the prayer before cashing the check.

Justice Stewart grasped this essentiality when he devoted his dissent to collecting examples of references to God in the National Anthem, on coins, and in the Pledge of Allegiance. In so doing he raised counterexamples that would ultimately prove troubling to his position in *Schempp*.

Engel was widely scored in both the lay and professional commentary. Not surprisingly, when a few months following the controversy and harsh attacks surrounding *Engel* the Court confronted a case that appeared to present the opportunity for the construction of a sturdier rationale, while being similar enough to *Engel* to be governed by that case, it granted certiorari.

At the outset it should be observed that *Schempp* went to the Supreme Court as something of a patchwork. Its first trip up, the three judge panel and apparently all the litigants had treated the case as principally a free exercise problem. The *Schempp* children could not exercise their freedom *not* to repeat doctrines that were distasteful to them. *Barnette,* the flag salute case holding that Jehovah's Witnesses have a First Amendment right not to say the Pledge of Allegiance, was thought an attractive precedent. What establishment claims there were could be settled by relying on the compulsion element in *McCollum*. But by amending the statute, the Pennsylvania legislature deftly removed the common element which held the *McCollum* and free exercise theories together. Or so one would have thought.

The three-judge panel, however, was undeterred:

> The statute now sub judice provides . . . that a child may be excused from attendance at the Bible reading on the written request of his parent or guardian. But since, as will appear hereinafter, we decide this controversy on the Establishment of Religion clause of the First Amendment the exculpatory phrase cannot aid the defendants' argument . . . for . . . there is religious establishment in this case whether pupils are or are not excused from attendance at the morning exercises.[9]

In the Supreme Court this holding was affirmed. Justice Clark wrote for the majority. He wrote a purely doctrinal argument, distilling a test from earlier cases and wholly ignoring the lengthy historical arguments which had characterized earlier discussions of the First Amendment clauses at issue. His opinion is straightforward; roughly, the argument is as follows:

1. The applicable caselaw requires a "wholesome neutrality by the state".[10]

2. The test of this neutrality can be summed up from previous cases as a simple matter of legislative intent and statutory effect:

> The test may be stated as follows: what are the purpose and primary effect of the enactment? If either is the advancement or inhibition of religion then the enactment exceeds the scope of legislative power as circumscribed by the Constitution. That is to say that to withstand the strictures of the Establishment Clause there must be a secular legislative purpose and a primary effect that neither advances nor inhibits religion. . . .[11]

3. The three-judge panel's finding of fact that the readings which had occurred, even though not required by law, were a religious ceremony and constituted the promotion of "public religiousness" permits the Supreme Court to infer a compatible legislative motive consistent with such a finding. (The Court carefully did not adopt the lower court's finding as to legislative motivation *per se*.)

> The trial court . . . has found that such an opening exercise is
> a religious ceremony and was intended by the State to be so.
> We agree with the trial court's finding as to the religious char-
> acter of the exercise. Given that finding the exercises and the
> law requiring them are in violation of the Establishment
> Clause.[12]

Thus the Pennsylvania statute was struck down, the legislature
having been held to have established a religion in Abington
township.

There are many critical things one may say about this opinion,[13] and most have been said. Perhaps most damning to any
doctrinal argument is a dissent which relies on the same principle asserted in the majority. So it is troubling that Justice
Stewart announces that he too is asserting a "neutrality thesis."

Justice Stewart's dissent in *Schempp* proceeds by way of two
parallel arguments: that no substantial Establishment issue exists on the record and that the construction required to render
such an issue significant would trigger the Free Exercise Clause,
which would save the statute. In other words, forbidding states
to take any measures which merely make available, without
compulsion, religious materials or exercises denies some parents the right to freely exercise their religious convictions. A
bona fide neutrality, on this view, is offended by the enforcement of religious exclusion, since it is hostile to and uses state
funds to inhibit religion. Those children whose parents can't
afford parochial schools are prevented from receiving an important element of their religious upbringing.

Here, Stewart sums up the first line of attack.

> To be specific, it seems . . . . clear that certain types of exercises
> would present situations in which no possibility of coercion on
> the part of secular officials could be claimed to exist. Thus, if
> such exercises were held either before or after the official school
> day, or if the school schedule were such that participation were
> merely one among a number of desirable alternatives, it could
> hardly be contended that the exercises did anything more than
> to provide an opportunity for the voluntary expression of reli-
> gious belief.[14]

> Viewed in this light, it seems to me clear the records in both of
> the cases before us are wholly inadequate to support an in-
> formed or responsible decision.[15]

This view depends on two assumptions that the majority rejected. First, Justice Stewart believes that religious exercises that reflect the diversity of the community are constitutionally permissible: "They become constitutionally invalid only if their administration places the sanction of secular authority behind one or more particular religious or irreligious beliefs." Second, Justice Stewart does not accept the noncoercive Establishment Clause rationale put forth by Justice Black in *Engel*. Thus, Stewart's call for a better record amounts to a smudging of the issue. While it does suggest what facts on remand might satisfy Justice Stewart of the impermissibility of the state practice, it fails to note that implicit in this statement is the concession that no further facts are necessary if one takes the Black view of anti-Establishment protection.

Even though Justice Stewart largely ignores the Black rationale, he might have been able to neutralize its force as precedent for *Schempp*. Given the doctrinal presumption of the constitutional validity of a statute, if a draw can be managed on the Establishment question, the Stewart view of the Free Exercise issue will, as we shall see, save the statute. So before making the Free Exercise Clause argument, Stewart attempts to entangle the Establishment issue with the Free Exercise claim.

> It is a fallacious oversimplification to regard [the Free Exercise and Establishment] provisions as establishing a single constitutional standard of 'separation of church and state,' which can be mechanically applied in every case to delineate the required boundaries between government and religion. The fact is that while in many contexts the Establishment Clause and the Free Exercise Clause fully complement each other, there are areas in which a doctrinaire reading of the Establishment Clause leads to irreconcilable conflict with the Free Exercise Clause.[16]

At this stage Justice Stewart is preparing the full-dress constitutional argument that eluded him in *Engel*: that striking down legislation that enables parents to provide religious exercises in the public schools denies parents the right to participate in a constitutionally recognized activity. The argument begins with broad assertions of a neutrality thesis and the proposition that the majority opinion establishes a kind of state secularism, an institutionalized hostility to religion.

Unlike other First Amendment guarantees, there is an inherent limitation upon the applicability of the Establishment Clause's ban on state support to religion. 'State power is no more to be used so as to handicap religions than it is to favor them.' A manifestation of such hostility would be at war with our national tradition as embodied in the First Amendment guaranty of the free exercise of religion. That the central value embodied in the First Amendment—and, more particularly, in the guarantee of 'liberty' contained in the Fourteenth—is the safeguarding of an individual's right to free exercise of his religion has been consistently recognized.[17]

After these preliminaries, Stewart proceeds to make the Free Exercise argument. It is a novel and interesting piece. He argues that the state has so occupied and organized the child's day, by compulsory attendance if he is not being educated privately, that his parents must provide for some religious instruction at the public school if there is to be any frequent and useful religious instruction. Implicit in this argument, but comprising a second, different tack, is the charge that to deny the legislature, and through them the parents, the right to provide such programs is to make a right contingent on the payment of money.

It might be argued here that parents who wanted their children to be exposed to religious influences in school could, under *Pierce*, send their children to private or parochial schools. But the consideration which renders this contention too facile to be determinative has already been recognized by the Court: 'Freedom of speech, freedom of the press, freedom of religion are available to all, not merely to those who can pay their own way.'

For there is involved in these cases a substantial free exercise claim on the part of those who affirmatively desire to have their children's school day open with the reading of passages from the Bible.

It might also be argued that parents who want their children exposed to religious influences can adequately fulfill that wish off school property and outside school time. . . . [But] a compulsory state educational system so structures a child's life that if religious exercises are held to be an impermissible activity in schools, religion is placed at an artificial and state-created disadvantage. Viewed in this light, permission of such exercises for those who want them is necessary if the schools are truly to be neutral in the matter of religion. And a refusal to permit religious exercises thus is seen, not as the realization of state neutrality, but rather as the establishment of a religion of secularism, or at the least, as government support of the beliefs of those who think that religious exercises should be conducted only in private.[18]

Viewed in the context that compulsion is both required to invoke anti-Establishment protection and may be present, on the Free Exercise side, when such anti-Establishment protection is improperly but successfully invoked, Justice Stewart's conclusion becomes clearer.

The records before us are so fundamentally deficient as to make impossible an informed or responsible determination of the constitutional issues presented[19]

It is not so much that the records are incomplete as that a remand would recognize the requirement of compulsion to present an Establishment claim and thereby much limit *Engel* and provide school boards all across the country with a variety of escapes from Establishment claims. These evasive maneuvers would consist not only of various modifications to include other religious studies, different texts, meetings at noncurricular hours, and so forth but also the preparation of a record that could put forward the Free Exercise argument. Such a remand would undoubtedly not have saved *Schempp*, as Stewart must have known from the record sent to the Court prior to the first remand. A remand would, however, have held out the possibility of constitutionally permissible prayers in the schools, a possibility not only significant in the context of litigation but a saving alternative in the context of defiance.[20]

It is disturbing that both Clark and Stewart are willing to advance neutrality theses drawing on the case law to bring about opposite results. This can partly be understood by appreciating Stewart's Free Exercise move, which acts as an inhibiting boundary for the operation of the neutrality thesis, a boundary that Clark does not recognize. Of course, Clark and Stewart are also using similar doctrinal arguments in service of different functions: Clark to check the state, Stewart to remand to the legislature. Yet there is a further explanation for the lack of decisiveness in the doctrinal rule. It is that a doctrinal approach itself is inadequate to decide this case.

A fundamental error in the use of these competing theses is that relying on the principle each asserts provides us with no way to choose between them. As a principle, a neutrality thesis is no help in this matter, because we have no adequate notion of generality on which a neutrality thesis, if it is to guide decision, must depend.

Recently a litigant has challenged the use of the motto "In God We Trust" engraved on United States coins.[21] It may seem simple to say that the primary purpose of the coins is to provide a medium of exchange and not to advance a particular sectarian view. But that statement assumes that the level of generality is fixed on the coin. One could just as legitimately ask what the primary purpose of the motto is.

Robbed of a standard of generality, the rule of neither advancing nor inhibiting religion is crippled. On some level of generality religions are always being affected by political acts, sometimes in both positive and negative ways by the same act. Something of this notion is captured in Stewart's comment that the Free Exercise and Establishment Clauses may conflict.

Suppose a conscientious objector is allowed to absent himself from military training. If a legislature does this it is plainly open to the charge of affording special status to that particular set of religions whose scruples include objection to war. But if a legislature refuses to make such provisions the objector can quite plausibly go to court and say that induction and service will infringe his rights of conscience. The Stewart dissent argues that this is the result of an artificial and aggressive restriction on alleged Establishment activities, but I think it is more difficult than that. It is hard to see any decision with respect to religious groups or individuals that would not commit or withdraw a resource from them. The recent news stories of men allowing themselves to be bitten by poisonous snakes remind us not only that a simple game statute may have an anti-religious effect on some sects but that its purpose may be so perceived as well.[22]

What is wrong with majority and dissent in *Schempp* is what is wrong with doctrinal argument generally when it is not supplemented by a method establishing the purpose and direction of doctrine. That Clark and Stewart should have determined that the First Amendment's purpose was the enforcement of neutral principles was a fatal, if ironic, step in pursuit of a satisfactory doctrine. Such a pursuit is indispensable if the checking function is to be adequately performed and hardly superfluous in service of the referring function. In either case, guidance must be given to others, namely the lower courts and the legislatures.

Assume for a moment, though, that a different function is to be served, an expressive function. We would then want a statement which characterizes the society and its rules but which does not attempt to set up a general rule for development in the lower courts outside the school prayer context. The First Amendment's religious clauses are particularly well-suited by their history to be the vehicle of the Court's expressive function.

American attitudes towards the role of the church in the state underwent deep and lasting change between 1600 and 1800. This change was accompanied by the liquidation by the heirs of the Enlightenment of the accumulated emotional assets of seven centuries, an inheritance that had capitalized the Puritan state. Knowing that fears of a national church and deep religious strife were concerns in a society at least as interested in getting ahead as in getting into heaven, the politicians of the First Congress mortgaged their legacy, forsaking the potential for making political profit out of religious endorsement in the process of building a nation. The great self-restraints against Congress making a law respecting the Establishment of Religion or prohibiting the Free Exercise thereof did not apply to the states, where established churches were a live possibility and in some states a reality. The Religion Clauses had significance because so many generations had suffered in the absence of such protections but also because the post-Revolutionary generation deliberately refused to allow the new nation to redress that suffering or claim identity with it. The value of these clauses was heuristic. It is doubtful that Jefferson feared an American Inquisition; he had written while in France that he expected all the thinking men of the next generation to be deists. Rather he sought that elevation of opportunity into virtue by which nations are often forged.

It is useful to remember that the text of the Constitution contains only three references to God and religion. Two of them are quite remote while the third scarcely suggests endorsement:

(1) the clause exempting Sundays as days to be counted in determining the period of time within which the President must exercise his veto;

(2) the dating of the document as "in the year of our Lord one thousand seven hundred and eighty seven," and

(3) the crucial clause of Article VI proscribing religious tests for office.

As Richard Morgan wrote after noting this paucity of religious reference:

> The absence of any positive reference to God was not accidental. It was . . . much remarked on at the time and blamed, by that dour Federalist Timothy Dwight, President of Yale, on Jefferson. . . . Under Washington's chairmanship [of the Constitutional Convention] there were no invocations, and when Benjamin Franklin (himself no orthodox Christian) moved that the meeting pray for divine guidance, he was defeated.[23]

With such a background, it is hardly surprising that the debate in the First Congress about the adoption of the Religion Clauses did not center on their usefulness *per se* as checks on likely national abuses. Thus, from the very start these clauses held the potential for an heuristic, expressive use.

It would be idle to draft an opinion for *Schemp* here. I will simply say that if this function, rather than either of the ones chosen by the majority or the dissenter in that case, had been adopted, the resulting opinion would have been quite different. The holding would have been based on the uniqueness of that unusual American institution, the public school, and its crucial role in our culture as framer and builder of the attitudes by which we, its products, characterize ourselves and our relation to organized society.

It is not the religiosity of these prayers—mostly mumbled by sleepy children or ignored by adolescents preoccupied with less pious pursuits—that should disturb us. It is their inclusion in the school context. It is not that neutrality in and of itself but abstinence, in such a context, that is required. The Court's decision, however, calls into question—indeed summons into litigation—everything from charitable donations to the designation of Army chaplains.

It is important for our study to note that even with the weak and uncompelling doctrines of both sides in *Schempp* and an erroneous choice of functions that case has nevertheless come to exercise a powerful expressive function. It is the statement of a new, secular national society. The fact that even though its mandate has been largely ignored in the public schools, the Court has shown little inclination to exploit its checking potential further suggests to me that the Court now perceives the importance of the case as principally an expressive one.

Many commentators have asked why the Court would grant certiorari in such sensitive, controversial cases as the school prayer cases when the justices must have known that their decision would be met with hostility by the vast majority of Americans. After posing this question, having to do with popular response, analysts answer it in a highly non-popular way: whatever the reaction, it is said, "for most Americans . . . the vitality of these . . . decisions must depend on [the] intrinsic persuasiveness" of the constitutional arguments offered.[24] It seems to me this answer is just as unlikely as the opposite view, that the arguments of an opinion are largely irrelevant and that only popular acceptance of the result can justify a particular exercise of judicial review.[25]

For if we accept the expressive function of the Court, then it must sometimes be in advance of and even in contrast to, the largely inchoate notions of the people generally. The Court's role in the exercise of this function, after all, is to give concrete expression to the unarticulated values of a diverse nation. We must approach decisions that have this function as their principal justification with an eye for their peculiar arguments. We need not entertain the fiction that the opinions will be pored over in every hamlet and town meeting. Nor need we abandon care for craft. To the contrary, once we recognize the function, we will know better how to evaluate the argument.

Consider, for example, the decision in *United States* v. *Nixon,* the Tapes Case, which can hardly be understood, much less justified, on any other than an expressive basis. In contrast to other weak doctrinal opinions, the Tapes Case has been charitably treated by commentators. Yet I venture to say that it is the worst set of doctrinal arguments—the least convincing, the most easily refuted, brief but repetitious, bombastic but unmoving—one is likely to encounter in the recent volumes of the United States Reports. Yet it can be shown that the decision is not wrong, once its correct function is recognized.

Early in March 1974 a federal grand jury indicted seven men, all of whom had previously held positions either on the White House staff or with the Committee to Re-Elect the President. In a separate, sealed report the grand jury also named the President as an unindicted co-conspirator. Prior to the trial arising from these indictments, the district court granted the Special Prosecutor's motion[26] for a subpoena dueces tecum ordering the President to produce tapes, papers, transcripts, and other writings containing or relating to conversations between himself and the defendants or potential witnesses. The President moved to quash the subpoena; this motion was denied. Before the Circuit Court could hear an appeal on this issue, the Special Prosecutor sought, and the Supreme Court granted, a writ of certiorari before judgment. In an opinion for a unanimous Court, the Chief Justice upheld the district court order.

This historic case can only be understood if one fully appreciates both the family of functions exercised by the Court—each function sharing features with other functions but no single feature present in all—and the dominant role of the expressive function here. Notice first that the Court had a prudential argument available that would have served a referring or remanding function. Since the Special Prosecutor was an officer of the Executive Branch, it was certainly arguable that no sufficient adversity could exist between him and a President to the obedience of whose orders he was constitutionally committed. Such a holding would have transferred the matter to Congress where an impeachment inquiry was already underway. While the court resolved this matter in a highly instrumental way, it refused to satisfy itself with a coordinate remand, that is to say, a prudential approach was used in service of a non-referring function. By regarding the departmental regulations[27] adopted to insure political autonomy of the Special Prosecutor as also establishing his independence as a matter of law, the Court avoided the fact that the President could simply have ordered the Justice Department to repeal the regulations. In this the Court relied on its political assessment, doubtless correct, that public sentiment would render such a repeal a political impossibility. This move illustrates one shortcoming of prudential argument: while it is available to allow courts not to have to make close political calls, it often requires just such a judgment as a condition to its being evaluated as argument.

What the Court purported to exercise was its legitimating function.[28] In bypassing the Circuit Court and offering an extended opinion on the merits, the Court had to give persuasive reasons why the Special Prosecutor's insistence on the order was consonant with constitutional authority. These reasons, however, are so flimsy and so unconvincing that one doubts that *United States* v. *Nixon* will in fact be read by lower courts and prosecutors as legitimating the practice its holding validates.

The Court begins its discussion of the central issue in the case, the claim of presidential privilege, by setting forth the two grounds on which that privilege is asserted. First, the privilege is said to be necessary to the functioning of the presidential office by allowing full and free discourse, the weighing of unpopular alternatives, and the assessment of political personalities and motivations. Second, the privilege is thought to derive from that necessary independence with respect to the judicial branch which protects a President either from indictment, on the one hand, or from being summoned before a Congressional Committee, on the other (except, of course, by the impeachment procedures). In either situation a President may not be thwarted in the execution of his responsibilities by the threat of these actions.

The Court responds to the first of these grounds with the following assertion:

> Absent a claim of need to protect military, diplomatic, or sensitive national security secrets, we find it difficult to accept the argument that even the very important interest in confidentiality of Presidential communications is significantly diminished by production of such material for *in camera* inspection with all the protection that a district court will be obliged to provide.[29]

That is, without relying on evidence or precedent on this point, and giving no reasons, the Court has determined that presidential confidentiality is not too much diminished if the only people privileged to intrude upon it are federal district judges. Apart from the wanting basis for this assessment, one wonders whether it occurred to the Chief Justice that he was assuming that no *in camera* inspections would lead to the production of documents and conversations, an assumption which, if true in fact, would largely negate the empirical basis for the inspection in the first place and which, if false, leaves the President's asserted position wholly unanswered. After all, it is not inconceivable that a court might be presented with material whose publication would tend to change the entire character of presidential conversations in the future, which might nevertheless be highly relevant to, say, a criminal prosecution for antitrust violations. (I do not dwell for the moment, on the Chief Justice's second assumption— that federal courts are the only ones likely to employ this procedure since the rationale for the holding—that the integrity of the criminal process be maintained—rather subverts this assumption, almost all criminal prosecutions being in state courts.)

From the assessment that the President's need for confidentiality will be only a little damaged by such intrusions, the Court moves to put weight onto the other side of the scale. Against what, we are asked, is the President's trivial inconvenience being measured? We are told it is being measured against the duty of the Judicial Branch to do justice in criminal prosecutions. Since the Chief Justice locates this duty in Article III, he has at once answered both the first and the second objections of the President. Not only is the President's interest in confidentiality outweighed by the interest in achieving a just criminal process, but his objections to a coordinate branch's enforcing this weighing is answered by the Constitution's commitment of responsibility to the courts in Article III. There are difficulties with this view arising from the fact that Article III makes no mention of such a responsibility and that to place it so seems to exclude the state courts, who have the primary duty to do justice in criminal prosecutions, but let us assume that the Constitution does charge federal courts with doing justice in criminal prosecutions. What does this imply with respect to a claim of privilege?

The Court writes, "To ensure that justice is done, it is imperative to the function of courts that compulsory process be available for the production of evidence needed either by the prosecution or the defense."[30] Of course, this statement is either plainly false, since the prosecution has never been able to avail itself of compulsory process to get privileged material, or an inadvertent but grave indictment of the entire system as so insufficiently helpful to the prosecution as to amount to a denial of justice or the statement is trivial, since it means what it says plus an unstated qualification, "except when the evidence is privileged."

How then does the Court determine whether the present material is privileged? The Court suggests that matters of foreign and defense policy are privileged. It observes that there is no precedent precisely in point. Then it announces surprisingly that Executive conversations and papers are privileged—indeed this privilege is *constitutionally* based—only to the extent that they relate to the effective discharge of the President's powers. In this regard, the Court reasserts its frank disbelief that the present claim is really related in this way:

> However, we cannot conclude that advisers will be moved to
> temper the candor of their remarks by the infrequent occasions
> of disclosure because of the possibility that such conversations
> will be called for in the context of a criminal prosecution.[31]

At this point, the Court must still go on to establish why they are the ones to make the determinate assessment. Accordingly, the Court concludes, in a mere repetition of the arguments made two pages prior, that to permit a privilege (one must supply the missing term that it would effectively be permitted but for the Court's intervention) would gravely impair the function of the courts: "The Constitutional need for production of relevant evidence in a criminal proceeding is specific and central to the . . . administration of justice."[32] Of course, the constitutional bases for such production of evidence, in the Fifth and Sixth amendments which the Court cites, adhere to defendants, not against them. It is always true that a privilege may discommode the prosecution. Nevertheless, the Court tells us that "without access to specific facts, a criminal prosecution may be totally frustrated."[33] How true. But has anyone ever thought that there was a constitutional *right* on the part of the prosecutor to obtain evidence? Finally, the Court generalizes this right as inhering in "due process of law," thus dragging the state courts back into the fray. With this, the discussion of the merits ends.

If this opinion is an example of doctrinal argument in service of the legitimating function it should be counted a complete, whole failure. Its arguments, if such they be, amount to little more than assertions, repeated to supply the force they lack in themselves. As an authoritative precedent it provides a fragile model. It decides a question it was not asked—whether there is a constitutional privilege to withhold information regarding foreign policy—and ignores the one precedent arguably on point. Marshall's opinion in the *Burr* case is quoted for points diametrically opposite to that of the Court, and his words followed by disclaimers.[34] Moreover, it relies on arguments which put forward in other circumstances would do much mischief. For example, should marital privilege be qualified by an assessment of how damaging the disclosures would be to a particular marriage? Can a prosecutor now claim a constitutional right to information withheld by a defendant, also on constitutional grounds, so that the interests of each must be "balanced"?

Most importantly, the holding in the case cannot be used as precedent. The Court succinctly states that holding:

> We conclude that when the ground for asserting privilege as to
> subpoenaed materials sought for use in a criminal trial is based
> only on the generalized interest in confidentiality, it cannot pre-
> vail over the fundamental demands of due process of law in
> the fair administration of criminal justice. The generalized as-
> sertion of privilege must yield to the demonstrated, specific need
> for evidence in a pending criminal trial.[35]

Can any court take this holding seriously (which is what it means
to rely on it as precedent)? Does anyone really think this holding means that any time a prosecutor reasonably demands the
private tapes and papers of a sitting President, a district judge
must be given them to examine and determine their relevancy?
For if not he, then what of Article III? And if not a prosecutor,
then surely the grand jury, which it would seem has a constitutional right to examine such materials when, in the Court's
words, they "have some bearing on . . . pending criminal
cases."[36]

It is difficult to bring oneself to believe this is what the holding means. I do not think, however, that the outcome in the
Tapes Case is wrong. I do not think the outcome is correct for
the reason sometimes offered by the former Special Prosecutor, that it "broke the case open." The tapes would inevitably
have been either turned over to the Impeachment Inquiry or
withheld from them, in either case leading to the same result.

No, the outcome in *United States* v. *Nixon* is right because it
expresses a national goal captured by the clichés "a government
of laws, not men" and "equal justice under law." The holding
in the Tapes Case is not the preposterous one stated by the
Court that an assertion of privilege must be balanced against a
prosecutor's need for evidence, the balance to be struck by a
preliminary inspection of the very documents and tapes as to
which the privilege is asserted. The real holding is that a President, as Chief Executive Officer, may not manipulate the instrumentalities of law enforcement both to prevent the law's
enforcement and to acquit himself. To have ruled in the opposite way would have forever given strength to the view that
the President is the sole and ultimate arbiter of the prosecution
of the law even when it means that he sits as judge in his own

case. This is a rather narrow holding since it is at once confined
to the rare facts of a President's appointment of someone with
the unique task of prosecuting him and his claims that the very
material he said was privileged would exculpate him. Yet, as a
principle, it is as unconfined as any great national ideal. This is
the serious and difficult point of constitutional law which Marshall had in mind when, sitting as a trial judge in the *Burr* case,[37]
he wrote, "In no case of this kind would a court be required to
proceed against a President as against an ordinary individual."[38] There are two sides to this caution: a President may by
his own acts place in jeopardy not only his occupancy, for which
the remedy is impeachment, but also his office. So, as the Court's
opinion reminds us, it is right that a President is not above the
law. *Nixon* was a unique case, for the self-referential manner in
which the Executive was turned on itself. The arguments by
which the case's statement of principle was made should have
reflected this, but the important thing is, I think, the expression itself.

There are other decisions which may also be usefully analyzed in this way. The magnificent statements that "legislators
represent people, not trees or acres" and that they "are elected
by voters, not farms or cities or economic interests"[39] are
scarcely accurate as descriptions. But they do fulfill an expressive role. We may disagree as to whether the issue is best thought
of as one involving Equal Protection or the Guaranty of Republican Government (although an appreciation of the expressive
function would make the abacus of equal protection doctrine
far less attractive and the simple straightforwardness of the
Guaranty Clause highly appealing).[40] By either approach, however, we may at the same time call for "one man, one vote"
without being reduced to mathematical formulae if we remember that the role of the Court in such a case is principally expressive. Such a case is no less effective if it relies on constitutional actors other that the courts to give it life.

Justice Hans Linde of the Oregon Supreme Court, then a
law professor, wrote with characteristic insight when he de-
rided the narrow view of the Court's effectiveness and called
for a recognition of the significance of a constitutional holding
for its own sake.[41] What would be the implications for the Con-

stitution, in its role as primary national symbol, Linde asks, of a decision saying that a bit of organized public prayer never hurt anyone? Or of a decision that a little inequality of voting rights did not matter as long as the state thought it served a useful purpose in some larger political scheme of things? Or that it was no injustice to ransack someone's home or wire it from floor to ceiling if the evidence obtained proved him guilty of a crime? Or that difficulties of effective schooling, of peaceful public recreation, or of mixed-race families might on occasion justify even-handed segregation? The values at stake in these cases are far more than programmatic effectiveness. Linde recognizes that such holdings "would shape people's vision of their Constitution and of themselves."[42] This would be a result of the operation of that function of the Court's work that I have been calling "expressive."

If one has the predictable reactions to Linde's imaginary holdings, one might ask oneself why that is. Of course no Court, deciding the famous cases to which he refers, need have supported the opposite decisions to the actual holdings by simply negating their rationales. I think that we have these reactions because the Court's expressive role has already worked its way into our constitutional sense. Thus Linde's questions are not only examples of the effect of the expressive function but, taken as a whole, reinforce that function.

CHAPTER 16

ARGUMENTS AND THE EXPRESSIVE FUNCTION

Borges has written, "Sometimes at evening there's a face that sees us from the deeps of a mirror. Art must be that sort of mirror, disclosing to each of us his face."[1] The Constitution is that sort of mirror for our society. How is this mirror, that creates as it discloses, related to the various sorts of argument discussed in Book I? Whenever a legitimate argument is advanced in an appropriate situation, the very fact of its avowal and assertion serves an expressive function. It says, "We are such people as would decide matters on this basis."

Listen for example to the arguments of the majority in *Reynolds* v. *Sims*, the reapportionment case I have previously mentioned in connection with the expressive function. After acknowledging the historical argument that the states anteceded the United States and were the model from which representative institutions came, the Court makes a different sort of argument.

> But representative government is in essence self-government through the medium of elected representatives of the people, and each and every citizen has an inalienable right to full and effective participation in the political processes of his State's legislative bodies. Most citizens can achieve this participation only as qualified voters through the election of legislators to repre-

sent them. Full and effective participation by all citizens in state government requires, therefore, that each citizen have an equally effective voice in the election of members of his state legislature. Modern and viable state government needs, and the Constitution demands, no less.[2]

And later,

A citizen, a qualified voter, is no more or less so because he lives in the city or on the farm. . . . This is an essential part of the concept of a government of laws and not men. This is at the heart of Lincoln's vision of 'government of the people, by the people, [and] for the people.'[3]

It is a notable feature of ethical argument that it may incorporate an address like Lincoln's even though it was delivered from no bench and ratified by no legislature. Ethical argument also changes through time as the constitutional ethos changes. This happens in part because of the expressive functions served by various constitutional actors, so there is a double relation here: Ethical argument is a powerful approach to the exercise of the expressive function, while the expressive function has in large measure determined the availability and force of ethical arguments.

Of course, there will be times when such arguments, and the consciousness of the power and commitment of this function will lead a Court to forbear their exercise. I am inclined to think this was the case in *Maher* v. *Roe*.[4] In *Maher*, a Connecticut regulation which restricted Medicaid payments to those abortions deemed "medically necessary" by a physician had been invalidated by a three-judge court.[5] In a companion case, *Poelker* v. *Doe*, the Eighth Circuit had struck down a municipal directive of the City of St. Louis prohibiting the performance of abortions in that city's municipal hospitals except where necessary to preserve the mother's physical health.[6] The Supreme Court reversed the lower court decisions in both cases, holding that state and local governments are not constitutionally required either to pay for abortions for indigents or provide abortion services, even when facilities for childbirth are maintained.

This holding, in my view, represents a deliberate decision

not to proclaim a national commitment in a situation highly fraught with moral ambiguity. The ethical argument by which it proceeds derives from our long-felt distinction between permitting someone to do something and paying them to do it, between regulation and bribery, coercion and inducement. It may be that from the standpoint of modern welfare economics there is no difference between a state refusing to permit wrecked out-of-state cars to be junkpiled in its borders and offering competitive bounties only for in-state wrecks; both would have the effect of shutting down out-of-state entrepreneurs.[7] And it may be that, in time, we will come to accept this real-world similarity. At present, however, the state's failure to commit additional resources will seldom be thought of in the same way as the provision for specific penalties, except of course when this failure is perceived as singling out some group arbitrarily or invidiously. A state could not provide scholarships for whites only. By contrast, we do not, as of this day, consider it inconsistent with our constitutional ethos that the availability of most goods is tied to wealth. Indeed, our ethos may be contrasted with those of other democratic and socialist societies on this very basis. For further evidence of this shared view recall President Carter's comment at the press conference following *Maher* and *Poelker*. "Life," said the President, "is unfair." This is the sort of perfunctory remark one expects when one encounters some customary rule which is not perceived as contradictory to the society's larger ethic.

The famous *Bakke* case offers another example. The expressive function of the Court is properly discharged by a statement that race, by itself, will not do as the basis by which people are to be judged. If you doubt this, imagine a different statement, such as "Race can sometimes be used to discriminate" or "Color can be used as a sole sufficient criterion for treating people differently if the color is black." Thus would the newly arrived African be entitled to a more favorable constitutional treatment than the American Indian or Chicano. I appreciate the persuasive arguments that may be advanced for affirmative action;[8] and I certainly think that black people and women and Indians each may claim a unique constitutional status. *Bakke* does not render affirmative action impermissible in an opinion that nevertheless is expressive of the color blind ideal. Indeed, the opinion by Mr. Justice Powell goes so far as to approve a particular preferential program not even a part of the record in the case—an extraordinary, expressive step.

I would not like to tie ethical argument and the expressive function too closely. There is no necessary convergence between them to the exclusion of other approaches and functions. As I emphasized at the close of Book I, my typology of conventions is neither comprehensive nor clear-cut. The arguments described often occur in combination; this is also true of the functions discussed in Book III. The relationship between argument and function is not representative, and not homological; the one does not stand for something in the other and they have not developed along identical lines. Indeed the arguments and functions, related in the way I have described, are critically disconnected, depending on the purpose of our inquiry and criticism. If we are interested in legitimacy, we must look to the argumentative conventions. If we want the justification for judicial review, we must address ourselves to its functions. If we wish to analyze the manner of a particular opinion, we must examine the relationship of argument to function.

Finally, the conventions which allow us to make arguments of different kinds are each themselves aspects of an expressive function which is reasserted whenever the relevant argument is used. Thus the simple assertion of an historical argument is also the expression of a continuity of tradition, a fidelity to our forefathers' legacy, an acknowledgment of the modesty of our perspective and the limits of our wisdom, a statement that constitutional institutions are faithful to the extent that they are constitutional. At the same time, while the existence of various arguments seems to depend upon the conflict of their approaches, their role in serving the various functions changes them.

In the same poem from which I quoted above, Borges also has written, "Art is endless like a river flowing, passing, yet remaining, a mirror to the same inconstant Heraclitus, who is the same and yet another, like the river flowing."

CHAPTER 17

CHANGE AND THE CONSTITUTION

Dying for the "Truth": We should not let ourselves be burnt for our opinions: we are not that sure of them. But perhaps for this: that we may have and change our opinions.

F. Nietzsche
The Wanderer and his Shadow

Change comes to the Constitution through many different channels and is mediated by different agencies. The most frequent processes are the incremental corrections in course that courts make as they confront unanticipated fact-situations and must apply old rules reconsidered in the light of new cases. Beyond this, sometimes courts use the earlier language in a new way to bring about the re-cognition of issues, the same clouds making a different face. Chief Justice Stone and Chief Judge Cardozo were masters of this re-conceptualization: recall, for example, Stone's punning use of the word "presence" in the *International Shoe*[1] case, transforming the Mercator-projection, "power" theories of *Pennoyer* v. *Neff*[2] into that modern day jurisdiction provided by a defendant's contacts with the forum.

As both the interstitial and the reviewed methods of change operate from the past, they also operate on the past. It has been remarked that every artist creates his own precursors.[3] I must read Keats differently having read Yeats and perhaps read both differently having read Auden. So I must read *Pierce* and *Meyer* differently having read *Griswold* and must read them all differently having read *Roe*.

Yet re-cognition differs from the incremental working out of doctrine because it acts to make available different arguments. The work of Calabresi may truly be called seminal because it brought to the academy a different analysis, which, in the pattern of ideas circulating between the three branches of our profession, will find its way into acceptable arguments in accepted opinions.[4] These arguments will come to be proffered by counsel who would otherwise lose or risk loss in the competition of previously accepted arguments. The accepted arguments will become opinions. The opinions will be accepted, first as fragments for higher courts mending their own internal conflicts, and later by lower courts seeking to explain the rules that are the products of such conflict, and later still in that temporary finality that occurs when a particular case is over. That acceptance will make such arguments part of lawyers' functioning perception of problems, "for reality in a world, like realism in a picture, is largely a matter of habit."[5]

There is also the rare, utterly transforming change which shatters the existing symmetry. In constitutional law, the Civil War was such a change. One of the principal analytical changes it brought about underscores the point that constitutional approaches often evolve in response to theoretical rather than practical needs. This was the development of substantive due process and the creative response this development called forth from the constitutional conventions of argument—the mistaken superimposition onto the states of the federal model of enumerated powers. The transforming constitutional event then becomes less important than the change by which we know it. (As it has been said that Thucydides' *Peloponnesian Wars*[6] has replaced the war itself since the event can't stay in print.)

Such constitutional transformations do not give us new conventions, new approaches. They change the context in which these conventions are applied and therefore the sense of "fit" which each will provide in a particular setting. This sense has been elsewhere discussed,[7] in the context of allocating scarce resources, creating great cultural drama. There exists a parallel phenomenon here. Our constitutional processes having created these conventions there is no one truth outside of them. This allows our constitutional institutions to take advantage of the insight captured by Niels Bohr's remark that "the opposite of a correct statement is a false statement. But the opposite of a profound truth may well be another profound truth."[8]

Within the conventions we may have correct or incorrect statements. For example, the position has been maintained that, as a matter of textual argument, the term "during such time" in the Emoluments Clause implies, as a matter of contemporary usage, "inclusive of the end of such period." Therefore a Senator nominated for a Cabinet post, the salary of which had been raised during the Senator's tenure, could nevertheless hold that office if, while still a Senator, he saw to it that the salary was lowered again. By this method, the nomination would avoid violating the provision of Article 1, § 6, that "No Senator shall, during the time for which he was elected, be appointed to any civil office under the Authority of the United States . . . the Emoluments whereof shall have been increased during such time."[9]

I think this is incorrect. But I cannot say that the further view that the text shouldn't govern at any rate is incorrect. We must test this solution against our larger sensibility to see if it comports comfortably with the other sorts of conventions for decision we have in this society, in law generally, and in Constitutional law. We must see if it is meet and right for us, as the people we are. Fortunately, this test is done by the case method,[10] and we may test one judgment in varying contexts, no one of which commits us irrevocably to a single approach. Indeed, I am inclined to paraphrase Constable's famous remark about painting and say that "law is a Science, of which cases are the experiments." By the case method doctrine tends to correctability within a stable convention and competing conventions gain ascendancy or decline with respect to particular sorts of problems.

This process of constitutional change is sometimes misunderstood by those unfamiliar with judicial review. For example, an article by the president of the Southwestern Political Science Association concludes that

> Our Constitutional system has become self-destructing. The
> source of this Constitutional destruction lies in the Constitution
> and its inappropriateness to modern society. Essentially, the
> Constitution provides no structure or function to Congress that
> would nurture internal power centralization and institutional
> cohesion. It merely assumes that these will be maintained by the
> natural operation of political life in an uncomplicated, agrarian
> society.[11]

The author would resolve this crisis by a "Constitutional
change." I have omitted his arguments since I do not intend to
answer them. They are by and large not really arguments at all
but highly questionable assertions about the cycles of power between the President and Congress, quite devoid of historical
evidence and flimsily buttressed by warnings that current ap-
pearances to the contrary are but illusion. What I am concerned with is the general view of constitutional change. Not
only does the article's author wish to reorient the relationship
between two branches of the federal government, something
no amendment has ever done, but he evidently believes that
such an external, imposed change will set measures right.

This attitude is nothing new in political science. In 1934,
Roger Pinto of the University of Paris in a monograph on the
dissenting opinions of the Supreme Court is said to have contended that judicial review of legislation of the American type
may have been useful and appropriate for a young and imma-
ture nation when the people were unwilling to trust themselves
or their elected representatives.[12] He then "[raised] the query
whether the American people have not grown up and whether
they are not at the present time able to stand upon their own
feet instead of continuing to depend in their economic and political conduct so largely upon the judgments of a few legal con-
servators."[13]

Such a view of the Constitution and of the institution of
judicial review would be impossible for someone holding the
positions I have described concerning arguments and functions
and the reflexive quality of each within the legal and more general culture. Such a view is, instead, the position of those who
think the Constitution and its institutions are models, blueprints as it were, and that blueprints are simplifications of

structures. One sees this view in the current (and to my mind misguided) call for a Constitutional Convention. This view is as naive and inattentive to the way in which the Constitution actually works as is its cynical counterpart, the view that the Constitution is irrelevant to the wholly "subjective" directions of judges and politicians. Both views begin with the notion that constitutional law is the appeal to declared rules.

The more carefully we examine the actual uses of the Constitution in constitutional decision, the sharper becomes the conflict between those uses and our requirement that they follow inexorably from a constitutional command. So if the investigator were looking for evidence of this, it is quite natural that he would be disillusioned. Sir George Thomas observed, "What it comes to when you say you repeat an experiment is that you repeat all the features of an experiment which a theory determines are relevant. In other words, you repeat the experiment as an example of the theory."[14] Thus the investigation of constitutional law by the leading Legal Realist disclosed that

> There is, in a word, one reason and one only, for turning in this day to the Text. A "written constitution" is a system of unwritten practices in which the Document in question, by virtue of men's attitudes, has *a little influence. Where it makes no important difference which way the decision goes,* the Text—in the absence of countervailing practice—is an excellent traffic-light. Aside from such cases, any Text of fifty years of age is an Old Man of the Sea.[15]

Llewellyn said he determined this by simple observation. All he was recounting he wrote, was the

> *tacit* doing of the Court, [drawing]from that doing conclusions not to be avoided by a candid child. The whole expansion of the due process clause has been an enforcement of the majority's ideal of government-as-it-should-be, running free of the language of the Document. Whatever the Court has *said,* it has departed from its own precedents whenever it saw fit to do so.[16]

This "observation" has given unjustifiable confidence to those who think constitutional judgment to be wholly without meaningful standards. Llewellyn certainly didn't believe this; and yet he didn't see the operation of the conventions there were, because he was captivated by the old pictures to whose discrediting he was devoted. Today this view is as true and yet as period-bound as a Braque or a Cubist Picasso. Of course, that doesn't mean one is any less likely to encounter vulgarized copies tacked up in the interiors of everyday life.

Someone must have noticed that the number of Supreme Court justices is the same as the number of the Muses. I have not seen this commented upon; perhaps it is thought that if judges are the artists of constitutional opinions, it would be unlikely that they could be inspirers and inspired at the same time. I have tried to show how this is possible. The Constitution is the principal medium by which the relationship between our society and our government is displayed in meaningful patterns. As there is nothing more revolting than a cynical lawyer deriding the constitutional process he scarcely comprehends, so there are few things more noble than the Constitution's work on all of us—and our work on it. Of this, too, one might say, "it is here before necessity that old morality is unmade and then remade into a new thing."[17] In the final chapters of this book, I shall explore the implication of this view for the question of the legitimacy and scope of the judicial review of constitutional questions.

CHAPTER 18

THE GENEALOGY OF ARGUMENTS

The various constitutional arguments and approaches I have discussed are made possible by corresponding features of our Constitution. A textual argument is possible only because we have a *written* Constitution; it is the Constitution's "written-ness," if you will, that enables textual approaches. Historical arguments are possible because the Constitution was proposed by a deliberative body, and campaigned for, and ratified by the People, instead of being imposed on the People or announced as law by fiat. Structural arguments work because the Constitution establishes three principal, fundamental structures of authority—the three-branch system of national government, the two-layer system of federalism, and the citizen-state relation. Prudential arguments are a result of our Constitution's rationalist superstructure of means and ends, of enumerated powers and implied methods, which impose a calculation of benefits. Doctrinal arguments are possible only because of the imposition of the federal courts onto the constitutional process. Ethical arguments arise from the ethos of limited government, from the "limited-ness" of our Constitutional grants of power.

In each of these features the American Constitution was unique. Because these features inhere in the Constitution and make the various approaches possible, each generation of constitutionalists will sort itself into styles corresponding to the different kinds of argument. I have mentioned Bruce Ackerman[1] in this regard as an exemplar of a prudential approach; I might also add his contemporaries, Paul Brest[2] and John Ely,[3] as representatives of the doctrinal and structural traditions, respectively. Hans Linde's articles[4] reflect a highly sophisticated textual approach. And so on.

A particular problem is more or less suited to a particular approach when the factual features of the problem bear a certain relationship to the corresponding factual feature of the Constitution which gives rise to that approach. For example, whether a state may enforce its own statute when this conflicts with a federal statute is a problem singularly appropriate to a textual approach since it shares a particular factual feature with a written rule in the Constitution. Article VI provides that the

> Laws of the United States . . . shall be the supreme Law of the Land; and the Judges in every State shall be bound thereby, any Thing in the Constitution or Law of any State to the Contrary notwithstanding.[5]

Similarly, we may sometimes test a problem to see which of several approaches is best suited to it by varying the significant factual features.

This is not to say that every constitutional problem presents a single question which will have a perspicuous factual feature that, on inspection, will turn out to be neatly paired with a particular constitutional feature and a particular sort of constitutional argument. I am arguing, instead, that the chance concatenation of numerous events makes one sort of constitutional argument work in a particular context. Of course, as you will see in the final chapter, I do not mean that chance alone governs constitutional decision. When we throw dice, it is often joked, we do not suspend the laws of dynamics.

I would also observe that one of the factual features of a constitutional problem is its posture as a potential decision. Therefore, a constitutional problem is different for a Congressman than for a judge. Once we realize this we may discard the absurd fiction that Congressmen pore over precedents and apply case law without our being led to the equally erroneous conclusion that only courts are proper deciders of constitutional issues. One way to understand, for example, the confusing and contradictory doctrines of the so-called Negative Commerce Clause is to stop treating such cases—if we ever truly have—as deriving from the affirmative grant of regulating commerce and to treat them instead as structural problems with the ultimate decision committed to Congress. Doing this from the outset would have spared us the doctrinal formulations of "local" problems, of "direct" and "indirect" burdens.

Moreover, a convention's development may make certain facts appear for the first time, or at least give them relevance for decisionmaking. Recall from earlier chapters, for example, the defensive maneuvers Bickel prescribed for the Supreme Court. Like the small fish, the photoblepharon,[6] who emit light from window-like openings beneath their eyes, the Court, when threatened or when unsure, was to swim in a zigzag fashion with lights on during the zig and lights off during the zag. The Court had been exploiting these passive virtues, Bickel said, but unconsciously and infrequently. Of course, once Bickel told the Court this is what they had been doing, they began doing it in earnest. The "fact" of arguable mootness in the *DeFunis* reverse discrimination case—a fact that Bickel himself ignored in his *amicus* brief[7] for the Anti-Defamation League, since it would hardly have detained the Court for a paragraph in another case—became the basis for the Court's ruling.[8]

This is the topological aspect of constitutional analysis—the correspondence between chance, factual features of constitutional problems, and features of the Constitution itself. This aspect does not, however, provide us with reasons for the legitimacy of such analysis by the courts. To that question the final chapter is devoted.

CHAPTER 19

LEGITIMACY AND REVIEW

In this book I have been engaged in a study of the legitimacy of judicial review. I have, however, gone about it in an odd way, beginning with the rejection of the usual justifications for this review and taking up instead a consideration of the kinds of argument that are customarily used in proving one justification or the other. I hope this approach has not reminded you, as it has sometimes reminded me, of Steinberg's first cartoon in the *New Yorker* magazine in 1941. In it a female art student faces a stern instructor and defends her painting of a centaur—equine head, human hindquarters—by saying, "But it *is* half man, half horse."[1]

I have gone about my investigation in a topsy-turvy, upside-down way because it really was an investigation. I did not impose on the cases, briefs, and oral arguments the requirement that they share some characteristics which would qualify them as being properly legitimate constitutional decisions. More importantly, I could not have begun with such a requirement since it would have derived from one of the various justifications for judicial review, which justification itself, I felt, was arrived at only by using a particular kind of argument as a vehicle. Each justification, it seemed, was the culmination of a proof in a competition of arguments played by rules which reflected a commitment to a particular form of argument. So I began instead with an examination of constitutional arguments—no, "examination" is misleading, is too strong; I began moving among different constitutional arguments. Now, we are almost finished with our tour. From our experience we ought to be able to give answers to some of the questions with which we began, questions which bear on the legitimacy of constitutional review by courts.

1. Do judges and commentators decide to adopt a particular approach or does the Constitution require one approach rather than another?

To the extent that one is attracted to natural law, it will perhaps seem that choosing a particular approach is a matter of finding that approach, latent in the Constitution, most suitable for a particular problem. To the extent that one is attracted to positivist or existentialist perspectives, it will often seem that choosing one of these approaches is a creative decision which, over time, yields an artifact that is the body of law expressing this approach. Some judicial activity appears to support both these views. I have discussed in the preceding chapter how particular factual features of a problem suit it to treatment by a particular approach. In the chapters preceding that, however, I discussed the relationship between a particular approach and the function served by a single decision displaying this approach. I concluded that the use of a particular function is made actual by the conventions.

To the layman, without these conventions, all legal opinions will appear to be creative acts, choices. To a judge or commentator working within a particular convention, its application will appear to be determined for us. This accounts for the genuine sincerity of judges who claim they only apply the law. Thus it is quite understandable but quite unfortunate that constitutional law will often appear to have a bewildering formlessness to, say, the Trusts and Estates lawyer who is nevertheless confident of particular rules and their operation within his or her own area of expertise.

Each is wrong. Legal truths do exist within a convention. But the conventions themselves are only possible because of the relationship between the constitutional object—the document, its history, the decisions construing it—and the larger culture with whom the various constitutional functions serve to assure a fluid, two-way effect on the ongoing process of constitutional meaning. We have, therefore, a participatory Constitution.

2. Is the Constitution a Realist's or a Formalist's institution?

Neither. Realism and Formalism are two different reactions which depend on a shared expectation. That expectation is that the statement of a legal rule is either true or false depending on whether it stands for a legal fact. For the Formalist as for the Realist, a law-statement is a proposition, the assertion of a state of affairs. If a law-statement is a true proposition, then it is true of something. The Formalist looks at the body of constitutional law and, trimming away inconsistent decisions as wrongly decided (as they must be if there is to be a set of true legal propositions) is confirmed in his view. If there were no legal truths, he asks, how would we know when a decision was wrongly decided? The Formalist is smug, reactionary, and suspicious of the motives of those who have forsaken his faith.

The Realist looks at law as what judges in fact do and, finding a mass of contradictory statements, concludes that legal truth can only have an arbitrary correctness. Since there are no legal objects in the world—there is not "sovereignty" unless a Court chooses to use that term as a way of resolving a case or, for that matter, "negligence" or "consideration"—the Realist concludes that legal rules are false statements about the world; they are illusions. The Realist is tough, battered, making a style out of despair. Some Realists are nihilists, refusing to claim a special validity for any set of rules. Others are constructivists trying to create a structure, admittedly imposed, within which a statement is either correct or incorrect. Perhaps Llewellyn's work on the Uniform Commercial Code was a response of this kind. By the same token, some Formalists are positivists, taking the law-statement to be true insofar as it corresponds with authoritatively declared law. Other Formalists are attracted by natural law, and they may take the Constitution to be its crystallization.

All this depends on treating legal rules as if they derived their validity from the truths they express about a world. This is a mistake. When we understand the notion of a participatory Constitution, we will reject both Formalism and Realism. The expression of law will be seen to be the formulation of rules and not propositions. These rules allow us to do constitutional law. They direct operations within the various conventions. Law consists of resolving questions in the context of the conventions that provide the methods for answering them.

In the opinion for the Court in *McCulloch* v. *Maryland,* Chief Justice Marshall proves, by means of structural arguments, that a national institution—a federal bank—is immune from state taxation. This holding may be roughly phrased as the proposition, "No state may tax a federal instrumentality *per se.*"

If we are interested in the legitimacy of judicial review, we will want to be able to establish the validity of its holdings by determining the source of this validity. So, it is thought, we must ask whether the constitutional proposition of law is true and, if it is true, how we know it is true.

One classic position is that judicial review is legitimate only if the holding is logically true, that is, if it follows necessarily from the Constitution. This is Thayer's Rule, announced in his famous article, "The Origin and Scope of the American Doctrine of Constitutional Law,"[2] first published in 1893 and excerpted countless times since. Thayer's Rule does not, I think, justify the holding in *McCulloch* v. *Maryland.*

Another view is that the holding in a constitutional case is true because the Court said so, and no other authoritative decisionmaker contradicted it. But courts have often disobeyed the Supreme Court with impunity, indeed without rebuke. In any event, this is scarcely a guide to a judge making a new decision: it tells him that whatever he decides will be correct while at the same time whatever was decided before, which he may now ignore or even overrule, was also correct.

Yet another reply is to say that the holding will become true as it becomes legitimate in the eyes of the public. A particular holding is therefore a kind of guess, and only time will say whether it is, or was, true. One more view is that a holding is true insofar as courts and others have agreed to call it true when it is arrived at within a certain system. The holding is true so long as the system is agreed upon and it is consistent with other holdings within that system. Thus a holding might be true only conventionally, *i.e.,* true in the Commonwealth of

Ames, or "true" for first-rate lawyers. Each of these views depends upon the holding being a proposition. I would like to say that a holding is not an assertion of a state of affairs, not a proposition at all (except for the single case in which it is stated). A holding is simply a rule for our future guidance. It may appear to us to be a proposition, an assertion about the Constitution or what courts will do or even what the People will accept. But it is not. Even when a holding seems to point to a reality outside itself, still it is only the expression of acceptance of a new measure of reality.[3]

This view of Constitutional law is not mere conventionalism (which is the source of the positivism of the Formalist and the constructivism of the Realist), because, as we shall see, a participatory Constitution is not an invention of judges. At the same time it is not a matter of finding law in the world, either (a task to which Formalists respond by "putting the Constitution next to a statute and seeing if it squares with it" and to which Realists respond by choking), because the resulting statements are not statements about the world and hence cannot be deduced from it.

The concepts which occur in Constitutional law must also occur and have a meaning in everyday life. We must argue in everyday life. We must arrive at decisions by way of arguments. It is the use of these concepts outside law (and this use is of course influenced by the reports of legal decisions, opinions, and so forth) that makes their use within constitutional law meaningful. "If there is a mystery to constitutional law," T. R. Powell once wrote, "it is the mystery of the commonplace and the obvious, the mystery of the other mortal contrivances that have to take some chances, that have to be worked by mortal men."[4] The rules of constitutional law are not *derived* from these everyday uses, however, but result from the operations of the various conventions.

3. What is the fundamental principle that legitimizes judicial review?

There is none. It follows from what I have said thus far that constitutional law needs no "foundation." Its legitimacy does not derive from a set of axioms which, in conjunction with rules of construction, will yield correct constitutional propositions.

Indeed, I would go further and say that the attempt to provide such a formulation for constitutional law will likely lead to the superimposition of a single convention on the Constitution, because only within this do we achieve the appearance of axiomatic derivation that the foundation-seeker is looking for. See, for example, John Ely's remarkable *Democracy and Distrust*. We do not have a fundamental set of axioms that legitimize judicial review. We have a Constitution, a participatory Constitution, that accomplishes this legitimation.

The physicist John Wheeler has told this story about the game of "Twenty Questions."

> You recall how it goes—one of the after-dinner party [is] sent out of the living room, the others agreeing on a word, the one fated to be questioner returning and starting his questions. "Is it a living object?" "No." "Is it here on earth?" "Yes." So the questions go from respondent around the room until at length the word emerges: victory if in twenty tries or less; otherwise, defeat.

> Then comes the moment when I am . . . sent from the room. [I am] locked out unbelievably long. On finally being readmitted, [I] find a smile on everyone's face, sign of a joke or a plot. [I] innocently start [my] questions. At first the answers come quickly. Then each question begins to take longer in the answering—strange, when the answer itself is only a simple "yes" or "no." At length, feeling hot on the trail, [I] ask, "Is the word 'cloud'?" "Yes," comes the reply, and everyone bursts out laughing. When [I was] out of the room, they explain, they had agreed not to agree in advance on any word at all. Each one around the circle could respond "yes" or "no" as he pleased to whatever question [I] put to him. But however he replied he had to have a word in mind compatible with his own reply— and with all the replies that went before.[5]

This story is an illuminating metaphor of the process of constitutional decision. Note that if Wheeler had chosen to ask a different question, he would have ended up with a different word. But, by the same token, whatever power he had in bringing a particular word—'cloud'—into being was only partial. The very questions he chose arose from and were limited by the answers given previously.

In Constitutional law the choice of a particular function will determine the effect of the analysis which results in a particular case. On the other hand, the choice of function is not wholly determinative of the mode of argument, since the chance facts of the case will make one convention rather than another appropriate for each question in the case. Moreover, these facts are partly a result of earlier constitutional decisions (just as the facts in *Colautti* are inconceivable without the opinion in *Roe* v. *Wade*) and partly a result of chance. If, as we saw in the previous section, concepts within a convention have a use outside law—as the words, "suspect classification" and "equal protection" have meaning in our ordinary lives—we must also remember that these ordinary uses are influenced by the way the concepts are used within legal conventions. Legal uses may operate formally, as it were, within the conventions. A "city" may be a "person" if we choose to call it so for constitutional purposes. But it is essential that these terms also have meaning in their ordinary, nonformal uses, so that the circuit of a participatory Constitution may be completed.

What are the features of this Constitution? First, the present must to some extent control the past. Otherwise one's decisions are either determined by precedent or we are forced to reject precedent and begin fresh. Second, the various conventions must have arisen, must have come into being, with the Constitution. They cannot be "natural" or have any *a priori* status. Third, the chance concatenations of facts which precipitate a constitutional decision must give rise to participation by observers, so that they are changed by it and they can communicate these changes in plain language. This participation, being two-way, is what gives tangible reality to the Constitution. By participation and observation I do not mean acquiescence. It is difficult to state just where this community of observer-participants ends, as the expressive function reminds us.

Our Constitution satisfies these conditions. The present does in part control the past. Justice Douglas's use in *Griswold* of the *Meyer* case as a First Amendment precedent might strike a law review editor as unprincipled; the First Amendment, after all, is not even cited in *Meyer*. But after such a use by the Court, *Meyer* becomes a First Amendment precedent and indeed may

now be seen as the decisive first step in the development of a
First Amendment doctrine of freedom of ideas. The present
use of precedent transforms it, and the earlier case must then
be read in light of the use to which it is later put. The conventions and types of argument we have discussed are reflections
of the Constitution itself and as such are not themselves
embedded in the nature of law. Finally, the Constitution is a
sort of self-excited circuit. As it is applied in the courts, among
other places, it gives rise to observer-participancy. Ask any
American adolescent what to look for to determine whether a
society is just, and he or she will answer, sooner or later, with
conceptions drawn from the applications of the Bill of Rights.
Judges, litigants, journalists, and juries are responsible for
what they often believe themselves merely to be witnessing. Out
of the chance collisions of interests, random acts of observer-
participancy arise. And so it was designed. Of the system of
judicial review one might say, as Washington once said of the
Constitutional system itself, that it,

> . . . the offspring of our own choice, uninfluenced and un-
> awed, adopted upon full investigation and mature deliberation
> completely free in its principles, in the distribution of its powers
> uniting security with energy, and containing within itself a pro-
> vision for its own amendment, has a just claim to [our] confi-
> dence and support.

CONCLUSION

In his masterpiece, *The Common Law Tradition*,[1] Karl Llewellyn gave us a semiclassical description of law. But because Llewellyn's jurisprudence requires us to give up rules beyond the parentheses of the common law method of deciding appeals, we know that that jurisprudence cannot be fundamental.

If law is predicting what a court will in fact do, then we have only statistical predictions. This is not because judges and legislators are corrupt or vapid, but because we cannot always say that one particular convention or argument is correct in a particular case. We are put to the choice as to what type of event it is, which is determined by which function is exercised. Only then can we evaluate the profferred argument. And so law is not just predicting what a court will do, but how it will do it.

The finality of such decisions is commonly misunderstood. A Moebius strip makes a better model for constitutional decisionmaking that does a motion picture. Our view is distorted owing to the various crises which begin, develop, and are resolved within the ongoing constitutional life. The constitutional crisis, begun in the 1930s by the assault of Legal Realists on the Court and given political urgency by the frustration of the New Deal on constitutional grounds, reached its climax in the case of *Brown* v. the *Board of Education of Topeka*.[2] The ratifying coda was sounded in the adoption of the 1964 Civil Rights Act. Not "guesses about the future," but the ordinary functioning of a participatory Constitution brought this about.

It may be that *Roe* v. *Wade* has begun another such crisis. The current calls for a constitutional convention attest to our bewilderment at our problems and to our deep faith in the constitutional instrument. Such a convention would be unwise, but it would scarcely be fatal. And it is unlikely that it would change the Constitution much. This is because the Constitution is in great measure what we are, and a convocation of this kind is unlikely to change us very much. We are, after all, in part what the Constitution is and, as such, we are resistant to programmatic efforts to change ourselves in ways incompatible with its premisses.

Law reflects and at the same time determines the fate and worth of our society. It has been our destiny to attempt what no society before ours has attempted, the making of justice through a Constitution. It is as we are; so it is not yet complete. I am prepared to believe it holds within it fates as yet unfolded, toward which we are working. Like the grub that builds its chamber for the winged thing it has never seen but is to be,[3] we labor within our forms of constitutional decision to bring into being a just society. Our constitutional fate is determined by the arguments by which the Constitution structures decision; yet we determine the power and result of these arguments by our choice of constitutional functions. The Framers could do no more than bequeath us such decisions, and the use of such conventions. In our theories shall be our fates.

AFTERWORD:

AMOR FATI

Political philosophy describes a world made of words, detached from, and yet engaged by, political life. Detached, as no one pretends that governments and parties are capable of a love of thought; engaged, because unlike the philosophy of science, for example, political philosophy persists in attempting to instruct practitioners how they ought to behave. It is the conceit of the present Age to believe its political thought to be motivated by a desire for explanation: just institutions, it is said, will come into being only when we know the conditions that account for justice. The life of the law however, has been the experience of its logic and not its words and therefore institutions do not stand beside this life, off to one side as it were. Accordingly there is no explanatory power in the abstract construction of institutions made only of words. It is as useless to say that we must experience law before we analyze it as it was to put the matter the other way round. Experiencing law is analyzing it; and the analysis of law is the experience that makes events lawful rather than arbitrary.

Constitutional Fate provides a study of the justification of a particular institutional arrangement of significance. It might have been titled, "The Rules of the Game" since it attempts a showing of how justification is brought forth from conventional practices. But the book goes about this study in an indirect way, since it aims to show the reader something that cannot be seen directly: justice to be done, it is often said, must be seen to be done; but justice to be established, cannot be seen to be established. If one tries to locate a particular object in a darkened room, one must not look at it straight on. Otherwise, the focal point of the image will coincide with that part of the surface of the retina at which the optical nerve enters. One may look indirectly at the object; there is enough information provided by the visual context generally to allow the brain to fill in the blank spot. If, however, your interest is in seeing truly what the blank spot cannot disclose, then the wholly integrated, rich field of well-lit context is a sort of moving palimpsest, erasing precisely the thing one is staring for, painting over it its copy. One must design a way of looking that isolates the mechanism that performs the inference.

That is one aim of this book, to isolate a phenomenon that is customarily obscured by our very sight of it. We want an explanation of the justification of Constitutional legitimacy while avoiding the conventions that are responsible for the usual explanations and the usualness of the legitimacy. To do this, the reader is taken through a series of encounters with legal arguments sprung from their contexts. I do not examine the relation between constitutional argument, on the one hand, and social, political and economic interests, on the other. For the position my formulation of the problem tries to gain is that theoretical requirements have driven law; that judicial review is legitimated by these theoretical moves and not by its congruence with what are thought to be more fundamental social and class motives; that the vocabulary of social and economic interests is itself just one more set of theoretical conventions, and indeed one of no particular fundamentality with respect to constitutional decisionmaking; that the constitutional types of argument are not determined by political and economic theory.

Constitutional Fate is written for those in sympathy with its spirit. This is not the spirit of the current vogue in American constitutional philosophy, which seems to believe that law is in need of a foundation constructed from political theory. I am not interested in constructing such a foundation, but instead in having a perspicuous view of the structures that make justification possible. To this aim *Tragic Choices* was directed; and so also *Constitutional Fate*. The latter work explicitly discards the notion that law takes place within a framework that is independent of the structure of legal argument. It rejects the view that a set of legal presuppositions exists that are discoverable in the absence of legal argument, upon which legal argument is supposed to depend. The entire enterprise in which others are engaged seems to be based on a confusion between the justification for judicial review—which is that legitimation that results from the operation of the various conventions discussed in this book—and a hypothesized causal explanation for judicial review derived from socio-political theories. Those engaged in this enterprise believe that such theories exist on a privileged plane and are not themselves simply other, stylized moves within another convention bound and largely irrelevant game. I present Constitutional law as a set of relations to argument. Legitimation is that relation among arguments (advanced by advocates) and other arguments from which the former may be inferred (e.g., precedent, the text of the Constitution, and so forth). In contrast to my approach, one might think of the legitimation of Constitutional law as a particular state occurring when law and argument bear a certain relationship to social facts (or metaphysical ones) that are thought to underlie law. If we accept the approach I offer, we will not feel the need to ground the series of arguments brought forward in support of other arguments: the very functioning of the argumentative modes works to insure that there is consensus among those persons operating within the conventions. Where there is a choice between arguments this will come about also as a matter of agreement guided by and determining legal conventions. But if we think of law in the way contrasted to mine, we will want to get behind arguments to causes. If we are motivated by this idea, we shall want to escape the argumentative structure with its inevitable choices to get to a compulsion from social facts, measuring our arguments against the social and political realities that are thought to account for them in the first place. Then, it is believed, we will arrive at a situation in which further argument is not merely unnecessary but is impossible. An appreciation of the facts will determine the correct conclusion. This latter view accounts for such otherwise disparate phrases as "the self-evident truth of a political reality characterized by equality of care" and "the incomplete hegemony of the ruling class," that is, normative theories standing in a justificatory relationship to Constitutional decisions, and empirical theories standing in a causally explanatory relationship to them. It is a view rejected, not simply ignored, in my work.

Constitutional Fate is organized into three books. Together they comprise an investigation of the question of the legitimacy of judicial review. This question may be roughly put: How can one group of unelected officials—a court—legitimately render void the acts of a legislative body of elected officials in a political society that derives legal authority from the consent of the governed? The first result of this investigation is the rejection of the customary method of examination by which an answer is provided, for the usual justifications for judicial review are made out by means of arguments that assume a particular role for review, that is, arguments that conceal commitments to a particular basis for judicial review. Book I is therefore devoted to a study of constitutional arguments and their assumptions. Constitutional arguments are displayed through the use of sketches showing important Constitutional actors and critics responding to the great theoretical crisis in the development of twentieth century Constitutional law. I did not wish to write a descriptive account of this development, but I hope that those of my contributions that are descriptive are sufficiently my own to show that no natural history of constitutional events exists outside of analysis.

Constitutional argument is the method by which the competition for legitimate decision is carried on. *Constitutional Fate* names six types of argument: historical, textual, structural, prudential, doctrinal and ethical. The presentation of these arguments has not been separated from the description of the personal and theoretical histories that have made the arguments actual and given them their particular cast in our era. Indeed many significant developments in the morphology of Constitutional law have come in response to theoretical rather than practical requirements; perhaps the most important of these is the derivation of the doctrine of incorporation from the theoretical requirements of textual argument. But because the archetypal arguments are ideological rather than formally logical (an ideology in a different field), they are embedded in and can provide no independent justification for judicial review. This is commonly disregarded. I have earlier stated my rejection of the commentary that seeks to superimpose political theories on the doctrine of judicial review. A different tack attempts to derive a doctrine for the use of judicial review from some element of its practice. Impressed by a certain feature of the Constitution, the contemporary critic makes that feature a model for the description of all Constitutional law. This accounts for the current interest in the celebrated *Carolene Products* footnote. It is the result of recognizing a form of Constitutional argument but, at the same time, being trapped within it and declaring this perspective to be the only legitimate one. Book I will perhaps suggest to some readers the reason this temptation is embraced. In Book II ethical arguments are discussed. A method of distinguishing constitutional ethical arguments—that is, those with a demonstrable basis in the constitutional ethos—from moral arguments is offered. The legal application of this distinction to the federal judicial review of state statutes is made through the use of various cases, and a generative principle is derived to supply rules protecting the unspecified rights implied by the Constitutional text. A construction of the Privileges and Immunities Clause, based on this principle, is given and applied in various contexts. The constitutional basis for ethical argument provides an account of the historical development of substantive due process. Ethical argument, like the other forms of argument, offers a mapping in understanding an opinion differentiated from its purposeful use, that is, from the *functions* of Constitutional decision. Function and argument operate, according to the rules of these two different operations, to integrate judicial review into the pattern of Constitutional decisionmaking and to assure legitimacy, respectively. This peculiar disconnectedness, between related subjects, is the assumption of Book III. Book III is devoted to the identification of functions of Constitutional decisionmaking. To the neo-classiclassical functions of checking, legitimating, and referring are added the cueing and expressionist functions, presented in the context of their role in constitutional cases. The Book concludes with a depiction of the interplay among the types of argument—each type derived from a feature of the Constitution—and choices as to which function is to be exercised. The account of this interplay is offered as a response to such questions as whether Constitutional law is found or made, whether Realism or Formalism most appropriately fits the Constitution, and, the question with which Book I began, how the legitimacy of judicial review is established and maintained.

Because this is an unusual approach I have provided, against my better judgment, this skeletal summary of the structure of *Constitutional Fate*. It is nothing more than a checklist so that the reader can avoid some of the more extravagant conclusions to which my unintended remarks might lead him.

There remain to be done in constitutional law two kinds of activity. First, there is the ongoing "normal science" as it were, the exchange of arguments within the conventions I have discussed, the game of scissors/paper/stone with its circular hierarchy that brings different values to a decisive but momentary preeminence and is then replayed. To this are devoted the law reviews, the professional lives of the members of the bar, and the intellectual energies of our judges.

Second, there will be essays depicting individuals and societies responding to the theoretical requirements of the legal conceptions with which they must cope. These essays, be they historicist or anthropological or economic, perhaps even fictive, can enhance our awareness of the force field of Constitutional law and will by their example, one hopes, rid us of the illusion that a social or theological mechanics explains our constitutional life. They will not purport to offer meta-theories about the basis of law in political philosophy to enable us to measure law against the theories of justice we concoct.

The Constitutional law of the United States is not a snapshot; like the mirrored wall behind a ballet dancer's rail, it is not placed so to reflect a particular image but to enable, through patient practice, the creation of an unbroken sequence of images. Thus is the dancer made inseparable from the unceasing changes in the light. We have been taught to think that this mirror showed back only ourselves, just as we were once taught that it would yield nature's secret arrangement. Our teachers were wrong, captivated by a picture of a dancing class, ignoring the inseparable unribboning relationship between the motion that law must be and the participant-spectators whose presence makes the motion meaningful. In the work that preceded this Afterword, we follow the body of thought as we might that of a dancer. The Book is organized to make the reader attentive to the postures and attitudes learned at the mirror so painfully.

NOTES

I: CONSTITUTIONAL ARGUMENT

CHAPTER 1: A TYPOLOGY OF CONSTITUTIONAL ARGUMENTS

1. 347 U.S. 483 (1954).
2. L. Hand, *The Bill of Rights* (1958).
3. 410 U.S. 113 (1973).
4. *See,* e.g., L. Hand, *The Bill of Rights;* A. Bickel, *The Least Dangerous Branch* (1962); C. Black, *The People and the Court* (1960); Wechsler, "Toward Neutral Principles of Constitutional Law," *Harvard Law Review* 73 (1959): 1; Deutsch, "Neutrality, Legitimacy, and the Supreme Court: Some Intersections Between Law and Political Science," *Stanford Law Review* 20 (1968): 169; Grey, "Do We Have an Unwritten Constitution?," *Stanford Law Review* 27 (1975): 703; R. Berger, *Government by Judiciary* (1977); Wellington, "Common Law Rules and Constitutional Double Standards: Some Notes on Adjudication," *Yale Law Journal* 83 (1973): 221; J. H. Ely, *Democracy and Distrust* (1980); Monaghan, "Constitutional Adjudication: The Who and the When," *Yale Law Journal* 82 (1973): 1363.
5. Or what individual justices have said, *see,* e.g., T. R. Powell, *Vagaries and Varieties in Constitutional Interpretation* (1956), p. 21, quoting a speech by Mr. Justice Holmes: "I do not think the United States would come to an end if we lost our power to declare an act of Congress void. I do think the Union would be imperiled if

we could not make that declaration as to the laws of the several states."

6. C. Black, *The People and the Court* (1960), p. 6.

7. J. Butzner, *Constitutional Chaff* (1941), p. 147.

8. A. Bickel, *The Least Dangerous Branch* (1962).

9. *See* U.C.C. § 2–209 (9th Ed. 1978), comment 2: "[M]odifications . . . must meet the test of good faith imposed by this Act. The effective use of bad faith to escape performance on the original contract is barred, and the extortion of a 'modification' without legitimate commercial reason is ineffective . . ."

10. "[N]o society can make a perpetual constitution . . . The earth belongs always to the living generation . . . They are masters too of their own persons, and, consequently, may govern them as they please. But persons and property make the sum of the objects of government. The constitution and the laws of their predecessors extinguished [the objects], in their natural course, with those whose will gave them being. This could preserve that being till it ceased to be itself, and no longer. Every constitution, then, and every law naturally expires. . . . If it be enforced longer, it is an act of force and not of right." Letter from Thomas Jefferson to James Madison (September 5, 1789), reprinted in *Annals of America,* vol. 3 (Encyclopedia Britannica, Inc., 1968), pp. 389, 391.

11. *Compare* J. Rawls, *A Theory of Justice* (1971).

12. L. Fuller, "Positivism and Fidelity to Law—A Reply to Professor Hart," *Harvard Law Review* 71 (1958): 138.

13. See discussion in Berger, *Government by Judiciary,* pp. 118–119.

14. Home Building & Loan Ass'n. v. Blaisdell, 290 U.S. 398, 453 (1933) (Sutherland, J. dissenting).

15. It was to maintain this distinction that Justice Story wrote, "Is the sense of the Constitution to be ascertained, not by its own text, but by the "probable meaning" to be gathered by conjectures from scattered documents . . . ? Is the Constitution of the United States to be the only instrument, which is not to be interpreted by what is written, but by probable guesses, aside from the text?" J. Story, *Commentaries on the Constitution of the United States* (1st ed., Boston 1833), vol. 1, § 405, p. 390, n. 1.

CHAPTER 2: HISTORICAL ARGUMENT

1. Quoted in R. Berger, *Government by Judiciary* (1977), p. 287. *See also Massachusetts Constitution of 1780;* Murphy notes that these words were "paraphrased in several other early state constitutions" in "Book Review," *Yale Law Journal* 87 (1978): 1752, 1763, note 60.

2. *Writings of James Madison,* ed. G. Hunt (1900), vol. 6, p. 272. *See also Writings of James Madison,* vol. 9, pp. 71–72, 477. For examples of recourse to the state ratifying conventions, *see* Pollack v. Farmers Loan and Trust Co., 157 U.S. 427, 565 (1865), on the original understanding of "direct tax"; Twining v. N.J., 211 U.S. 78, 107–110 (1908), on whether "due process" was understood to include privilege against self-incrimination; Monaco v. Mississippi, 292 U.S. 313, 323–24 (1933), on whether the Constitution bars suits by foreign governments against unconsenting states. *See also* Wesberry v. Sanders, 376 U.S. 1, 15–16 (1964); Duncan v. Louisiana, 391 U.S. 145, 174–75 (1967) (Harlan, J., and Stewart, J., dissenting); Powell v. McCormack, 395 U.S. 486, 540–41 (1968).

3. T. Cooley, *Constitutional Limitations* (8th ed., 1927), p. 124. *See also* Bell v. Maryland, 378 U.S. 226, 288–89 (1964) (Goldberg, J., concurring): "Our sworn duty to construe the Constitution requires . . . that we read it to effectuate the intent and purposes of the framers."

4. *See* Twining v. New Jersey, 211 U.S. 78 (1908).

5. Rhode Island v. Massachusetts, 37 U.S. (12 Pet.) 657, 721 (1838).

6. Veazie Bank v. Fenno, 75 U.S. (8 Wall) 533, 540–541 (1869).

7. Knowlton v. Moore, 178 U.S. 41, 100 (1900).

8. Myers v. United States, 272 U.S. 52, 116–118 (1926).

9. Cramer v. United States, 325 U.S. 1, 22–26 (1945); Justice Jackson erroneously states that the requirement of two witnesses to the same overt act was an original invention of the Convention of 1787. It originated with the British Treason Trials of 1695: 7 Won. III, c. 3.

10. Wesberry v. Sanders, 376 U.S. 1, 8–14 (1964).

11. Powell V. McCormack, 395 U.S. 486, 532–541 (1969). *See also* Gannett Co. v. DePasquale, 44 U.S. 368, 385–391 (1979); *id.* at 418–427 (Blackmun, J., dissenting).

12. A. Bickel, *The Least Dangerous Branch* (1962), pp. 98–110.

13. Madison tells us that George Read of Delaware objected to a draft of the Guaranty Clause which guaranteed Republican government and territory to each state. Read said, "(I)t abetted the idea of distinct states [which] would be a perpetual source of discord. There can be no cure for this evil but in doing away [with] States altogether and uniting them all into one great Society." J. Madison, *Notes of Debates in the Federal Convention of 1787* (Ohio Univ. Press, 1966), p. 105. Surely, no one would argue that alteration of the draft to delete the term 'territory' means the Framers intended to make easy "doing away [with]" states altogether.

14. Missouri v. Illinois, 180 U.S. 208, 223 (1901). It may, however, always be possible that some members may have voted against the

rejected proposal because they thought it unnecessary, i.e., that the text unamended would provide for the proposed course.

15. Myers v. U.S., 272 U.S. 52, 294 (1926). For a similar argument, see Palmore v. United States, 411 U.S. 389, 412–413 (1973) (Douglas, J., dissenting).

16. *The Records of the Federal Convention of 1787,* ed. M. Farrand (1966), vol. 2, p. 550.

17. Holmes, "The Theory of Legal Interpretation," Harvard Law Review 12 (1899): 417–418.

18. *See Branch Historical Papers* (June 1908), vol. 2, pp. 51–52, 56–57, for criticism by Roane of Marshall's historical arguments in Martin v. Hunter's Lessee. *See* argument of counsel in McCulloch v. Maryland, 17 U.S. (4 Wheat.) 315, 372–374 (1819), for Martin's view that Congress had no implied power to charter a bank because "the scheme of the framers intended to leave nothing to implication."

19. Kalven, "Our Man From Wall Street," *Univ. of Chicago Law Review* 35 (1968): 229.

20. Ibid.

21. Gregory, "William Winslow Crosskey—As I Remember Him," *Univ. of Chicago Law Review* 35 (1968): 243, 244.

22. W. Crosskey, *Politics and the Constitution in the History of the United States* (1953), p. 77.

23. Rheinstein, "Book Review," *Univ. of Chicago Law School Record* 2 (1953): 6 (quoting Schlesinger).

24. Krock, "Book Review," *Univ. of Chicago Law School Record* 3 (1954): 8.

25. Rheinstein, "Book Review," *Univ. of Chicago Law School Record* 2 (1953): 6.

26. Corbin, "Book Review," *Univ. of Chicago Law School Record* 2 (1953):14,*see also* Corbin, "Book Review," Yale Law Journal 62 (1953): 1137.

27. Sharp, "Book Review," *Columbia Law Review* 54 (1954): 439.

28. Brant, "Book Review," *Columbia Law Review* 54 (1954): 443, 450.

29. Goebel, "Book Review," *Columbia Law Review* 54 (1954): 450–51.

30. Brown, "Book Review," *Harvard Law Review* 67 (1954): 1439.

31. Hart, "Book Review," *Harvard Law Review* 67 (1954): 1456, 1457.

32. Ibid., p. 1458.

33. Ibid., p. 1461.

34. Ibid., p. 1474.

35. Rheinstein, "Book Review," *Univ. of Chicago Law School Record* 2 (1953): 16.

36. Michelin Tire Corp. v. Wages, Tax Comm'r, 423 U.S. 276, 290–

291 (1976). The Court later questioned even the slight reliance in *Michelin,* see Dept. of Revenue v. Ass'n. of Wash. Stevedoring Cos., 435 U.S. 734, 760 n.26 (1978).

37. 347 U.S. 483, 489 (1954).

38. It is clear that Crosskey recognized his approach as such a "variant." See, e.g., his criticism of the Fairman article mentioned infra at TAN 16 in Chapter 3, Book I: "[E]ntirely apart from questions of the adequacy, and of the handling, of the evidence which Mr. Fairman presents, it is to be remembered that a recurrence to evidence of the sort he presents, is illegitimate in the case of a provision, like the first section of the Fourteenth Amendment, which is clear in itself, or clear when read in the light of the prior law. It is doubly illegitimate when it is remembered that most of what the first section of that amendment requires, was also required by Amendments II–VIII. *Cf.,* discussion herein in chapters xxx and xxi. Mr. Fairman apparently forgets that the ultimate question is not what the legislatures meant, any more than it is what Congress or the more immediate framers of the amendment meant: it is what the amendment means." *Cf.,* Holmes, "The Theory of Legal Interpretation," 12 *Harvard Law Review* 417 (1899). *See also* Crosskey, *Politics and the Constitution,* p. 1381.

39. Chisholm v. Georgia, 2 U.S. (2 Dall.) 419 (1793).

40. G. Gunther, *Constitutional Law Cases and Materials* (9th ed., 1975), p. 49.

41. *The Federalist, No. 81* (A. Hamilton) (Bourne ed., 1937), pp. 119, 125–26.

42. Larson v. Domestic & Foreign Commerce Corp., 377 U.S. 682, 708 (1949) (Frankfurter, J., dissenting).

43. Hans v. Louisiana, 134 U.S. 1 (1890).

44. Ibid., at 10.

45. *See,* e.g., Principality of Monaco v. Mississippi, 292 U.S. 313 (1934); but this does not apply to suits by sister states or by the United States. See North Dakota v. Minnesota, 263 U.S. 365, 372–73 (1923); United States v. Mississippi, 380 U.S. 128, 140–41 (1965).

46. 134 U.S. at 15.

47. *See* Edelman v. Jordan, 415 U.S. 651 (1974) and cases cited therein.

48. R. Dworkin, "The Jurisprudence of Richard Nixon," *New York Review of Books,* May 4, 1972, p. 27.

49. Bickel, "The Original Understanding and the Segregation Decision," *Harvard Law Review* 69 (1955): 1.

50. Carey v. Population Services International, 431 U.S. 678, 717 (1977) (Rehnquist, J., dissenting).

CHAPTER 3: TEXTUAL ARGUMENT

1. J. Story, *Commentaries on the Constitution of the United States,* 1st ed. (Boston, 1833), vol. 1, § 407, p. 390, n. 1.
2. Ibid., § 451, pp. 436–37.
3. H. Black, Jr., *My Father: A Remembrance* (1975), p. 160.
4. T. R. Powell, *Vagaries and Varieties in Constitutional Interpretation* (1956), pp. 19–20, quoting H. Fielding, *The History of the Life of Mr. Jonathan Wild the Great,* Bk. III, ch. vii (1743).
5. *Roosevelt and Frankfurter,* ed. Freedman (1967) p. 392.
6. United States v. Butler, 297 U.S. 1, 62 (1936).
7. In his Charpentier Lectures, Thomas Reed Powell had written with heavy sarcasm of this passage, "Of course lawyers and students of constitutional law have known this for a long time. There was no need to call the point to the attention of any educated man. But Mr. Justice Roberts was evidently fearful that the farmers might not be fully aware of it. So he told them, and so they knew." *Vagaries and Varieties in Constitutional Interpretation,* p. 43, n. 4.
8. Ibid., p. 28.
9. "Justice Black and the Bill of Rights," CBS News Special (broadcast Dec. 3, 1968), 9 *Sw. L. Rev.* 937, 938 (1977).
10. Ibid.
11. Ibid.
12. Ibid.
13. Ibid.
14. Ibid., p. 940.
15. Ibid.
16. Adamson v. California, 332 U.S. 46, 71–72 (1947) (Black, J., dissenting).
17. Fairman, "Does the Fourteenth Amendment Incorporate the Bill of Rights?," *Stanford Law Review* 2 (1949): 5.
18. *See,* generally, Annot., 23 L.Ed.2d 985 (1970).
19. CBS News Special, p. 941.
20. *See,* e.g., Katz *v.* United States, 389 U.S. 347, 364 (1967) (Black, J., dissenting); Berger *v.* New York, 388 U.S. 41, 70 (1966) (Black, J., dissenting).
21. 433 U.S. 425 (1977). One justice even went so far as to concur specially on the ground that he had taken judicial notice of the fact that the former president had been pardoned—thereby confusing a reason with a rationale.
22. Holmes to T. R. Powell; for an example of such arguments in the constitutional context, *see* B. Ackerman, *Private Property and the Constitution* (1977); for a recognition of their incompatability with

textual arguments, *see* Sagoff, "Review of Ackerman," *Environmental Ethics* 1 (1979): 89.

23. Connecticut General Life Ins. Co. v. Johnson, 303 U.S. 77, 85–90 (1938) (Black, J., dissenting).

24. T. R. Powell, "Insurance as Commerce," *Harvard Law Review* 57 (1944): 937, 982.

25. Furman v. Georgia, 408 U.S. 238, 380 (1972) (Burger, C. J., dissenting).

26. Richardson v. Ramirez, 418 U.S. 24, 55 (1973).

27. Ibid.

CHAPTER 4: DOCTRINAL ARGUMENT

1. Morehead, Warden v. New York ex rel. Tipaldo, 298 U.S. 587 (1936).

2. Adkins v. Childrens' Hospital, 261 U.S. 525 (1923).

3. West Coast Hotel Co. v. Parrish, 300 U.S. 379 (1937).

4. Frankfurter, "Mr. Justice Roberts," *Univ. of Penn. Law Review* 104 (1955): 310, 312.

5. Ibid., p. 315.

6. J. Alsop and T. Catledge, *The 168 Days* (1938), p. 18.

7. Smith v. Allwright, Election Judge, et al., 321 U.S. 649 (1944).

8. Grovey v. Townsend, 295 U.S. 45 (1935).

9. United States v. Classic et al., 313 U.S. 299 (1941).

10. Smith v. Allwright, 321 U.S. 649, 669 (1944).

11. H. Hart and A. Sacks, *The Legal Process* (tentative ed., 1958), p. 4.

12. Ibid., p. 666, quoting Professor Fuller.

13. *See* G. Dunne, *Hugo Black and the Judicial Revolution* (1977), pp. 225, 235–48, for an example of a philosophical dispute between Justice Black and the doctrinalist Justice Jackson which escalated into a personal conflict and made front-page headlines across the country. At issue was Black's refusal to abstain in Jewell Ridge Coal Corp. v. Local 6167 U.M.W., 325 U.S. 161 (1945).

14. By the spring of 1979, the United States Supreme Court had cited the Hart and Wechsler casebook fifty-seven times.

15. Hart, "The Supreme Court 1958 Term—Forward: The Time Chart of the Justices," *Harvard Law Review* 73 (1959): 84.

16. Ibid., p. 99.

17. Ibid., pp. 96–98.

18. Irvin v. Dowd, 359 U.S. 394 (1959).

19. Hart, "Supreme Court 1958 Term," p. 123.

20. Wechsler, "Toward Neutral Principles of Constitutional Law," *Harvard Law Review* 73 (1959): 1.

21. *See* Griswold, "The Supreme Court 1959 Term—Forward: Of Time and Attitudes—Professor Hart and Judge Arnold," *Harvard Law Review* 74 (1960): 81, 85.

22. *See,* e.g., Rogers v. Missouri Pacific Railroad, 352 U.S. 500, 506 (1957).

23. Hart, "Supreme Court 1958 Term," p. 97, n. 29.

24. But cf. Allegheny College v. National Chatauqua County Bank of Jamestown, 246 N.Y. 369, 159 N.E. 173 (1927) and International Shoe Co. v. Washington, 326 U.S. 310 (1945), for examples of radical departures in doctrine derived from the doctrines they replace.

25. Rogers v. Missouri Pacific Railroad, 352 U.S. 500 (1957).

26. Arnold, *Professor Hart's Theology, Harvard Law Review* 73 (1960): 1298.

27. Hart, "The Power of Congress to Limit the Jurisdiction of Federal Courts: An Exercise in Dialectic," *Harvard Law Review* 66 (1953): 1362, reprinted in P. Bator, P. Mishkin, D. Shapiro, and H. Wechsler, *Hart and Wechsler's The Federal Courts and the Federal System,* 2nd ed. (1973).

28. American Law Institute, *The American Law Institute 50th Anniversary,* 2nd ed. (1973), p. 11.

29. Ibid., p. 276.

30. Florey, *The Restatement of Torts in Pennsylvania* 1939–1949, 22 Penn. B.A.Q. 79, 81 (1950).

31. *The ALI Annual Report,* "Citations to the Restatement of the Law," (Table), (1981), 20–21.

32. *American Law Institute 50th Anniversary,* p. 279, n. 31.

33. The one, partial, exception to this is the Restatement on Foreign Relations.

34. Youngstown Sheet & Tube Co. et al. v. Sawyer, 343 U.S. 579 (1952).

35. Ibid., p. 587.

36. H. Hart and A. Sacks, *The Legal Process* (tentative ed., 1958), p. 1072.

37. Ibid.

38. Simson, "A Method for Analyzing Discriminatory Effects Under the Equal Protection Clause," *Stanford Law Review* 29 (1977): 663, 681.

39. Wechsler, "Toward Neutral Principles of Constitutional Law," supra n.20.

40. Friendly, "Federal Administrative Agencies: The Need for Better Definition of Standards," *Harvard Law Review* 75 (1962): 863, 1055, 1263.

41. Henry, "Hart Converses on Law and Justice," *Harvard Law School Record,* 36 (Feb. 28, 1963): p. 7.

CHAPTER 5: PRUDENTIAL ARGUMENT

1. Black, "The Bill of Rights," *N.Y.U. Law Review* 35 (1960): 865.
2. Ibid., pp. 877–878.
3. For an interesting comment on a contemporary prudential approach to the takings clause, see Sagoff, "Book Review," *Environmental Ethics* 1 (1979): 89, 92–93.
4. Act of September 1, 1916, Public Law No. 249, 39 Stat. 675.
5. Hammer v. Dagenhart, 247 U.S. 251 (1918).
6. Child Labor Tax Act, Pub. Law No. 65-254, 40 Stat. 1138 (1919).
7. Child Labor Tax Case, 259 U.S. 20 (1922).
8. Atherton Mills v. Johnston, 259 U.S. 13 (1922).
9. A. Bickel, *The Unpublished Opinions of Mr. Justice Brandeis* (First Phoenix ed., 1967), pp. 13–14.
10. Ibid., p. 18.
11. Ibid., p. 15.
12. Ibid., p. 17. *See also* Pennsylvania v. West Virginia, 262 U.S. 553, 611 (1923) (Brandeis, J. dissenting) and Chastelton Corp. v. Sinclair, 264 U.S. 543, 549 n. 1 (1923) (Brandeis, J., dissenting).
13. Chief Justice Stone shared this view of *Atherton Mills, see* CIO *v.* McAdory, 325 U.S. 472, 475 (1945); Coffman v. Breeze Corps., 323 U.S. 316, 324 (1945).
14. Bickel, *Unpublished Opinions of Justice Brandeis,* p. 19.
15. Ashwander v. TVA, 297 U.S. 288, 341 (1936) (Brandeis, J., concurring).
16. Ibid. at 346.
17. The Brandeis-Frankfurter Conversations manuscript in the Library of the Harvard Law School, quoted in Bickel, *Unpublished Opinions of Brandeis,* p. 17.
18. A. Bickel, *The Least Dangerous Branch* (1962), p. 71.
19. This is not to say that Brandeis advocated the wide-ranging consideration of policy that characterizes contemporary prudentialist thought: "It would preposterously mistake the judicial philosophy of a Brandeis . . . to suppose that he was at one with the majority in a cheerful desire to make social and economic policy and differed only about the particular policy that should be made. Brandeis believed and said that it was not the business of judges to enunciate such policy. . . . In Brandeis' philosophy the labor cases were of a piece with such a case as International News Serv. v. Associated Press. He resisted in that case the admittedly reason-

able, indeed enlightened and proper, formulation of a common-law rule to prevent the pirating of news. He resisted not because he disagreed with the rule or thought it unauthorized but because he was convinced that in formulating it the Court was assuming a task it would prove unfit to discharge. Bickel and Wellington, "Legislative Purpose and the Judicial Process: The Lincoln Mills Case," *Harvard Law Review* 71 (1957): 1, 29 (citations omitted).

Nevertheless, arguments over such institutional arrangements are policy arguments and Brandeis did refuse to apply the doctrinal approach of Hand in the cases discussed by Bickel and Wellington. *See also* the Frankfurter dissent in Lincoln Mills, 353 U.S. at 464–65.

20. Bickel, "The Passive Virtues," *Harvard Law Review* 75 (1961): 40; Bickel, *The Least Dangerous Branch*, p. 111.
21. *See* TAN 34 Chapter 4 supra.
22. Bickel, *The Least Dangerous Branch*, p. 132.
23. Ibid.; Youngstown Sheet & Tube Co. v. Sawyer, 343 U.S. 579, 937–38 (1952).
24. F. Frankfurter, "A Note on Advisory Opinions," *Harvard Law Review* 37 (1924): 1002, 1006.
25. See TAN 16 Chapter 6 infra.
26. F. Frankfurter, "Advisory Opinions," in *Encyclopedia of the Social Sciences* pp. 475, 478. Note the "dialectical" nature of Hart's "Dialogue," the "Conversations" and the question form of the Hart & Wechsler casebook.
27. Bickel, *The Least Dangerous Branch*, p. 116.
28. Ibid., p. 126.
29. J. Lash, *From the Diaries of Felix Frankfurter*, (1975), p. 174.
30. Ibid., p. 175.
31. *See The Least Dangerous Branch*, p. 112.
32. Gunther, "The Subtle Vices of the 'Passive Virtues—A Comment on Principle and Expediency in Judicial Review' " *Columbia Law Review* 64 (1964): 1, 3.
33. Ibid., p. 7.
34. Ibid., p. 28.
35. Jaffe, "Was Brandeis an Activist? The Search for Intermediate Premises," *Harvard Law Review* 80 (1967): 986, 992.
36. *Holmes-Pollock Letters*, ed. M. Howe (1942), vol. 2, p. 13.
37. Olmstead v. United States, 277 U.S. 438 (1928).
38. Gilbert v. Minnesota, 254 U.S. 325 (1920).
39. Casey v. United States, 276 U.S. 413 (1928).
40. Meyer v. Nebraska, 262 U.S. 390 (1923).
41. L. Hand, The Bill of Rights (1958).

42. A. Bickel, *The Supreme Court and the Idea of Progress* (1978, revised).

43. Bickel, *The Supreme Court and the Idea of Progress,* p. 98, quoting Hart, "The Supreme Court 1958 Term—Forward: The Time Chart of the Justices," *Harvard Law Review* 73 (1959): 84, 99. But *see* U.S. v. Richardson, 418 U.S. 166 (1974), for the current effect of prudential argument.

44. Bickel, "Reconsideration: Edmund Burke," *New Republic* (March 17, 1973), pp. 30, 31.

45. G. Calabresi, *The Common Law Function in an Age of Statutes* (forthcoming Harvard Univ. Press).

46. B. Ackerman, *Private Property and the Constitution* (1977).

CHAPTER 6: STRUCTURAL ARGUMENT

1. B. Ackerman, *Private Property and the Constitution* (1977).

2. 426 U.S. 833 (1976).

3. *See,* e.g., Nowak, Rotunda, and Young, *Constitutional Law* (1978), p. 53; Barber, National League of Cities v. Usery: New Meaning for the Tenth Amendment, *Supreme Court Rev.* 1976: 183.

4. 17 U.S. (4 Wheat.) 316 (1819).

5. 314 U.S. 160 (1941).

6. 73 U.S. (6 Wall.) 35 (1868).

7. C. Black, *Structure and Relationship in Constitutional Law* (1969).

8. T. S. Eliot, "Introduction," in *Seneca: His Tenne Tragedies,* ed. T. Newton (anno. 1581, 1927), pp. xlix–l.

9. J. Bronowski, *Magic, Science, and Civilization* (1978), p. 5.

10. 380 U.S. 89 (1965), discussed in Black, *Structure and Relationship in Constitutional Law,* pp. 8–13.

11. Black, *Structure and Relationship,* pp. 10–11.

12. Ibid.

13. 17 U.S. (4 Wheat.) at 427.

14. A textualist, to take a third position, might prefer to rely on the language, without more, of the Supremacy Clause; but it is not easy to see why the mere fact of legal superiority in the conflict of statutes can settle whether there is in fact such a conflict.

15. Blasi, "Creativity and Legitimacy in Constitutional Law," *Yale Law Journal* 80 (1970): 176, 182.

16. Black, *Structure and Relationship,* p. 43.

17. 2 U.S. (2 Dall.) 419 (1793): discussed *supra* in Book I, Chapter 2, TAN 39.

18. Abourezk, James, "The Congressional Veto: A Contemporary Response to Executive Encroachment on Legislative Perogatives," *Indiana Law Journal* 52 (1977): 323, 323–24.

19. Ibid., p. 324.
20. Mendelson, Wallace, "Separation, Politics, and Judicial Activism," *Indiana Law Journal* 52 (1973): 313.
21. Stewart, "Constitutionality of the Legislative Veto," *Harvard Journal of Legislation* 13 (1976): 593.
22. Watson, "Congress Steps Out: A Look at Congressional Control of the Executive," *California Law Review* 63 (1975): 983.
23. *The Federalist, No. 77* (Cooke ed., 1961), p. 515.
24. J. Story, *Commentaries on the Constitution*, C, 388 n. 1.
25. *New York Times*, April 14, 1976, p. 21. *See* Kennedy v. Jones, 412 F. Supp. 353 (D.C. 1976); Kennedy v. Sampson, 364 F. Supp. 1075 (D.C. 1973), aff'd., 511 F.2d 430 (1974); and Bordallo v. Camacho, 416 F. Supp. 83 (Dist. Guam 1973).
26. Blasi, "Creativity and Legitimacy in Constitutional Law."
27. P. Brest, *Processes of Constitutional Decisionmaking, Cases and Materials* (1975), p. 172.
28. Blasi, "Creativity and Legitimacy," p. 184.
29. Alexander Bickel, *The Morality of Consent* (1975).
30. 60 U.S. (19 How.) 393 (1856).
31. Bickel, *The Morality of Consent*, p. 53.
32. Perez v. Brownell, 356 U.S. 44, 64–65 (1957) (Warren, C. J., Black, J., Douglas, J., dissenting) *overruled*, Afroyim v. Rusk, 387 U.S. 253 (1967).
33. Bickel, *The Morality of Consent*, p. 53.
34. Ibid.
35. Ibid., p. 36.
36. Ibid., p. 53.
37. 60 U.S. (19 How.) 393 (1856).
38. Bickel, *The Morality of Consent*, pp. 51–52.
39. Perez v. Brownell, 356 U.S. 44, 64 (1957) (Warren, C. J., Black, and Douglas, J. J., dissenting).
40. Bickel, *The Morality of Consent*, pp. 47–51.
41. C. Black, "The Unfinished Business of the Warren Court," *Washington Law Review* 46 (1970): 3, 10.
42. It is helpful here to compare this structural approach with the doctrinal arguments that have usually been used in such cases, *see* e.g., Anbach v. Norwick, 47 U.S.L.W. 4388 (4/1/79); Foley v. Connelie, 435 U.S. 291 (1978).
43. Baker v. Carr, 369 U.S. 186 (1962); Reynolds v. Sims, 377 U.S. 533 (1964).
44. N.Y. Times v. Sullivan, 376 U.S. 254 (1964).
45. Powell v. McCormack, 395 U.S. 486 (1969).
46. Shelton v. Tucker, 364 U.S. 479 (1960).
47. Goldberg v. Kelly, 397 U.S. 254 (1970).

48. Loving v. Virginia, 388 U.S. 1 (1967).
49. Griswold v. Connecticut, 381 U.S. 479 (1965).
50. Pierce v. Society of the Sisters and Pierce v. Hill Military Academy, 268 U.S. 510 (1925).
51. *Compare* Black, "Unfinished Business of the Warren Court," p. 10.
52. *Cf.* Michelman, "The Advent of a Right to Housing: A Current Appraisal," *Harvard Civil Rights Review* 5 (1970): 207, 209–211.
53. Bickel, *The Morality of Consent,* p. 53.
54. Black, "Unfinished Business of Warren Court," p. 10.
55. Black, *Decision According to Law,* p. 20b.
56. "In all the other cases before mentioned, the Supreme Court shall have appellate jurisdiction, both as to law and fact, with such exceptions, and under such regulations as the Congress shall make." U.S. Constitution, Art. 3, § 2.
57. Black, *Decision According to Law,* pp. 77–78.
58. Black, "Alexander Mordecai Bickel," *Yale Law Journal* 84 (1974): 199.
59. Ibid.

CHAPTER 7: ETHICAL ARGUMENT

1. Although even as to this list, I should like to observe that at the time of my preparation of the Doughterty Lectures, and their publication, no typology of listing these five types *as argument,* was in use. I include in this statement trivial variations that retain the definitions I have identified.
2. Moore v. City of East Cleveland, 431 U.S. 494 (1977).
3. Village of Belle Terre v. Boraas, 416 U.S. 1 (1974).
4. Moore v. City of East Cleveland, 431 U.S. 494, 503 (1977) (footnote omitted).
5. Ibid. at 504–05 (footnote omitted).
6. L. Tribe, *American Constitutional Law* (1978), p. 990 (emphasis in original).
7. Ibid., p. 990, note 30.
8. Meyer v. Nebraska, 262 U.S. 390 (1923).
9. "The problem for our determination is whether the statute as construed and applied unreasonably infringes the liberty guaranteed to the plaintiff in error by the 14th Amendment." Ibid. at 399.
10. Ibid.
11. *But see* generally, R. Berger, "From Natural Law to Libertarian Due Process," in *Government by Judiciary* (1977): 249.
12. Pierce v. Society of Sisters, 268 U.S. 510 (1925).
13. Ibid. at 535.

14. *Compare* Kurland, The Supreme Court, Compulsory Education, and the First Amendment's Religion Clauses, *West Va. Law Review* 75 (1973): 213, 218–220.

15. Black, "The Unfinished Business of the Warren Court," *Washington Law Review* 46 (1970): 3, 35.

16. C. Rice, *Freedom of Association* (1962), p. 58, note 95.

17. New York Times Co. v. U.S., 403 U.S. 713 (1971) (per curiam).

18. Ibid. at 746.

19. *See also* Charles Black's following list of hypotheticals which he thinks might either be candidates for textual disregard or victims of a petty literalism: "Take the First Amendment. What if 'Congress' did not 'make' the 'law' you are talking about, and it isn't even a law—say a judge's overbroad gag order, or a lawless police chief's turning his dogs loose on demonstrators? Suppose the 'people' didn't really 'assemble,' but peaceably corresponded, or peaceably sent in their dues. Going on, suppose—as in Brown v. Maryland—the tax is not really on imports, as commonly understood, but on the occupation of being an importer. Is it a 'search' or a 'seizure' when the police tap your telephone? Are the rules of double jeopardy applied to those trials that do not result in a judgment either of death or of mutilation because the chance of a long prison term is a 'jeopardy of life,' or because it is a 'jeopardy of limb?' " C. Black, *Decision According to Law,* p. 30.

20. Trop v. Dulles, 356 U.S. 86 (1958).

21. Ibid. at 125 (Frankfurter, J., dissenting).

22. *See* Roche, "The Loss of American Nationality," *Univ. of Penn. Law Review* 99 (1950): 25, 60–61.

23. *See* Vance *v.* Terrazas, 444 U.S. 252, 258–263 (1980).

24. Rochin v. California, 342 U.S. 165 (1952).

25. Ibid. at 175 (Black, J., concurring).

26. Schmerber v. California, 384 U.S. 757 (1966).

27. Skinner v. Oklahoma, 316 U.S. 535 (1942).

28. Ibid. at 541.

29. Ibid. at 543–45 (Stone, C. J., concurring).

30. *See generally* G. Calabresi and P. Bobbitt, *Tragic Choices* (1978), pp. 26, 74–75.

31. Fletcher v. Peck, 10 U.S. (6 Cranch) 87 (1810).

32. Ibid. at 135.

33. Ibid.

34. Ibid. at 143 (Johnson, J., concurring).

35. Terrett v. Taylor, 13 U.S. (9 Cranch) 43 (1815).

36. Ibid. at 50.

37. Wilkinson v. Leland, 27 U.S. (2 Pet.) 627 (1829).

38. Ibid. at 658.

39. The facts and decision are printed in the *Richmond Enquirer,* December 9, 1830, p. 4, col. 1.

40. Cherokee Nation v. Georgia, 30 U.S. (5 Pet.) 1 (1831).

41. Worcester v. Georgia, 31 U.S. (6 Pet.) 515 (1832).

42. Fletcher v. Peck, 10 U.S. (6 Cranch) 87 (1810).

43. Chisholm v. Georgia, 2 U.S. (2 Dall.) 419 (1793).

44. A. Beveridge, *The Life of John Marshall,* vol. III: *Conflict and Contruction 1800–1815* (1919), p. 556, note 1.

45. Fletcher v. Peck, 10 U.S. (6 Cranch) 87 (1810).

46. Phillips, *"Georgia and State Rights,"* in *American Historical Assn. Annual Report* 2 (1901): 15, 65.

47. Ibid. at 72.

48. "Andrew Jackson, State Rightist: The Case of the Georgia Indians," *Tennessee Historical Society,* 11 (1952): 329, 334.

49. Ibid., p. 335.

50. Cherokee Nation v. Georgia, 30 U.S. (5 Pet.) 1 (1831).

51. U.S. Constitution, Art. 7, § 8; Cherokee Nation v. Georgia, 30 U.S. (5 Pet.) 1, 13 (1831).

52. Burke, "The Cherokee Cases: A Study in Law, Politics and Morality," *Stanford Law Review* 21 (1969): 400, 519.

53. Ibid.

54. *Niles Weekly Register* (Baltimore), (June 25, 1831), p. 297.

55. "Andrew Jackson, State Rightist," p. 340.

56. Worcester v. Georgia, 31 U.S. (6 Pet.) 515 (1832).

57. "Andrew Jackson, State Rightist," p. 342, note 48.

58. Ibid., p. 343.

59. Phillips, "Georgia and State Rights," p. 83, note 46.

60. Letter from Jackson to John Coffee, April 7, 1832, *Jackson, IV Correspondence,* p. 430.

61. "Andrew Jackson, State Rightist," p. 344, note 48.

62. Phillips, "Georgia and State Rights," p. 83, note 46.

63. Ibid., p. 83–84.

64. Ibid., p. 85.

65. Ibid., p. 86.

66. A. Beveridge, *The Life of John Marshall,* Vol. IV: *The Building of the Nation 1815–1835* (1919), p. 546.

67. Burke, "The Cherokee Cases," pp. 530–531, note 52.

68. Cherokee Nation v. Georgia, 30 U.S. (5 Pet.) 1, 17 (1831).

69. Ibid.

70. Burke, "The Cherokee Cases," p. 516, note 52.

71. Cherokee Nation v. Georgia, 30 U.S. (5 Pet.) 1, 17 (1831).

72. Burke, "The Cherokee Cases," p. 518, note 52.

73. L. Baker, *John Marshall, A Life in Law* (1974), p. 732.
74. Ibid.

II: CONSTITUTIONAL ETHICS

INTRODUCTION

1. *See generally* L. Wittgenstein, *Philosophical Investigations* (1958).
2. One might say that all doctrinal arguments are historical, since they comprise the history of the Court. Or that all the various arguments are doctrinal because they proceed from and embody doctrine: we know them by cases, that is, and they become approaches once they become doctrines for construction. But we would say these things if we were *trying* to assimilate the approaches into each other, while I have been trying to disentangle these to see them from, and to construct, an argument-perspective.

CHAPTER 8: ETHICAL PERSPECTIVE

1. 1 U.S. (3 Dall.) 386 (1798).
2. Ibid. at 388.
3. U.S. Constitution, Amend. XIV.
4. 83 U.S. (16 Wall.) 36, 114–19 (1872) (Bradley, J., dissenting).
5. Ibid. at 114, 118–19.
6. Ibid. at 97 (Field, J., dissenting).
7. *In re* Quackenbush, 156 N.J. Super. 282, 383 A.2d 785 (1978). *See also* Satz v. Perlmutter, 362 So.2d 160 (Fla. Dist. Ct. App. 1978), and cases cited therein.
8. United States v. Rutherford, 439 U.S. 1128 (1979).
9. Rutherford v. United States, 438 F. Supp. 1287 (W.D. Okla. 1977), *modified* 582 F.2d 1234 (10th Cir. 1978), *cert. denied*, 439 U.S. 1128 (1979).
10. 438 F. Supp. at 1298–1301.
11. 582 F.2d at 1237.
12. 408 U.S. 606 (1972).
13. United States v. Nixon, 418 U.S. 683 (1974).
14. U.S. Constitution, Art. I, § 6, cl. 1.
15. 43 U.S.L.W. 3010 (Jul. 16, 1974).
16. *See Speak for Yourself, Daniel: A Life of Webster in His Own Words,* ed. N. Lewis (1969); M. Baxter, *Daniel Webster and the Supreme Court* (1966).
17. 383 U.S. 663 (1966).
18. 34 U.S.L.W. 3261 (Feb. 1, 1966).

19. Ibid.
20. Ibid.
21. U.S. Constitution, Art. IV, § 4.
22. 48 U.S. (7 How.) 1 (1849).
23. Brief for the United States, Harper v. Virginia State Board of Elections (1966).
24. 394 U.S. 618 (1969).
25. 37 U.S.L.W. 3153 (Oct. 29, 1968).
26. The term is Ronald Dworkin's. *See,* e.g., "Three Concepts of Liberalism," in *New Republic,* April 14, 1979, pp. 41, 47.
27. 37 U.S.L.W. 3154 (Oct. 29, 1968).
28. E. Leonard, *The Early History of English Poor Relief* (Am. ed., 1965).
29. Ibid.
30. 37 U.S.L.W. 3154 (Oct. 29, 1968).
31. 372 U.S. 144 (1963).
32. 31 U.S.L.W. 3191 (Dec. 11, 1962).
33. Ibid.
34. Ibid. at 3193.
35. Quoted in 372 U.S. at 197 (Brennan, J., concurring).
36. 354 U.S. 1 (1957).
37. 25 U.S.L.W. 3252 (Mar. 5, 1957).
38. Ibid.
39. Ibid. (emphasis added).
40. 367 U.S. 497 (1961).
41. 29 U.S.L.W. 3259 (Mar. 7, 1961).
42. Ibid.
43. Ibid.
44. Ibid.
45. Ibid.
46. Ibid.
47. Ibid.
48. Ibid.
49. Griswold v. Connecticut, 381 U.S. 479 (1965).
50. 364 U.S. 507 (1960).
51. United States v. Murdock, 284 U.S. 141 (1931).
52. 29 U.S.L.W. 3142 (Nov. 15, 1960).
53. Ibid.
54. Ibid.
55. Brennan, "Chief Justice Warren," *Harvard Law Review* 88 (1974): 1, 3.
56. The famous question is widely quoted, but less easily verified. *See,* e.g., Bartlett, "Earl Warren—A Tribute" *California Law Review* 58 (1970): 17, 17n. 8; Traynor, "Chief Justice Warren's Fair Question," *Georgia Law Journal* 58 (1969): 1, 4.

57. Cox, "Chief Justice Earl Warren," *Harvard Law Review* 83 (1969): 1, 2.

CHAPTER 9: GOOD AND BAD / GOOD AND EVIL

1. 394 U.S. 618 (1969).
2. G. Harman, *The Nature of Morality* (1977).
3. *See* Kuhn, "Logic of Discovery or Psychology of Research," in *Criticism and the Growth of Knowledge*, eds. I. Lakatos and A. Musgrave (1970), p. 1.
4. A. de Tocqueville, *Democracy in America*, eds. J. Mayer and M. Lerner (1966), p. 248.
5. Robinson, "The Chomsky Problem," *New York Times*, Book Review, February 25, 1979, p. 3.
6. Story is reported to have said that he saw tears on the face of Chief Justice Marshall at the close of Wirt's argument in *Cherokee Nation* v. *Georgia*. See J. Marshall, *My Dearest Polly: Letters of Chief Justice Marshall to His Wife, 1779–1831*, ed. F. Mason (1961).

CHAPTER 10: DERIVING ETHICAL ARGUMENTS

1. Black, "The Unfinished Business of the Warren Court," *Washington Law Review* 46 (1970): 3, 38–39.
2. *See,* e.g., Comment, "Eugenic Sterilization Statutes: A Constitutional Reevaluation," *Journal of Family Law* 14 (1975): 280, 289–90.
3. West Virginia State Board of Education v. Barnette, 319 U.S. 624, 634–35 (1943).
4. "The enumeration in the Constitution of certain rights, shall not be construed to deny or disparage others retained by the people." U.S. Constitution, Amend. IX.
5. *The Federalist*, No. 84 (A. Hamilton) (Tudor ed., 1937), p. 156.
6. *The Federalist*, No. 84 (A. Hamilton) (Tudor ed., 1937), p. 157.
7. *Annals of Congress,* eds. Gales and Seaton (1789) vol. 1. Reprinted in B. Schwartz, *The Bill of Rights: A Documentary History* 2 (1971): 1031.
8. G. Ryle, *The Concept of Mind* (1949), pp. 16–17. *See* Ely, "Toward A Representation-Reinforcing Mode of Judicial Review," *Maryland Law Review* 37 (1978) 451, 471–85.
9. *See* Zenith Radio Corp. *v.* Matsushita Electric Industrial Co., 478 F. Supp. 889 (E.D. Pa. 1979) (*vacated*), 631 F.Zd 1069 (3 Cir. 1980).
10. *See* Black, "The Unfinished Business of the Warren Court, pp. 3, 38–39.

11. *See,* e.g., Coppage v. Kansas, 236 U.S. 1 (1915); Adair v. United States, 208 U.S. 161 (1908); Lochner v. New York, 198 U.S. 45 (1905); Allgeyer v. Louisiana, 165 U.S. 578 (1897).

12. *The Federalist,* No. 84 (A. Hamilton) (Tudor ed., 1937), p. 155.

13. The Court eventually spoke of that era with distaste. *See, e.g.,* Lincoln Federal Labor Union v. Northwestern Iron & Metal Co., 335 U.S. 525, 536–37 (1949).

14. 268 U.S. 510 (1925).

15. E.g., R. Berger, *Government By Judiciary: The Transformation of the Fourteenth Amendment* (1977); L. Lusky, *By What Right?* (1978); Bork, "Neutral Principles and Some First Amendment Problems," *Indiana Law Journal* 47 (1976): 1; Rehnquist, "The Notion of a Living Constitution," *Texas Law Review* 54 (1976): 693.

16. E.g., Moore v. City of East Cleveland, 431 U.S. 494 (1974); Roe v. Wade, 410 U.S. 113 (1973); Shapiro v. Thompson, 394 U.S. 618 (1969); Griswold v. Connecticut, 381 U.S. 479 (1965).

17. Counsel for the State of Virginia argued to the contrary at oral argument in Harper v. Virginia State Board of Elections, 383 U.S. 663 (1966), 34 U.S.L.W. 3262 (February 1, 1966).

18. U.S. Constitution, Amend. X.

19. 298 U.S. 238 (1936).

20. 42 U.S.C., § 2000a (1976).

CHAPTER 11: APPLYING ETHICAL ARGUMENTS

1. 410 U.S. 113 (1973).

2. 1907 Tex. Gen. Laws, ch. 33, § 1, at 55 (held unconstitutional); 1858 Tex. Gen. Laws, ch. 121, at 17 (held unconstitutional). The companion case, Doe v. Bolton, 410 U.S. 179 (1973), struck down a Georgia abortion statute.

3. *See,* e.g., Destro, "Abortion and the Constitution: The Need for a Life-Protective Amendment," *California Law Review* 63 (1975); Ely, "The Wages of Crying Wolf: A Comment on Roe v. Wade," *Yale Law Journal* 82 (1973): 920; Epstein, "Substantive Due Process By Any Other Name: The Abortion Cases," 1973 *Supreme Court Review* 159; O'Meara, "Abortion: The Court Decides A Non-Case," 1974 *Supreme Court Review* 337; Veira, "Roe and Doe: Substantive Due Process and the Right of Abortion," *Hastings Law Journal* 25 (1974): 867.

4. 410 U.S. 113, 152 (1973).

5. Ibid. at 153.

6. Ibid. at 155.

7. Ibid. at 163.

8. Ibid. at 158.

9. Ibid. at 159.

10. Griswold v. Connecticut, 381 U.S. 479 (1965).

11. *See* W. Prosser, *Handbook of the Law of Torts,* 4th ed. (1971), § 56, pp. 338–43.

12. *See* ibid., § 56, p. 343; *see,* e.g., California Business and Professional Code, §§ 2144, 2727.5 (1969); New York Education Code 6527 (Supp. 1976).

13. Thomson, "A Defense of Abortion," *Philosophy & Public Affairs* 1 (1971): 47.

14. The Court, of course, has not yet embraced this, *see,* e.g., Paris Adult Theatre I v. Slaton, 413 U.S. 49 (1973); Miller v. California, 413 U.S. 15 (1973).

15. E.g., Ely, "The Wages of Crying Wolf: A Comment on Roe v. Wade," pp. 920, 922.

16. *See* note 3 above.

17. Poelker v. Doe, 432 U.S. 519 (1977); Maher v. Roe, 432 U.S. 464 (1977); Beal v. Doe, 432 U.S. 438 (1977).

18. 439 U.S. 379 (1979).

19. Roe v. Wade, 314 F. Supp. 1217, 1223 (N.D. Tex. 1970).

20. 422 U.S. 563 (1975).

21. 400 U.S. 869 (1970); 390 U.S. 971 (1968); 371 U.S. 806 (1962); 364 U.S. 808 (1960).

CHAPTER 12: CONSTITUTIONAL CONSCIENCE

1. Griswold v. Connecticut, 381 U.S. 479, 520 (1965) (Black, J., dissenting).

2. Eric Railroad v. Tompkins, 304 U.S. 641 (1938); see also United States v. Hudson and Goodwin, 11 U.S. (7 Cranch) 32 (1812) which authoritatively established that there can be no federal common law crimes, a holding that doubtless would be placed on due process grounds today. The power which Congress possess to create courts of inferior jurisdiction necessarily implies the power to limit the jurisdiction of those courts to particular objects. Accordingly, when a court is created and its jurisdiction confined it is without power to assume further jurisdiction.

3. Griswold v. Connecticut, 381 U.S. 479 (1965).

4. 268 U.S. 510 (1925).

5. 262 U.S. 390 (1923).

6. 381 U.S. at 482.

7. Ibid. at 483.

8. E.g., NAACP v. Button, 371 U.S. 415 (1963); NAACP v. Alabama, 357 U.S. 449 (1958).

9. 381 U.S. at 484.

10. "Association in that context is a form of expression of opinion; and while it is not expressly included in the First Amendment *its existence is necessary in making the express guarantees fully meaningful.*" Ibid. at 483 (emphasis added).
11. Ibid. at 484.
12. Ibid. at 485.
13. Ibid. at 483.
14. 381 U.S. at 508 (Black, J., dissenting).
15. Ibid. at 510.
16. Ibid. at 509.
17. Ibid. at 486 (Goldberg, J., concurring).
18. Ibid. at 495.
19. Ibid. at 486, 492.
20. Ibid. at 492.
21. Ibid. at 492, 493.
22. Ibid. at 494 (quoting Olmstead v. United States, 277 U.S. 438, 478 (1928) (Brandeis, J., dissenting).
23. Ibid. at 494.
24. Poe v. Ullman, 367 U.S. 497, 551–52 (1961) (Harlan, J., dissenting, *quoted in* 381 U.S. at 495).
25. Ibid. (emphasis added).
26. 367 U.S. 497 (1961).
27. 381 U.S. at 500 (Harlan, J., concurring in the judgment).
28. 367 U.S. 497, 547 (Harlan, J., dissenting).
29. Ibid. at 547–48.

CONCLUSION

1. *See,* e.g., United States v. O'Brien, 391 U.S. 367 (1968); Dennis v. United States, 341 U.S. 494 (1951); Abrams v. United States, 250 U.S. 616 (1919). The Supreme Court never ruled on the constitutionality of either the Alien Act, ch. 58, 1 Stat. 570 (1798) (expired 1800) (giving the President the power to deport aliens dangerous to the peace and safety of the United States) or the Sedition Act, ch. 74, 1 Stat. 596 (1798) (expired 1801) (outlawing numerous, supposedly seditious activities including writing, printing, uttering, or publishing anything false, scandalous, and malicious with the intent to bring the government, the Congress, or the President into contempt or disrepute). The constitutional validity of the Sedition Act, however, was sustained by the lower federal courts and by three Supreme Court Justices sitting on circuit. *See* T. Emerson, D. Haber & N. Dorsen, *Political and Civil Rights in the United States* 1 (3d ed. 1967) 38.
2. New York Times Co. v. United States, 403 U.S. 713 (1971).

III: CONSTITUTIONAL EXPRESSION

CHAPTER 13: CONSTITUTIONAL REVIEW

1. G. Calabresi, *The Cost of Accidents* (1970).
2. *See,* e.g., A. Kronman and R. Posner, *The Economics of Contract Law* (1979).
3. Orbell and Wilson, "Institutional Solutions to the N-Prisoners' Dilemma," *American Political Science Review* 72 (1978): 411.
4. Ibid.
5. Tribe, "The Supreme Court, 1972 Term—Foreword: Toward a Model of Roles in the Due Process of Life and Law," *Harvard Law Review* 87 (1973): 1, 33–41.
6. G. Gilmore, *The Ages of American Law* (1977), pp. 110–11.
7. E.g., "For a score of kingdoms you should wrangle,/And I would call it fairplay." *The Tempest,* act V, scene i, lines 1974–75.
8. *All's Well That Ends Well,* act II, scene iii, line 58.
9. *Pericles, Prince of Tyre,* act II, scene v, line 36.
10. A. Lincoln, "First Inaugural Address," *Messages and Papers of the President* 7 (1897): 3206.
11. Ibid. at 3208.
12. *See* Seddig, "John Marshall and the Origins of Supreme Court Leadership," *Univ. of Pittsburgh Law Review* 36 (1975): 785, 800; *cf.* D. Morgan, *Justice William Johnson: The First Dissenter,* Appendix II (1954), p. 306.
13. The average length of service for Supreme Court Justices, not including those serving at present, is approximately 16 years. *See* A. Blaustein & R. Mersky, The First One Hundred Justices app. at 104–09 (1978) (table one). The average length of service for the 25 most senior Senators and the 75 most senior Representatives of the 96th Congress, as of January 1979, was approximately 21 years. *See* Cong. Q. Weekly Rep. 37 (1979): 52, 52–55.
14. Glass v. The Sloop Betsey, 3 U.S. (3 Dall.) 6 (1794).
15. *See* J. Shirley, *The Dartmouth College Cases and the Supreme Court of the U.S.* (1895), pp. 309–10.
16. Seddig, "John Marshall and the Origins of Supreme Court Leadership," pp. 785, 796.
17. Indeed, there is no discussion of this point in Mason v. Eldred, 73 U.S. (6 Wall.) 231 (1867), which unanimously overruled Sheehy v. Mandeville, 10 U.S. (6 Cranch) 253 (1810), the first express overruling nor in the controversial Legal Tender Cases, 78 U.S. (11 Wall.) 682; in 79 U.S. (12 Wall.) 457 (1870), overruling Hepburn v. Griswold, 75 U.S. (8 Wall.) 603, decided only the previous year, the Court says merely "it is no unprecedented thing in courts of

last resort, both in this country and in England, to overrule decisions previously made." 79 U.S. (12 Wall.) at 554.

18. G. Calabresi and P. Bobbitt, *Tragic Choices* (1978), pp. 195–99.

19. A. MacIntyre, *A Short History of Ethics* (1966), pp. 256–57.

20. Ibid., p. 257.

21. Quoted in J. Updike, *Picked Up Pieces* (1966), p. 29.

CHAPTER 14: FUNCTIONS OF REVIEW

1. C. L. Black, Jr., *The People and the Court* (1960), p. 223.

2. Ibid., pp. 223–25.

3. Ibid., p. 224.

4. P. Kurland, "Book Review," *Univ. of Chicago Law Review* 28 (1960): 188.

5. A. Bickel, *The Least Dangerous Branch* (1962), pp. 29–33.

6. Bobbitt, "The Dougherty Lectures," *Univ. of Texas Law Review* 58 (1980) 695, 757–759.

7. 426 U.S. 833 (1976).

8. *See,* e.g., Comment, "At Federalism's Crossroads: National League of Cities v. Usery," *Boston Univ. Law Review* 57 (1978): 178. Note, "Federalism and the Commerce Clause: National League of Cities vs. Usery," *Iowa Law Review* 62 (1977): 1189; *Rutgers Law Review* 30 (1976): 152; *Texas Tech Law Review* 8 (1976): 403; *Emory Law Review* 25 (1976): 937; Note, "National League of Cities v. Usery: State Sovereignty as a Limitation on Federal Powers, *Creighton Law Review* 10 (1977): 488; *Univ. Pennsylvania Law Review* 125 (1977): 665; *see also* Choper, "The Scope of National Power vis-a-vis the States: The Dispensability of Judicial Review," *Yale Law Journal* 86 (1977): 1552.

9. 426 U.S. at 856 (Brennan, White, and Marshall, J. J., dissenting); ibid. at 880 (Stevens, J., dissenting).

10. 312 U.S. 100 (1941).

11. 426 U.S. at 855.

12. 392 U.S. 183 (1968).

13. Fry v. United States, 421 U.S. 542 (1975).

14. *See* Linde, "Without 'Due Process,' " *Oregon Law Review* 49 (1970): 125, and P. Brest, *Processes of Constitutional Decisionmaking* (1975).

15. 312 U.S. 100, 115 (1941).

16. Wechsler, "The Political Safeguards of Federalism: The Role of the States in the Composition and Selection of the National Government," *Columbia Law Review* 54 (1954): 543, 546–52.

17. *See The Federalist, No. 45* (Lodge ed., 1888), pp. 288–89, and No. 46, p. 294.

18. An imaginative defense of National League of Cities has been made by Professor Tribe suggesting that it is really a decision in favor, not of the states, but of individual rights, taken in fifty aggregate chunks. *See* Tribe, "Unraveling National League of Cities: The New Federalism and Affirmative Rights to Essential Governmental Services," *Harvard Law Review* 90 (1977): 1065.

19. 426 U.S. at 877 (Brennan, J., dissenting).

20. 317 U.S. 111 (1942).

21. *See* H.B. 13040, introduced April 5, 1976. The National League of Cities decision was also frequently invoked by proponents of the successful effort in Congress to halt a plan which, by use of the spending power, would have induced the states to adopt no-fault auto insurance plans. And the recent Executive debate regarding the extension of FLSA regulations to mass transit workers was squarely the result. See Defendants' Motion for Partial Summary Judgment at 19–23, San Antonio Metro Transit Auth. v. Marshall, Civ. Act. No. SA-79-CA-457 (W.D. Tex., filed Nov. 21, 1979).

22. Indeed the Court has only acted when lower courts have mistaken relied on *National League of Cities* to strike down statutory applications to states, see Hodel v. Virginia Surface Mining & Reclamation Assoc., Inc., 101 Sp.Ct. 2352 (1981), and United Transportation Union v. Long Island Rail Road Co., 50 U.S.L.W. 4135 (1982).

23. 435 U.S. 389 (1978). *See* discussion in *Preview of United States Supreme Court Cases,* No. 6 (October 10, 1977): 6, for a typical example of the commentators' expectations. Naturally enough the commentators were taken aback.

24. In a footnote, Justice Brennan wrote, "[O]ur emphasis today in our conclusion, that municipalities are 'exempt' from antitrust enforcement when acting as state agencies implementing state policies to the same extent as the State itself, makes it difficult to see how *National League of Cities* is even tangentially implicated." 435 U.S. 389, 413 n. 42 (1977).

But it does not follow that, even if this statutory construction permits the Court to avoid reaching the constitutional issue, that *National League of Cities* underlying rationale can be so effortlessly limited to states and not their subdivisions when the latter are anything other than "state agencies implementing state policies to the same extent as the State itself." (*See also* the avoidance maneuvers in EPA v. Brown, 431 U.S. 99 (1977).

CHAPTER 15: EXPRESSIVE FUNCTION

1. 374 U.S. 203 (1963).
2. *See* Katz, "Patterns of Compliance with the Schempp Decision," *Journal of Public Law* 14 (1965): 396, 402.
3. Pennsylvania Education Code, § 1516 (West 1949; amended 1959).
4. Pennsylvania Education Code, § 1516 (West 1962). Current version at Penn. Educ. Code, § 1516 (West Supp. 1978–79).
5. Engel v. Vitale, 370 U.S. 421 (1962).
6. McCollum v. Board of Education, 333 U.S. 203 (1948).
7. 370 U.S. at 430–31.
8. 370 U.S. at 438–39 (Douglas, J., concurring).
9. Schempp v. School District of Abington Township, Pa., 201 F. Supp. 815, 818 (E.D. Penn. 1962).
10. 374 U.S. at 217–22.
11. Ibid. at 222.
12. Ibid. at 223.
13. 374 U.S. at 308 (Stewart, J., dissenting).
14. Ibid. at 318.
15. Ibid. at 319 (Stewart, J., dissenting).
16. Ibid. at 308–309.
17. Ibid. at 311, 312 (Stewart, J., dissenting).
18. Ibid. at 312–313 (Stewart, J., dissenting).
19. Ibid. at 308.
20. *See* Katz, "Patterns of Compliance with the Schempp Decision."
21. O'Hair v. Blumenthal, 462 F. Supp. 19 (1979).
22. Such subtleties are not to be confused with the more obvious efforts to prescribe "Creationism" as a topic for biology lectures.
23. Contrast Perry Miller's description of the early Massachusetts colony with Peter Gay's and Richard Morgan's description of the attitudes of the Framers:
    "The government of Massachusetts, and of Connecticut as well, was a dictatorship, not of single tyrant, or of an economic class, or of a political faction, but of the holy and regenerate. Those who did not hold with the ideals entertained by the righteous or who believed God had preached other principles, or who desired that in religious belief, morality, and ecclesiastical preferences all men should be at liberty to do as they wished—such persons had every liberty, as Nathaniel Ward said, to stay away from New England. If they did come, they were expected to keep their opinions to themselves; if they discussed them in public or attempted to act upon them, they were exiled; if they persisted in returning, they were cast out again; if they still came

back, as did four Quakers, they were hanged on Boston Common, and from the Puritan point of view it was good riddance. . . ."

Morgan's observations are from R. Morgan, *The Supreme Court and Religion* (1972), pp. 20–21.

24. Pollak, "Public Prayers in Public Schools," *Harvard Law Review* 77 (1963): 62, 64.
25. Deutsch, "Neutrality, Legitimacy, and the Supreme Court," *Stanford Law Review* 20 (1968): 235–36.
26. Fed. R. Crim. P. 17(c).
27. *See* 38 Fed. Reg. 30738–39 (1973).
28. C. Black, Jr., *The People and the Court* (1960), p. 6.
29. United States v. Nixon, 418 U.S. 683, 706 (1974).
30. Ibid. at 709.
31. Ibid. at 712.
32. Ibid. at 713.
33. Ibid.
34. Ibid. at 715.
35. Ibid. at 713.
36. Ibid.
37. United States v. Burr, 25 F. Cas. 30 (C.C.D. Va. 1807) (No. 14,692d).
38. Ibid. at 37.
39. Reynolds v. Sims, 377 U.S. 533, 562 (1964).
40. W. Wiecek, *The Guarantee Clause of the U.S. Constitution* (1972): 270–281.
41. Linde, "Judges, Critics, and the Realist Tradition," *Yale Law Journal* 82 (1972): 227.
42. Ibid., p. 238.

CHAPTER 16: ARGUMENTS AND THE EXPRESSIVE FUNCTION

1. Borges, *The Art of Poetry,* trans. Anthony Kerigan.
2. 377 U.S. 533, 565 (1964).
3. Ibid., p. 568.
4. 432 U.S. 464 (1977).
5. Roe v. Norton, 408 F. Supp. 660 (D. Conn. 1975).
6. Doe v. Poelker, 515 F.2d 541 (8th Cir. 1975).
7. Hughes v. Alexandria Scrap Corp., 426 U.S. 794 (1976).
8. *Cf.* Calabresi, "Bakke: Lost Candor," *New York Times,* July 6, 1978, p. 19; Calabresi, "Bakke as Pseudo-Tragedy," *Catholic Law Review* 28 (1979): 427.

CHAPTER 17: CHANGE AND THE CONSTITUTION

1. International Shoe Co. v. Washington, 326 U.S. 310 (1945).

2. 95 U.S. 714 (1877).

3. *See*, e.g., H. Bloom, *The Anxiety of Influence* (1973); W. J. Bate, *The Burden of the Past and the English Poet* (1970).

4. *See*, e.g., G. Calabresi, *The Cost of Accidents* (1970); Calabresi, "Transaction Costs, Resource Allocation and Liability Rules: A Comment," *Journal of Law and Economics* 11 (1968): 67; Calabresi, "The Decision for Accidents: An Approach to Nonfault Allocation of Costs," *Harvard Law Review* 78 (1965): 713.

5. N. Goodman, *Ways of Worldmaking* (1978): 20.

6. Thucydides, *History of the Peloponnesian War,* trans. T. Hobbes, ed. D. Grene (1959).

7. G. Calabresi and P. Bobbitt, *Tragic Choices* (1978), pp. 195–99.

8. N. Bohr, "Discussion with Einstein on Epistemological Problems in Atomic Physics," in *Atomic Physics and Human Knowledge* (1958): 66.

9. U.S. Constitution, Art. 1, § 6.

10. K. Llewellyn, *The Common Law Tradition: Deciding Appeals* (1960).

11. Dodd, "Congress and the Quest for Power," in *Discovery* (Univ. of Texas Publication) pp. 8–11 (1979).

12. R. Pinto, *Des Juges Qui Ne Gouvernement pas: Opinions Dissidentes à la Cour Supreme des Etats-Unis, 1900–1933* (1934).

13. I quote from the paraphrase of Pinto's article by yet another political scientist, C. Ct. Haines, who shares this perspective. *See* Haines, "Judicial Review of Acts of Congress and the Need for Constitutional Reform," *Yale Law Journal* 45 (1936): 816, 852.

14. *See* Goodman, *Ways of Worldmaking.*

15. Llewellyn, "The Constitution as an Institution," *Columbia Law Review* 34 (1934): 1, 39.

16. Ibid., p. 40.

17. W. Arrowsmith, "The Criticism of Greek Tragedy," in *Tragedy: Vision and Form,* ed. W. Corrigan (1965), p. 342.

CHAPTER 18: THE GENEALOGY OF ARGUMENTS

1. *See*, e.g., B. Ackerman, *Private Property and the Constitution* (1977).

2. *See*, e.g., P. Brest, *Processes of Constitutional Decisionmaking* (1975).

3. *See*, e.g., Ely, "Toward a Representation-Reinforcing Mode of Judicial Review," *Maryland Law Review* 37 (1978): 451. And J. H. Ely, *Democracy and Distrust* (1980).

4. *See*, e.g., Linde, "Judges, Critics, and the Realist Tradition," *Yale Law Journal* 82 (1972): 227.

5. U.S. Constitution, Art. 6.
6. *See* discussion of the "passive virtues" in Book I, Chapter 5.
7. *See* Brief of Anti-Defamation League of B'Nai B'rith as Amicus Curia in Support of Jurisdictional Statement, or, in the Alternative, Petition for Certiorari, 1 DeFunis v. Odegaard, The University Admissions Case (A. Ginger ed., 1974), and Brief of the Anti-Defamation League of B'Nai B'rith Amicus Curiae, 2 ibid. 465 (A. Ginger, ed.)
8. 416 U.S. 312 (1974) (per curiam).

CHAPTER 19: LEGITIMACY AND REVIEW

1. *The New Yorker,* Oct. 25, 1941, at 15.
2. J. B. Thayer, *Legal Essays* (1908), p. 1; originally in *Harvard Law Review* 7: 129.
3. R. Fogelin, *Wittgenstein* (1976).
4. Paraphrasing Holmes, who said, "Constitutional law, like other moral contrivances, has to take some chances." T. R. Powell, "The Logic and Rhetoric of Constitutional Law," in *Essays in Constitutional Law,* ed. R. McCloskey (1957), pp. 88, 89.
5. Lecture by Professor John Archibald Wheeler, February 9, 1979, University of Texas.

CONCLUSION

1. K. Llewellyn, *The Common Law Tradition* (1960).
2. 347 U.S. 483 (1954).
3. The figure is from Holmes's Speech at a Dinner of the Harvard Law School Association of New York on February 15, 1913, reprinted as *Law and the Court: The Occasional Speeches of Justice Oliver Wendell Holmes,* ed. M. Howe (1962), pp. 168, 174.

INDEX